Reworking the Student Departure Puzzle

Reworking the Student Departure Puzzle

Edited by

John M. Braxton

Vanderbilt University Press

Nashville

04 03 02 01 00 5 4 3 2 1

Library of Congress Cataloging-in-Publication Data

Reworking the student departure puzzle / edited by John M. Braxton.—
1st ed.
p. cm. — (Vanderbilt issues in higher education)
Includes bibliographical references and index.
ISBN 0-8265-1308-5
1. College dropouts—United States. 2. College attendance—
United States. 3. Tinto, Vincent. I. Braxton, John M. II. Series.
LC148.15 .R48 2000
378.1'6913—dc21   00-010641

Contents

Reworking the Student Departure Puzzle

Introduction

Reworking the Student Departure Puzzle

John M. Braxton

The national rate of student departure from colleges and universities has remained constant at 45 percent for over one hundred years (Tinto 1982). Why has this rate remained constant over such a long period of time? More perplexing is an average first-year departure rate of 8 percent at highly selective colleges and universities (Tinto 1993). The emergence of the use of private counselors, tutors, and SAT enhancement services by students who strive for admission to highly selective colleges and universities (McDonough 1994) makes this rate of departure particularly surprising. Moreover, Tinto (1993, p. 82) estimates that academic dismissals account for 15 to 25 percent of student departures from college. Why do so many college students depart voluntarily from their institutions? What accounts for student departure? Through efforts to understand this "departure puzzle" we have much to learn about colleges and universities as organizations, the college experience of students, and the interpretations students make of these experiences.

The departure puzzle has been the object of empirical inquiry for over seventy years. Summerskill (1962) and Pantages and Creedon (1978) mark the longevity of this line of inquiry. Summerskill reviewed research dating back to Johnson (1926), whereas Pantages and Creedon reviewed studies conducted between 1950 and 1975. Tinto (1975) also reviewed the research literature on this problem and criticized the lack of theoretical formulations to account for college student departure. To remedy this

1

deficiency, Tinto (1975) postulated an interactionalist theory of college student departure.

In addition to Tinto's theory economic, organizational, psychological, and sociological theoretical perspectives have been advanced to account for the departure puzzle (Tinto 1986, 1993). Tinto's interactionalist theory, nevertheless, enjoys near paradigmatic stature in the study of college student departure. Such stature manifests itself in more the 400 citations and 170 dissertations pertinent to this theory (Braxton, Sullivan, and Johnson 1997).

Tinto's Interactionalist Theory

Tinto (1975) states that students enter college with various individual characteristics that play roles in the college student departure process. These student entry characteristics include family background factors, individual attributes, and precollege schooling experiences. Family background characteristics include family socioeconomic status, parental educational level, and parental expectations. Individual attributes identified by Tinto are academic ability, race, and gender. Precollege schooling experiences include the characteristics of the student's secondary school and record of high school academic achievement.

Such student entry characteristics directly influence the student's initial commitment to an institution and to the goal of college graduation. Tinto also hypothesizes that student entry characteristics also directly affect the departure decision. Initial commitment to an institution and to the goal of graduation in turn affects the student's degree of integration into the academic and social systems of the college or university.

Structural and normative dimensions define academic integration. Tinto (1975, p. 104) states that structural integration involves the meeting of explicit standards of the college or university, whereas normative integration pertains to an individual's identification with the normative structure of the academic system. Academic performance indexes the student's degree of structural integration into the academic system of a college or university given that grades offer assessments of a student's ability to meet an institution's standards for student academic achievement. According to Tinto, normative integration manifests itself in student intellectual development because it reflects the student's appraisal of the institution's academic system (1975, p. 104). Tinto also adds that normative integration takes the form of congruency between the individual's intellectual development and the intellectual environment of the college or university (1975, p. 106).

Social integration pertains to the degree of congruency between the individual student and the social system of a college or university. Tinto indicates that mechanisms of social integration include informal peer group associations, extracurricular activities, and interactions with faculty and administrators (1975, p. 107).

Academic and social integration affect the formation of subsequent commitments to the institution and to the goal of college graduation. To elaborate, the greater the student's level of academic integration, the greater the level of subsequent commitment to the goal of college graduation. Moreover, the greater the student's level of social integration, the greater the level of subsequent commitment to the focal college or university (Tinto 1975, p. 110). Both subsequent commitments are also shaped by the student's initial level of commitments. The greater the levels of both subsequent institutional commitment and commitment to the goal of college graduation, the greater the likelihood the individual will persist in college. These formulations yield thirteen testable propositions.

Recently Braxton, Sullivan, and Johnson (1997) assessed the extent of empirical support for each of these thirteen propositions. In making these assessments, both multi-institutional and single-institutional tests of these propositions were used. Four propositions received strong empirical backing by multi-institutional tests, whereas single-institutional appraisals provide strong empirical affirmation for five propositions. As a consequence Braxton, Sullivan, and Johnson (1997) conclude that Tinto's theory is partially supported and lacks empirical internal consistency.

Given such a conclusion, scholars may elect one of two decidedly different courses of action. Serious revision of Tinto's theory constitutes one course of action, whereas abandonment of Tinto's theory and pursuit of new theoretical perspectives is the other course of action. The pursuit of either course of action will serve to reinvigorate scholarly inquiry on the departure puzzle. Thus, this edited volume offers various approaches to the revision of Tinto's theory as well as new theoretical directions.

This volume, however, is limited in two ways. First, the authors of the chapters herein have, with few exceptions, neither described the measurement of the constructs they present nor recommended methodological approaches. The choice of methodological approaches and the measurement of constructs are left to the scholarly community to develop. Second, the authors of the chapters of this edited volume have selected a theoretical perspective(s) for discussion rather than the range of theories that might be classified under their underlying theoretical orientation (e.g., economic, psychological, or sociological). Put differently, the theoretical perspectives advanced are not exhaustive of theories scholars might select to study the process of college student departure.

In addition to this introduction and a concluding chapter, two parts comprise the structure of this volume. Part 1 contains chapters that suggest approaches to the revision of Tinto's theory, while chapters postulating new theoretical directions make up part 2.

Part 1, "Revising Tinto's Theory," is made up of six chapters. In chapter 1 John M. Braxton and Leigh A. Lien explore the viability of academic integration as a core construct in Tinto's theory. Braxton, Sullivan, and Johnson's (1997) assessment of empirical support for the propositions of Tinto's theory indicates that the hypothesized positive influence of academic integration on subsequent goal commitment fails to garner strong empirical support. Thus, questions arise concerning the viability of this core construct. Accordingly, Braxton and Lien assess empirical support for academic integration's possible influence on subsequent institutional commitment or the departure decision. Based on this assessment, they recommend one of two courses of action: the abandonment of academic integration or rethinking its theoretical specification and measurement.

Theory elaboration offers an approach to the revision of Tinto's interactionalist theory. Theory elaboration involves the use of constructs derived from other theoretical perspectives to explain the phenomenon of interest (Thornberry 1989). The remaining five chapters of part 1 advance various constructs derived from other theoretical perspectives—economic, psychological, and sociological—that may assist in revising Tinto's theory. Tinto (1986) recognizes that a shortcoming of his theoretical schema is its failure to take into account other theoretical perspectives. Thus, the revisions of his theory through the use of constructs derived from economic, psychological, and sociological theoretical perspectives offer the possibility of a more explanatory interactionalist theory of college student departure.

In chapter 2 Edward P. St. John, Alberto F. Cabrera, Amaury Nora, and Eric H. Asker review studies that incorporated finance variables into models of student retention. From this review they advance some "new understandings" of the ways economic forces affect institutional commitment, academic integration, and social integration. St. John, Cabrera, Nora, and Asker also suggest some directions for further research using financial variables to revise Tinto's theory.

Chapters 3 and 4 offer psychological perspectives. In chapter 3 John P. Bean and Shevawn Bogdan Eaton present a psychological model of college student retention. Four psychological theories—attitude-behavior, coping behavior, self-efficacy, and attribution—undergird this model, which seeks to account for social integration, institutional commitment, and student departure decisions. Thus, this model suggests a way to revise Tinto's theory using the psychological constructs.

The model proposed by Bean and Eaton focuses on psychological processes at the level of the individual student. In contrast, Leonard L. Baird concentrates in chapter 4 on such processes at the level of the environment of colleges and universities. Baird argues that student perceptions of the collegiate environment or climate lead to various behaviors that in turn affect their degree of academic and social integration. He presents a representative schema for assessing the psychological character of climates, describes lessons learned from efforts to assess campus climates, and discusses the consequences of such research for theory, measurement, and research design, and for policy.

Chapters 5 and 6 advance sociological perspectives on college student departure. In chapter 5 Vincent Tinto contends that the social structure of college classrooms plays a role in the student retention process. He asserts that college classrooms function as smaller academic and social communities that link students to the broader academic and social systems of their colleges and universities. Faculty pedagogical behavior shapes such social structures. Tinto presents some formulations that describe the linkages among classrooms as communities and academic integration, social integration, and persistence.

In chapter 6 Joseph B. Berger extends Bourdieu's notion (1973, 1977) of cultural capital to the college student departure process. Berger contends that individual students and individual colleges and universities possess varying degrees of cultural capital. Through his extension of Bourdieu's formulations to college student departure, Berger advances a set of two organizational-level and two student-level propositions. Implications for further research are also presented.

Part 2, "New Theoretical Directions," consists of six chapters. These chapters represent an admixture of directions: a critique of Tinto's theory as it pertains to the departure of minority students, a methodological approach to generating new theory, and three new theoretical perspectives. In chapter 7 Laura I. Rendón, Romero E. Jalomo, and Amaury Nora critically assess the explanatory power of Tinto's theory to account for minority student departure. Their critique focuses not only on Tinto's 1975 formulations regarding academic and social integration, but also on his more recent (1993) postulations regarding the separation and transition stages in the process of student integration (incorporation) into the community of a college or university. The critical analysis of Rendón, Jalomo, and Nora takes issue with the assimilation/acculturation framework that underlies Tinto's interactionalist perspective. Based on their critique, Rendón, Jalomo, and Nora urge scholars to take retention theory to a higher level, and they suggest that a new "helper" theory may be necessary to take Tinto's theory to a higher level to adequately account for the collegiate experience of minority students.

Robert M. Johnson, Jr., contends in chapter 8 that discourse analysis offers a methodological approach to the generation of new theory, grounded and predicated on the socially constructed reality of college students. Discourse analysis entails the observation or evocation of speech to determine how individuals construct their realities. Johnson describes the various categories of speech attended to by discourse analysis. He contends that by focusing on culture, cognition, and the structure of meaning scholars can radically "rethink the departure puzzle."

Some scholars (Attinasi 1989; Braxton, Vesper, and Hossler 1995; Hamrick and Hossler 1996; St. John, Paulsen, and Starkey 1996; Stage and Rushin 1993) recognize that linkages may exist between the processes of college choice and college student departure. However, few if any scholars have formulated a theoretical perspective on such linkages. In chapter 9 Frances K. Stage and Don Hossler develop such a perspective. They propose a theory that links the educational process from predisposition to college to college persistence. In formulating this theory Stage and Hossler postulated inter-relations among the precollege characteristics, attitudes, and behaviors of students; college experiences and behaviors; and the interactions among these factors that result in college persistence or departure.

In chapter 10 George D. Kuh and Patrick G. Love argue that the notion of culture affords an alternative to studying college student departure. Using the lens of culture, they pose eight propositions to guide scholarly inquiry. Kuh and Love also discuss the implications of using the cultural perspective for institutional policy and practice and for research on college student departure.

Writing from a critical theory perspective, William G. Tierney in chapter 11 advances a model predicated on the notions of power and community.

The underlying premise of this approach is that retention of students defined as "at risk" for departure depends on the extent to which the identities of such students are affirmed and incorporated into the cultures of colleges and universities. Tierney also holds that colleges and universities need to modify the cultures of their institutions to accommodate individuals or groups of students who are at risk of departure. He offers this model as a blueprint for interventions for students at risk for college departure—low income, urban black, and Hispanic students.

In chapter 12 Berta Vigil Laden, Jeffrey F. Milem, and Robert L. Crowson apply new institutional theory to the contours of the departure puzzle at the systems level of higher education. They apply this theory to address two important questions posed in this chapter: Is retention in school an inadequately institutionalized feature of higher education? and Is student departure itself an institutionalized feature of higher education? Laden, Milem, and Crowson conclude that college student departure may be an institutionalized property of higher education.

In the concluding chapter to this edited volume, John M. Braxton asserts that Tinto's interactionalist theory should be seriously revised, with the four strongly backed propositions serving as a foundation. He proposes a process of inductive theory revision that would use the findings of research using economic, organizational, psychological, and sociological theoretical perspectives to explain social integration, subsequent institutional commitment, and student departure decisions. Other recommendations for research are also advanced, as is a set of issues needing resolution.

Closing Thoughts

Research on the departure puzzle stalled in the mid 1990s because of the near-paradigmatic stature of Tinto's theory. This edited book, however, hopefully will serve as an important impetus to reinvigorating research on college student departure. Such research may take the direction of seriously rethinking the specification and measurement of academic integration or revising Tinto's interactionalist formulations through theory elaboration using the economic, psychological, or sociological perspectives advanced in part 1 of this book. The new theoretical directions described in the chapters comprising part 2 may also be embraced by scholars studying college student departure. Through such efforts in either direction we may make some headway in unraveling the departure puzzle. Such headway may include but transcend the confidence we hold in those propositions of Tinto's theory that boast strong empirical affirmation.

References

Attinasi, L. C. 1989. Getting in: Mexican Americans' perceptions of university attendance and the implications for freshman year persistence. *Journal of Higher Education* 60: 247–277.

Bourdieu, P. 1973. Cultural reproduction and societal reproduction. In R. Brown(ed.), *Knowledge, Education and Cultural Change.* pp. 487–510, London: Tavistock.

Bourdieu, P. 1977. *Outline of a Theory of Practice.* Translated by Richard Nice. Cambridge, U.K.: University Press.

Braxton, J. M., A. S. Sullivan, and R. M. Johnson. 1997. Appraising Tinto's theory of college student departure. In J. C. Smart (ed.), *Higher education: A handbook of theory and research,* vol. 12, pp. 107–164. New York: Agathon Press.

Braxton, J. M., N. Vesper, and D. Hossler. 1995. Expectations for college and student persistence. *Research in Higher Education* 36: 595–612.

Hamrick, F. A., and D. Hossler. 1996. Active and passive searching in postsecondary educational decision making. *Review of Higher Education* 19 (2): 179–198.

Johnson, J. B. 1926. Predicting success in college at time of entrance. *School and Society* 23: 82–88.

McDonough, P. M. (1994). "Buying and Selling Higher Education: The Social Construction of the College Applicant." *Journal of Higher Education,* 65:427—446.

Pantages, T. J., and C. F. Creedon. 1978. Studies of college attrition: 1950–1975. *Review of Educational Research* 48 (1): 49–101.

St. John, E. P., M. B. Paulsen, and J. B. Starkey. 1996. The nexus between college choice and persistence. *Research in Higher Education* 37 (2): 175–220.

Stage, F. K., and P. W. Rushin. 1993. A combined model of student predisposition to college and persistence in college. *Journal of College Student Development* 34: 276–281.

Summerskill, J. 1962. Dropouts from college. In N. Sanford (ed.), *The American college: A psychological and social interpretation of the higher learning,* pp. 627–657. New York: John Wiley and Sons.

Thornberry, T. P. 1989. Reflections on the advantages and disadvantages of theoretical integration. In S. F. Messner, M. D. Krohn, and A. E. Liska (eds.), *Theoretical integration in the study of deviance and crime,* pp. 51–60. Albany: State University of New York Press.

Tinto, V. 1975. Dropout from higher education: A theoretical synthesis of recent research. *Review of Educational Research* 45: 89–125.

Tinto, V. 1982. Limits of theory and practice in student attrition. *Journal of Higher Education* 53 (6): 687–700.

Tinto, V. 1986. Theories of student departure revisited. In J. C. Smart (ed.), *Higher education: Handbook of theory and research,* vol. 2, pp. 359–384. New York: Agathon Press.

Tinto, V. 1993. *Leaving college: Rethinking the causes and cures of student attrition.* 2d ed. Chicago: University of Chicago Press.

Part I

Revising Tinto's Theory

The Viability of Academic Integration as a Central Construct in Tinto's Interactionalist Theory of College Student Departure

John M. Braxton and Leigh A. Lien

Tinto's interactionalist theory of college student departure needs revision. Braxton, Sullivan, and Johnson (1997) offer this conclusion from their assessment of empirical support for this near-paradigmatic theory of college student departure. Several logically interrelated propositions possessing strong empirical affirmation provide a basis for such revision. These propositions take the following form: student entry characteristics affect the level of initial institutional commitment; students' initial levels of institutional commitments also influence their degree of subsequent commitment to the institution; students' subsequent commitment to the institution is positively affected by their degree of social integration; the greater the degree of students' subsequent institutional commitment, the greater the likelihood of their persistence in college.

Academic and social integration are pivotal constructs to Tinto's interactionalist theory. Academic integration, however, plays little or no part in any revision of this theory based on Braxton, Sullivan, and Johnson's recommendations. To elaborate, in one core proposition of Tinto's theory academic integration is posited to wield a positive influence on subsequent commitment to the goal of college graduation. Braxton, Sullivan, and Johnson (1997) discerned only modest empirical affirmation for this proposition.

Perhaps academic integration performs a different role in the college student departure process than envisioned by Tinto. Academic integration

may lead to either subsequent institutional commitment or to student persistence in college. If either of these possibilities yields strong empirical
confirmation, then revisions to Tinto's interactionalist theory might include propositions pertinent to the role of academic integration in the college student departure process.

This chapter assesses empirical support for both of these possibilities.
More specifically, the questions addressed in this chapter are:

*What is the magnitude of empirical support, in the aggregate, for the
influence of academic integration on subsequent institutional commitment?*

*Does the magnitude of empirical support for the influence of aca-
demic integration on subsequent institutional commitment vary
across different types of colleges and universities?*

*What is the magnitude of empirical support, in the aggregate, for
the influence of academic integration on student departure decisions?*

*Does the magnitude of empirical support for the influence of aca-
demic integration on student departure decisions vary across different types of colleges and universities?*

We pursued these four questions by reviewing studies that have been subject to peer review. Peer review affords some confidence in the quality of
the scholarship of such studies. Accordingly, this chapter concentrates on
papers presented at annual meetings of scholarly and professional associations and articles published in refereed academic and professional journals.

Like Braxton, Sullivan, and Johnson (1997), we used the "box score"
method of assessing the magnitude of empirical support for the two possible forms of influence exerted by academic integration. We also employed
the same criteria that Braxton, Sullivan, and Johnson used for determining
the magnitude of empirical support. Accordingly we assessed the magnitude of empirical support as strong if 66 percent or more of three or more
tests of these possible influences demonstrate statistical significance.
Modest support was accorded if between 34 percent and 65 percent of three

or more tests of these possible influences exhibit statistical significance. Weak support was ascribed if 33 percent or less of three or more tests of these possible influences display statistical significance. Indeterminate support is indicated when fewer than three tests were performed because subsequent tests may be affirming or disconfirming.

Aggregate assessment of empirical support for these two possible forms of influence wielded by academic integration included all tests of these forms of influence. Put differently, tests executed in different types of colleges and universities and different groups of students were included. In contrast, assessments of empirical support for these two possible forms of influence across different types of colleges and universities include tests conducted in particular types of colleges and universities and for different groups of students nested within these particular types of institutions. Thus, the particular type of college or university is the unit of analysis.

Although some scholars (Hurtado and Carter 1997; Tinto 1997) question the ways in which integration has been measured in various studies of the college student departure process, little consensus exists among scholars on the meaning of academic integration. As a consequence, we included studies in our assessments if their measures of academic integration, subsequent institutional commitment, and departure exhibited reasonable face validity. Such an approach is also consistent with Lazarsfeld's (1959) notion of the interchangeability of indicators when measuring complex constructs.

Our assessments of empirical support include studies with samples that are either multi-institutional or single-institutional in their scope. Single-institutional studies, however, are more congruous with the underlying assumptions of Tinto's theory of college student departure. Tinto asserts that his theoretical perspective seeks to account for the longitudinal process of student withdrawal within a particular college or university. He reiterates this point by adding, "it is not a systems model of departure" (Tinto 1993, p. 112). Nevertheless, multi-institutional studies increase the variability in the measurement of theoretical constructs. The restricted variance in single-institutional studies can lead to a failure to identify empirical support for the two possible forms of influence academic integration may have on college student departure decisions. As a consequence, we include both multi-institutional and single-institutional tests in addressing the questions guiding this chapter. However, we make careful distinctions between these two types of tests.

The Influence of Academic Integration on Subsequent Institutional Commitment

Aggregated Support

Multi-institutional and single-institutional tests of the possible relationship between academic integration and subsequent institutional commitment yield different results. Multi-institutional tests provide strong support, whereas single-institutional appraisals accord modest empirical backing. More specifically, six of the eight (75 percent) multi-institutional tests that were carried out discerned a statistically significant relationship between academic integration and subsequent institutional commitment. In comparison, eighteen of the twenty-eight (64 percent) single-institutional assessments of this possible relationship yielded statistically significant findings. Table 1 shows the studies making the multi-institutional tests, and table 2 exhibits the studies performing the single-institutional assessments of a possible relationship between academic integration and subsequent institutional commitment.

Table 1
Multi-institutional Tests of the Influence of Academic Integration on Subsequent Institutional Commitment (Eight Tests)

Supportive Tests (six tests)
Braxton, Vesper, and Hossler (1995)
Munro (1981)
Pascarella and Chapman (1983) two tests
Pascarella, Smart, and Ethington (1986)
Pavel (1991)

Unsupportive Tests (two tests)

Pascarella and Chapman (1983)
Pascarella, Smart, and Ethington (1986)

Support by Institutional Type

Multi-institutional tests were carried out in residential institutions, commuter universities, two-year colleges, and unspecified types of four-year colleges and universities. Appraisals executed in unspecified types of four-year colleges and universities furnish strong empirical affirmation for a relationship between academic integration and subsequent institutional commitment. Of the four tests made, three of them discerned a statistically reliable relationship between academic integration and subsequent institutional commitment. However, those assessments made in commuter universities (one test), residential universities (two tests), and two-year colleges (one test) offer indeterminate empirical support. These multi-institutional tests by institutional type are displayed in table 3.

Table 2

**Single-Institutional Tests of the Influence of Academic Integration on
Subsequent Institutional Commitment
(Twenty-eight Tests)**

Supportive Tests (eighteen tests)
> Allen (1986)
> Braxton and Brier (1989)
> Braxton, Duster, and Pascarella (1988)
> Cabrera, Castañeda, Nora, and Hengstler
> (1992)
> Cash and Bissel (1985) four tests
> Fox (1986)
> Nora and Cabrera (1996) two tests
> Pascarella and Terenzini (1983) two tests
> Pascarella, Duby, and Iverson (1983)
> Pascarella, Terenzini, and Wolfle (1986)
> Pike, Schroeder, and Berry (1997) two tests
> Terenzini, Pascarella, Theophilides, and Lorang (1985)

Unsupportive Tests (ten tests)

> Allen and Nelson (1989) two tests
> Cabrera, Nora, and Castañeda (1992)
> Cabrera, Nora, and Castañeda (1993)
> Milem and Berger (1997)
> Stage (1988) two tests
> Stage (1989) three tests

Single-institutional evaluations of the relationship between academic integration and subsequent institutional commitment yield varying degrees of empirical support across residential colleges and universities, four-year commuter institutions, and two-year colleges. Tests conducted in commuter universities provide strong empirical affirmation given that seven of the ten tests conducted identified a statistically significant relationship between academic integration and subsequent institutional commitment. Single-institutional assessments enacted in four-year residential colleges and universities provide moderate empirical backing for a statistically verifiable relationship between academic integration and subsequent institutional commitment as ten of sixteen tests made affirm this relationship. Since two assessments were performed in two-year colleges, indeterminate empirical support is offered in this type of collegiate institution. These various single-institutional tests arrayed by institutional type are shown in table 4.

Table 3
Multi-institutional Tests of the Influence of Academic Integration on
Subsequent Institutional Commitment by Institutional Type
(Eight Tests)

Two-Year Colleges (three tests)

    Supportive Tests (two tests)
        Pascarella and Chapman (1983)
        Pascarella, Smart, and Ethington (1986)

    Unsupportive Tests (one test)
        Pascarella, Smart, and Ethington (1986)

Four-Year Commuter Universities (one test)

    Supportive Tests (one test)
        Pascarella and Chapman (1983)

Residential Colleges and Universities (one test)

    Unsupportive Tests (one test)
        Pascarella and Chapman (1983)

Unspecified Types of Four-Year Colleges and Universities (two tests)

    Supportive Tests (two tests)
        Braxton, Vesper, and Hossler (1995)
        Munro (1981)

Unspecified Types of Colleges and Universities (one test)

    Supportive Tests (one test)
        Pavel (1991)

Table 4
Single-Institutional Tests of the Influence of Academic Integration on Subsequent Institutional Commitment by Institutional Type
(Twenty-eight Tests)

Commuter Universities (ten tests)

Supportive Tests (seven tests)
Braxton and Brier (1989)
Braxton, Duster, and Pascarella (1988)
Cabrera, Castañeda, Nora, and Hengstler (1992)
Fox (1986)
Nora and Cabrera (1996) two tests
Pascarella, Duby, and Iverson (1983)

Unsupportive Tests (three tests)
Allen and Nelson (1989)
Cabrera, Nora, and Castañeda (1992)
Cabrera, Nora, and Castañeda (1993)

Four-Year Residential Colleges and Universities (sixteen tests)

Supportive Tests (ten tests)
Cash and Bissel (1985) four tests
Pascarella and Terenzini (1983) two tests
Pascarella, Terenzini, and Wolfle (1986)
Pike, Schroeder, and Berry (1997) two tests
Terenzini, Pascarella, Theophilides, and Lorang (1985)

Unsupportive Tests (six tests)
Milem and Berger (1997)
Stage (1988) two tests
Stage (1989) three tests

Two-Year Colleges (two tests)
Supportive Tests (one test)
Allen (1986)

Unsupportive Tests (one test)
Allen and Nelson (1989)

Influence of Academic Integration on Departure

Aggregated Support

A total of twenty multi-institutional and thirty-nine single-institutional tests of the direct influence of academic integration on student departure decisions were made. Of the twenty multi-institutional tests conducted, fifteen show that academic integration exhibits a statistically reliable effect on student departure. Thus, multi-institutional tests yield strong support. Table 5 exhibits the studies making these multi-institutional tests.

Table 5

Multi-institutional Tests of the Influence of Academic Integration on Persistence
(Twenty Tests)

Supportive Tests (fifteen tests)
    Cabrera, Stampen, and Hansen (1990)
    Donovan (1984)
    Munro (1981)
    Pascarella (1986) three tests
    Pascarella, Smart, and Ethington (1986) two tests
    Pavel (1991)
    Stoecker, Pascarella, and Wolfle (1988) four tests
    Williamson and Creamer (1988) two tests

Unsupportive Tests (five tests)
    Nora (1987)
    Pascarella (1985)
    Pascarella and Chapman (1983) three tests

In contrast, single-institutional tests provide modest empirical backing. Of the thirty-nine tests of this influence executed, twenty (51 percent) produced statistically reliable results. Table 6 displays the studies conducting these thirty-nine single-institutional appraisals.

Support by Institutional Type

Multi-institutional tests of a direct influence of academic integration on student persistence were made using student samples drawn from four-year residential universities, commuter universities, four-year colleges and universities of an unspecified type, and unspecified types of colleges and universities. The studies performing these tests are shown in table 7. Appraisals made in unspecified types of four-year colleges and universities (eleven of twelve tests) yield robust affirmation for a statistically significant relationship between academic integration and student withdrawal decisions. Those tests conducted in community colleges, however, offer modest support since two of the four tests made yielded statistically significant results. As evidenced by table 7, tests conducted in commuter universities, residential colleges and universities, and unspecified types of colleges and universities garner indeterminate empirical support.

Table 6

Single-Institutional Tests of the Influence of Academic Integration on Persistence
(Thirty-nine Tests)

Supportive Tests (twenty tests)

Allen (1986)
Allen and Nelson (1989)
Bers and Smith (1991)
Cabrera, Castañeda, Nora, and Hengstler (1992)
Cash and Bissel (1985)
Fox (1986)
Getzlaf, Sedlacek, Kearney, and Blackwell (1984)
Halpin (1990)
Nora, Attinasi, and Matonak (1990)
Pascarella and Terenzini (1980)
Pascarella and Terenzini (1983) two tests
Pascarella, Duby, and Iverson (1983)
Pike, Schroeder, and Berry (1997)
Stage (1988) two tests
Stage (1989) two tests
Terenzini, Lorang, and Pascarella (1981)
Terenzini and Pascarella (1978)

Unsupportive Tests (nineteen tests)

Allen and Nelson (1989)
Braxton and Brier (1989)
Braxton, Brier, and Hossler (1988)
Braxton, Duster, and Pascarella (1988)
Brower (1992)
Cabrera, Nora, and Castañeda (1992)
Cabrera, Nora, and Castañeda (1993)
Cash and Bissel (1985) three tests
Grosset (1991) two tests
Mallette and Cabrera (1991)
Nora and Cabrera (1996) two tests
Pascarella, Terenzini, and Wolfle (1986)
Pike, Schroeder, and Berry (1997)
Stage (1989)
Terenzini, Pascarella, Theophilides, and Lorang (1985)

Table 7
**Multi-institutional Tests of the Influence of Academic Integration on
Persistence by Institutional Type
(Twenty Tests)**

Two-Year Colleges (four tests)

　　Supportive Tests (two tests)
　　　　Pascarella, Smart, and Ethington (1986) two tests

　　Unsupportive Tests (two tests)
　　　　Nora (1987)
　　　　Pascarella and Chapman (1983)

Four-Year Commuter Universities (one test)

　　Unsupportive Tests (one test)
　　　　Pascarella and Chapman (1983)

Residential Colleges and Universities (one test)

　　Unsupportive Tests (one test)
　　　　Pascarella and Chapman (1983)

Unspecified Types of Four-Year Colleges and Universities (twelve tests)

　　Supportive Tests (eleven tests)
　　　　Donovan (1984)
　　　　Munro (1981)
　　　　Pascarella (1985) three tests
　　　　Stoecker, Pascarella, and Wolfle (1988) four tests
　　　　Williamson and Creamer (1988) two tests

　　Unsupportive Tests (one test)
　　　　Pascarella (1985)

Unspecified Types of Colleges and Universities (two tests)

　　Supportive Tests (two tests)
　　　　Cabrera, Stampen, and Hansen (1990)
　　　　Pavel (1991)

Single-institutional appraisals of the possibility of a relationship between academic integration and departure were enacted in four-year residential colleges and universities, commuter universities, and two-year colleges. The studies conducting these appraisals are shown in table 8. None of these three types of institutional settings affords robust empirical support for a relationship between academic integration and student departure decisions. As evidenced by table 8, all three types of settings yield modest empirical backing.

Table 8
Single-Institutional Tests of the Influence of Academic Integration on
Persistence by Institutional Type
(Thirty-nine Tests)

Commuter Universities (thirteen tests)

Supportive Tests (five tests)
Allen (1986)
Cabrera, Castañeda, Nora, and Hengstler (1992)
Fox (1986)
Nora, Attinasi, and Matonak (1990)
Pascarella, Duby, and Iverson (1983)

Unsupportive Tests (eight tests)
Allen and Nelson (1989)
Braxton and Brier (1989)
Braxton, Brier, and Hossler (1988)
Braxton, Duster, and Pascarella (1988)
Cabrera, Nora, and Castañeda (1992)
Cabrera, Nora, and Castañeda (1993)
Nora and Cabrera (1996) two tests

Four-Year Residential Colleges and Universities (twenty-one tests)

Supportive Tests (thirteen tests)
Brower (1992)
Cash and Bissel (1985)
Getzlaf, Sedlacek, Kearney, and Blackwell (1984)
Pascarella and Terenzini (1980)
Pascarella and Terenzini (1983) two tests
Pike, Schroeder, and Berry (1997)
Stage (1988) two tests

Table 8 *(continued)*

Stage (1989) two tests
Terenzini, Lorang, and Pascarella (1981)
Terenzini and Pascarella (1978)

Unsupportive Tests (eight tests)
Cash and Bissel (1985) three tests
Mallette and Cabrera (1991)
Pascarella, Terenzini, and Wolfle (1986)
Pike, Schroeder, and Berry (1997)
Stage (1989)
Terenzini, Pascarella, Theophilides, and Lorang (1985)

Two-Year Colleges (five tests)

Supportive Tests (three tests)
Allen and Nelson (1989)
Bers and Smith (1991)
Halpin (1990)

Unsupportive Tests (two tests)

Grosset (1991) two tests

Conclusion and Recommendations

We offer one primary conclusion from our assessments of the influence of academic integration on persistence and subsequent institutional commitment. We conclude that the magnitude of support for influence of academic integration on both subsequent institutional commitment and persistence varies between multi-institutional and single-institutional tests of these two relationships. Multi-institutional appraisals provide robust empirical backing for the effect of academic integration on both subsequent institutional commitment and student departure decisions. In contrast, single-institutional tests render modest empirical support for both of these forms of influence of academic integration.

Perhaps multi-institutional assessments yield vigorous backing because variability in the measurement of academic integration is enhanced by such tests. Also, measures of academic integration are consistent across the institutions included in a given multi-institutional study. As a consequence, statistically significant affirmation of these two forms of influence of academic integration occurs and strong support is afforded.

If we remain true to Tinto's assertions concerning the suitability of single-institutional tests of his interactionalist theory of college student departure, then we must put the greatest weight on single-institutional appraisals of the influence of academic integration on subsequent institutional commitment and persistence.

As a consequence, we propose two possible courses of action for scholars studying college student departure. The abandonment of the construct of academic integration from further research using Tinto's interactionalist theory represents one course of action. Scholars wishing to be consistent with Tinto's perspective on the suitability of single-institutional tests of his theory may elect to choose this particular course of action.

The misspecification of the measurement of academic integration may account for the failure of these various single-institutional tests to yield strong empirical confirmation of these possible sources of influence exerted by academic integration. Thus, rethinking the measurement of academic integration constitutes the other course of action scholars may select. Such a course seems warranted because single-institutional appraisals of the influence of academic integration on subsequent institutional commitment yield strong empirical support in four-year commuter universities. Because nonresidential or commuter colleges and universities offer few opportunities for social interaction necessary for social integration (Pascarella, Duby, and Iverson 1983), academic integration may offer the only way students can establish membership in the communities of such institutions. As a consequence, nonresidential colleges and universities afford a rigorous test for academic integration. Put differently, if academic integration fails to demonstrate some effects in these institutional settings, then it is unlikely to do so in residential colleges and universities. Such a rigorous test was passed with strong affirmation. As a consequence, academic integration remains a viable construct worthy of reconsideration of its measurement.

Tinto's (1975, 1993) extension of Durkheim's (1951) formulations surrounding egotistical suicide provides a basis for rethinking the measurement of academic integration. Durkheim postulated that egotistical suicide occurs when individuals are not integrated into the communities of society. Integration into the communities of society takes two forms: normative integration, or integration through similarity in beliefs and values; and integration through collective affiliation with other members of a community. By extension, college students depart from a particular college or university when their values and beliefs are different from prevailing attitudes and beliefs or when they experience isolation from other members of the campus community.

The notions of normative integration and collective affiliation may also be extended to the academic communities of colleges and universities. Thus students' departure and/or failure to form subsequent commitments to an institution occur when students experience incongruence with the beliefs and values inherent in the academic communities of an institution and/or when students feel a sense of intellectual isolation in such communities.

Tinto (1975), however, posits that the normative dimension of academic integration is indexed in both a student's intellectual development and the congruency between a student's intellectual development and the intellectual environment of a college or university. Thus, Tinto does not view normative academic integration as a student's degree of congruence with the prevailing attitudes, values, and beliefs inherent in the academic system.

Moreover, Tinto (1975) also views academic integration as having a structural dimension that is indexed in students' academic achievements. Students' academic achievements reflect structural integration because they indicate students' ability to meet the expectations of the institution for student achievement. Consequently, Tinto does not account for intellectual isolation or collective affiliation as a form of academic integration in his formulations.

Because of his perspectives on the components of academic integration, Tinto may have misspecified academic integration. As a consequence, we propose that scholars develop measures of academic normative integration and intellectual isolation more closely aligned with the formulations of Durkheim. Accordingly, we offer the following suggestions.

Academic normative incongruence may occur around students' incompatibility with the prevailing academic attitudes, values, and beliefs at various levels of the academic system: the general education dimension of the curriculum, the curriculum of the academic major, and individual courses offered by faculty. More palpable examples include the prevailing goals of the general education curriculum, academic majors, and individual faculty members as well as epistemological assumptions of various subject-matter areas, and the academic environments of various subject-matter areas constitute patterns of attitudes, values, and beliefs with which some students may feel incongruent.

To be more specific, the prevailing faculty instructional goals in a given college or university may emphasize such cognitively oriented goals as the mastery of the discipline, whereas some students may prefer an emphasis on vocational skills or job preparation after college. Such students would experience little or no academic normative congruence.

Another specific example of academic normative integration pertains to the academic environments formed by different subject-matter areas. One premise of Holland's (1985) theory of career choice is that academic environments emanate from personality types associated with the choice of academic majors. Realistic, investigative, artistic, social, enterprising, and conventional are types of academic environments that "psychologically resemble" the personality types associated with choice of major. Holland posits that student achievement and satisfaction in college are functions of the fit between the personality type of a student and the prevailing academic environment of a given college or university. By extension, academic normative congruence may also entail such a fit.

Intellectual isolation may stem from the individual student's failure to find a major field of study of interest. For example, a student wishing to create an individual interdisciplinary program of study would experience intellectual isolation if that student's institution does not support student-designed majors. Another form of intellectual isolation may arise from students' failure to find courses that are intellectually challenging to them. More specifically, students desiring courses that emphasize critical thinking would experience intellectual isolation if most of their courses emphasized the recall and recognition of content.

Thus, scholars are urged to consider the development of measures of academic normative congruence using faculty teaching goals and Holland's typology of academic environments. Scholars are also encouraged to develop ways of measuring intellectual isolation using the forms of isolation suggested above. However, these facets of academic normative integration and intellectual isolation are suggested with the intent of inviting scholars to delineate other indicators of these complex constructs.

The indexes of academic normative integration and intellectual isolation we suggest here require single-institutional tests of their influence on either subsequent institutional commitment or student persistence. Because such characteristics of academic normative integration and intellectual isolation vary from institution to institution, the development of a general set of indicators applicable to a wide range of colleges and universities is not possible.

The viability of academic integration as a central construct in revisions of Tinto's (1975, 1993) interactionalist theory of college student departure remains an open empirical question. Research using the suggested facets of academic integration should help scholars studying college student departure to resolve this vexing problem. Although the suggested indexes of academic normative integration and intellectual isolation should be tested across all types of colleges and universities, nonresidential collegiate settings offer a rigorous test of these recommended measures. Should these tests produce unreliable empirical affirmation, then the abandonment of academic integration seems warranted.

References

Allen, D. F. 1986. Attrition at a commuter institution: A path analytic validation of Tinto's theoretical model of college withdrawal. Paper presented at the meeting of the American College Personnel Association, Los Angeles, Calif.

Allen, D. F., and J. M. Nelson. 1989. Tinto's model of college withdrawal applied to women in two institutions. *Journal of Research and Development in Education* 22 (3): 1–11.

Bers, T. H., and K. E. Smith. 1991. Persistence of community college students: The influence of student intent and academic and social integration. *Research in Higher Education* 32 (5): 539–556.

Braxton, J. M., and E. M. Brier. 1989. Melding organizational and interactional theories of student attrition. *Review of Higher Education* 13 (1): 47–61.

Braxton, J. M., E. M. Brier, and D. Hossler. 1988. The influence of student problems on student withdrawal decisions: An autopsy on "Autopsy Studies." *Research in Higher Education* 28 (3): 241–253.

Braxton, J. M., M. Duster, and E. T. Pascarella. 1988. Causal modeling and path analysis: An introduction and an illustration in student attrition research. *Journal of College Student Development* 29: 263–272.

Braxton, J. M., A. S. Sullivan, and R. M. Johnson. 1997. Appraising Tinto's theory of college student departure. In J. C. Smart (ed.), *Higher education: A handbook of theory and research,* vol. 12, pp.107–164. New York: Agathon Press.

Braxton, J. M., N. Vesper, and D. Hossler. 1995. Expectations for college and student persistence. *Research in Higher Education* 36: 595–612.

Brower, A. M. 1992. The "second half" of student integration: The effects of life task predominance on student persistence. *Journal of Higher Education* 63 (4): 441–462.

Cabrera, A. F., M. B. Castañeda, A. Nora, and D. Hengstler. 1992. The convergence between two theories of college persistence. *Journal of Higher Education* 63 (2): 143–164.

Cabrera, A. F., A. Nora, and M. B. Castañeda. 1992. The role of finances in the persistence process: A structural model. *Research in Higher Education* 33 (5): 571– 593.

Cabrera, A. F., A. Nora, and M. B. Castañeda. 1993. College persistence: Structural equations modeling test of an integrated model of student retention. *Journal of Higher Education* 64 (2): 123–139.

Cabrera, A. F., J. O. Stampen, and W. L. Hansen. 1990. Exploring the effects of ability to pay on persistence in college. *Review of Higher Education* 13 (3): 303–336.

Cash, R. W., and H. L. Bissel. 1985. Testing Tinto's model of attrition on the church-related campus. Paper presented at the annual forum of the Association for Institutional Research, Portland, Oreg.

Donovan, R. 1984. Path analysis of a theoretical model of persistence in higher education among low-income black youth. *Research in Higher Education* 21 (3): 243–259.

Durkheim, E. 1951. *Suicide.* Translated by J. A. Spaulding and G. Simpson. Glencoe, Ill.: The Free Press. Originally published as *Le Suicide: Etude de Sociologie.* Paris: Felix Alcan, 1897.

Fox, R. N. 1986. Application of a conceptual model of college withdrawal to disadvantaged students. *American Educational Research Journal* 23 (3): 414–424.

Getzlaf, S. B., G. M. Sedlacek, K. A. Kearney, and J. M. Blackwell. 1984. Two types of voluntary undergraduate attrition: Application of Tinto's model. *Research in Higher Education* 20 (3): 257–268.

Grosset, J. M. 1991. Patterns of integration, commitment, and student characteristics and retention among younger and older students. *Research in Higher Education* 32 (2): 159–178.

Halpin, R. L. 1990. An application of the Tinto model to the analysis of freshman persistence in a community college. *Community College Review* 17 (4): 22–32.

Holland, J. L. 1985. *Making vocational choices.* 2d ed. Englewood Cliffs, N.J.: Prentice-Hall.

Hurtado, S., and D. F. Carter. 1997. Effects of college transition and perceptions of the campus racial climate on Latino college students' sense of belonging. *Sociology of Education* 70: 324–345.

Lazarsfeld, P. 1959. Problems in methodology. In R. K. Merton (ed.), *Sociology today.* New York: Basic Books.

Mallette, B. I., and A. F. Cabrera. 1991. Determinants of withdrawal behavior: An exploratory study. *Research in Higher Education* 32 (2): 179–194.

Milem, J. F., and J. B. Berger. 1997. A modified model of student persistence: Exploring the relationship between Astin's theory of involvement and Tinto's theory of student departure. *Journal of College Student Development* 38: 387–400.

Munro, B. H. 1981. Dropouts from higher education: Path analysis of a national sample. *American Educational Research Journal* 18 (2): 133–141.

Nora, A. 1987. Determinants of retention among Chicano college students: A structural model. *Research in Higher Education* 26 (1): 31–59.

Nora, A., and A. F. Cabrera. 1996. The role of perceptions of prejudice and discrimination on the adjustment of minority students to college. *Journal of Higher Education* 67 (2): 119–148.

Nora, A., L. C. Attinasi, and A. Matonak. 1990. Testing qualitative indicators of precollege factors in Tinto's attrition model: A community college student population. *Review of Higher Education* 13 (3): 337–355.

Pascarella, E. T. 1985. Racial differences in factors associated with bachelor's degree completion: A nine-year follow-up. *Research in Higher Education* 23 (4): 351–373.

Pascarella, E. T., and D. W. Chapman. 1983. A multi-institutional, path analytic validation of Tinto's model of college withdrawal. *American Educational Research Journal* 20 (1): 87–102.

Pascarella, E. T., and P. T. Terenzini. 1980. Predicting freshmen persistence and voluntary dropout decisions from a theoretical model. *Journal of Higher Education* 51 (1): 60–75.

Pascarella, E. T., and P. T. Terenzini. 1983. Predicting voluntary freshman year persistence/withdrawal behavior in a residential university: A path analytic validation of Tinto's model. *Journal of Educational Psychology* 75 (2): 215–226.

Pascarella, E. T., P. B. Duby, and B. K. Iverson. 1983. A test and reconceptualization of a theoretical model of college withdrawal in a commuter institution setting. *Sociology of Education* 56: 88–100.

Pascarella, E. T., J. C. Smart, and C. A. Ethington. 1986. Long-term persistence of two-year college students. *Research in Higher Education* 24 (1): 47–71.

Pascarella, E. T., P. T. Terenzini, and L. M. Wolfle. 1986. Orientations to college and freshman year persistence/withdrawal decisions. *Journal of Higher Education* 57 (2): 156–175.

Pavel, D. M. 1991. Assessing Tinto's model of institutional departure using American Indian and Alaskan native longitudinal data. Paper presented at the annual meeting of the Association for the Study of Higher Education, Boston.

Pike, G. R., C. C. Schroeder, and T. R. Berry. 1997. Enhancing the educational impact of residence halls: The relationship between residential learning communities and first-year college experiences and persistence. *Journal of College Student Development* 38 (6): 609–621.

Stage, F. K. 1988. University attrition: LISREL with logistic regression for the persistence criterion. *Research in Higher Education* 29 (4): 343–357.

Stage, F. K. 1989. Motivation, academic and social integration, and the early dropout. *American Educational Research Journal* 26 (3): 385–402.

Stoecker, J., E. T. Pascarella, and L. M. Wolfle. 1988. Persistence in higher education: A 9-year test of a theoretical model. *Journal of College Student Development* 29: 196–209.

Terenzini, P. T., and E. T. Pascarella. 1978. The relation of students' precollege characteristics and freshman year experience to voluntary attrition. *Research in Higher Education* 9: 347–366.

Terenzini, P. T., W. G. Lorang, and E. T. Pascarella. 1981. Predicting freshman persistence and voluntary dropout decisions: A replication. *Research in Higher Education* 15 (2): 109–127.

Terenzini, P. T., E. T. Pascarella, C. Theophilides, and W. G. Lorang. 1985. A replication of a path analytic validation of Tinto's theory of college student attrition. *Review of Higher Education* 8 (4): 319– 340.

Tinto, V. 1975. Dropout from higher education: A theoretical synthesis of recent research. *Review of Educational Research* 45: 89–125.

Tinto, V. 1993. *Leaving college: Rethinking the causes and cures of student attrition.* 2d ed. Chicago: University of Chicago Press.

Tinto, V. 1997. Classrooms as communities: Exploring the educational character of student persistence. *Journal of Higher Education* 68 (6): 599–623.

Williamson, D. R., and D. G. Creamer. 1988. Student attrition in 2– and 4–year colleges: Application of a theoretical model. *Journal of College Student Development* 29: 210–217.

Economic Influences on Persistence Reconsidered

How Can Finance Research Inform the Reconceptualization of Persistence Models?

Edward P. St. John, Alberto F. Cabrera, Amaury Nora, and Eric H. Asker

Financial assistance to college students increased from a meager $557 million in 1963–1964 (Lewis 1989) to a phenomenal $55.7 billion in 1996–1997 ("Average Cost of Tuition" 1997). Because of the enormity of this investment it is not surprising that a single policy question—How do prices and student subsidies influence the ability of students to persist?—has motivated much of the research on the economic aspects of persistence over three decades (St. John 1994). The economic studies examine how financial assistance equalized opportunities to persist in college for those students in need of financial support (St. John et al. 1994; Andrieu and St. John 1993; Astin 1975; Terkla 1985). However, because financial aid is not the only reason students persist in college (e.g., Stampen and Cabrera 1986, 1988), recently researchers have developed more complete models that seek to explain how finances interact with other factors that influence college persistence (e.g., Cabrera, Nora, and Castañeda 1993; St. John, Paulsen, and Starkey 1996). This recent line of inquiry can inform efforts to build a more complete understanding of the departure puzzle. In this chapter we first examine the evolution of economic models and then explore ways of integrating the logic of the new economic models into mainstream persistence research. We summarize by articulating a set of challenges facing persistence researchers.

The Evolution of Economic Models of Persistence

Research on factors believed to have an influence on college student persistence has been dominated by two distinct, yet overlapping, lines of inquiry: those studies that have focused on an economic perspective and
those that have based their investigative efforts along a student-institution
fit perspective. While both of these lines of inquiry address factors that
influence a student to stay in college, they do so through competing explanations. Academic and social collegiate experiences emerge as primary
determinants of persistence in studies that focus on student-institution fit
(Pascarella and Terenzini 1991), while financial need, student aid packaging, and adequacy of aid are of central concern in those studies that focus
on the economic perspective (Cabrera, Nora, and Castañeda 1992; Nora
and Horvath 1989; St. John, Paulsen, and Starkey 1996). Moreover, the
multiplicity of theoretical assumptions and conceptual frameworks has led
to the suggestions of a confusing array of intervention strategies. While financial aid from government and institutional sources supports access and
persistence in college (Wilcox 1991), enhancing the cognitive and affective development as they relate to student-departure decisions would be
stressed by those adhering to a student-institution fit model. Clearly, a better understanding of factors impacting student persistence in college
emerges when both of these lines of conceptualization inquiry are considered.

The Economic Approach

Reliance on price-response theories and their allied theory of targeted
subsidies is evident in research bringing about an economic approach to
the investigation of student persistence (e.g., Manski and Wise 1983; St.
John 1990; St. John, Kirshstein, and Noell 1991; Stampen and Cabrera
1986, 1988). Essentially, price-response theories focus in part on economic factors whereby the social and economic benefits of attending college are believed to outweigh any costs and benefits associated with
alternative activities (e.g., working full-time). A critical component in
these cost/benefit analyses is the student's perception of his or her ability
(or inability) to pay for college (Becker 1964). While price-response theories provide a conceptual foundation for examining persistence, the theory of targeted subsidies suggests that the means to influence such
behavior is through subsidies targeted at specific groups based on their

ability to pay. Reduced tuition, direct grants, low-interest loans, and subsidized work-study programs all seek to equalize students on their ability to pay for college education and to increase the benefits derived from attending college (Bowen 1977; Cabrera, Stampen, and Hansen 1990). This line of research has focused on the overall effect of financial aid on persistence (e.g., Astin 1975; Murdock 1987; Stampen and Cabrera 1986, 1988); the sensitivity of persistence decisions to charges along with tuition reduction, grants, loans, and work-study awards (e.g., Astin 1975; Nora 1990; St. John 1990, 1994; St. John, Kirshstein, and Noell 1991; Voorhees 1985); and the effectiveness of particular student aid packages in the retention of minorities (e.g., Astin 1975; Olivas 1985; Nora 1990; Nora and Horvath 1989; St. John 1990). These studies focus on actual effects of student aid rather than on perceptions of aid adequacy or the adequacy of aid relative to college costs.

However, economic studies provide an incomplete view of the true nature of financial influences on persistence in college, compared to recent integrative models. They focus on the influence of aid, along with the factors that need to be controlled to assess this effect, rather than attempting to construct a logical model that assesses interactions among all of the important factors that influence persistence. Two circumstances have handicapped this line of inquiry: methodological problems and shortcomings in the conceptualization of the persistence phenomenon.

First, some of the early economic studies on persistence were primarily impact-oriented (Cabrera, Stampen, and Hansen 1990; Nora 1990; Vorhees 1985).* While they took into account such important predictors of persistence as precollege motivational factors, precollege academic ability and achievement, demographic factors, students' socioeconomic status, and college performance, they did so with the purpose of controlling for sources of variance that substantially interact with the direct effects of prices and subsidies. The emphasis was on ascertaining the direct effects of financial aid on persistence, not the effects of noneconomic factors. This approach was limited in that it did not address the ways financial circumstances interacted with other factors in a manner more complex than would be evident from a measure of direct effect.

* Other researchers attempted to integrate variables related to commitments and college experiences (e.g., Andrieu and St. John 1993; St. John et al. 1994). This line of research provided the foundation for the nexus model (St. John, Paulsen, and Starkey 1996) discussed below.

Second, the economic-impact approach underestimated the role that the institution plays in shaping persistence decisions. Factors such as student-support systems, interaction with faculty, and affective outcomes associated with college, while known to play a role (Pascarella and Terenzini 1991), were seldom sufficiently considered in economic-impact studies. Indeed the extant data sets typically used in this research usually do not include variables related to some of these forces. Further, to address the question of fit, which is important from an institutional perspective, most persistence researchers conducted supplemental surveys.

Student-Institution Fit Approach

Research utilizing this approach views persistence decisions as the end product of a successful match between a student and his or her academic and social environment in a higher-education setting (Bean 1980; Spady 1970, 1971; Tinto 1987, 1993). Experiences with the academic and social realms of an institution are seen as playing a key role in the cognitive and affective development of the student. In turn, these developmental changes are presumed to affect a student's commitments to an institution and to college completion. The stronger these commitments are, the greater the probability that a student will remain enrolled in college (Tinto 1987, 1993).

With the exception of Bean (1982), the early proponents of this approach did not incorporate finances as an independent variable. The underlying assumption was that personal or family finances were important only in helping to shape students' educational aspirations and their subsequent selection of institutions. In other words, once students enrolled in college, finances were disregarded as instrumental in playing a role in persistence decisions (Tinto 1987). The implicit assumption being made was that financial need was met.

In 1993 Tinto revisited his student integration model and included student finances as a key component in the adjustment of the student to college. Such a revision, while consistent with the mounting evidence highlighting the role of financial aid on persistence (e.g., Cabrera, Nora, and Castañeda 1992; Olivas 1985; Stampen and Cabrera 1986, 1988; Murdock 1987; Nora 1990; St. John 1989; St. John, Kirshstein, and Noell 1991; Voorhees 1985), did not substantially influence subsequent research. Most of the persistence research using the institutional-fit model continued to disregard finances (Braxton, Sullivan, and Johnson 1997). Below we review integrative studies that are an exception to this pattern of ignoring the crucial role of finances.

Integrative Approaches

Efforts at integrating both lines of research have followed two paths. Early studies by Voorhees (1985), Moline (1987), and Nora (1990) sought to explore the interconnections between financial aid and other variables (e.g., student grades) found to have an effect on student persistence. Later approaches, such as the ability-to-pay model (Cabrera, Stampen, and Hansen 1990; Cabrera, Nora, and Castañeda 1992) and the college choice–persistence nexus model (St. John, Paulsen, and Starkey 1996), have attempted to clarify the process by which ability to pay and financial aid are interrelated with collegiate experiences and the reenrollment decisions of students. Relying on path analysis, structural equation modeling, and sequential logistic regressions, the major thrust of this approach has been to uncover the interconnections that link financial factors and nonfinancial factors as much as documenting the direct and indirect effects of finances on persistence decisions.

The Early Integrative Models

In 1985 Voorhees examined the association between federal campus-based aid programs and the persistence of high-need first-year college students. His model of persistence reflected withdrawal decisions as the by-product of a two-stage process whereby financial resources that students bring to college, students' demographic characteristics, and academic ability would determine the type of campus-based financial aid programs granted, their academic performance in college, and, ultimately, persistence. Moline (1987), while examining persistence decisions among students also enrolled in a commuter institution, found that merit aid exerted an indirect effect on students' departure through the academic performance of students. Nora (1990) examined the effect of campus-based resources on the retention of Chicano community college students. Nora's model approached persistence decisions as a three-stage process involving the academic ability of students as they entered college, the financial need of those students, different forms of campus-based financial aid, and the academic performance of students during their first year in college. His model also explained three-quarters of the variance in the persistence process and highlighted the complex interplay among financial aid (both campus- and non-campus-based) and the academic performance of students.

While the notion of examining the process involved in the withdrawal of students from college furthered research on finances (the economic perspective) by stressing the need for a simultaneous analysis of numerous constructs, a common problem of this early research was not addressed; the adjustment of students to college in the persistence process was totally disregarded. For example, current institutional commitments were omitted. Nora and Horvath (1989), as well as Stampen and Cabrera (1986), noted that the role of finances in the adjustment process needed to be explicitly examined from both conceptual and empirical bases.

The Ability-to-Pay Model

Cabrera, Stampen, and Hansen (1990) also argued that a more comprehensive view of college persistence could be secured by merging economic theory with persistence theory. They reasoned that researchers should disentangle the indirect and direct effects of finances from intellectual and nonintellectual factors related to collegiate experiences. Building upon educational attainment theory, organizational theory, cost/benefit theory, and institution-student fit theory, the model they advanced portrayed persistence as the product of a complex longitudinal process involving the interaction between the student and the institution. While acknowledging that prior academic skills, positive interactions with faculty and peers, as well as goals and institutional commitments are key for explaining persistence, they also recognized that such factors as encouragement and support from significant others and ability to pay could moderate the adjustment of the student with the institution. In this context they postulated that ability to pay was a precondition for the attainment of the cognitive and noncognitive outcomes, due to its role in removing or reducing a student's barriers to participate in the college academic and social dimensions of the institution while freeing such a student of the need to work long hours and from financial concern. Testing the model on a sample of college students drawn from the National Center for Educational Statistics (NCES) High School and Beyond 1980 Senior Cohort, Cabrera, Stampen, and Hansen (1990) found that adding college-related variables increased the proportion of variance explained over and above a model that presumed that persistence was primarily affected by economic factors (22.9 percent vs. 14.1 percent). They also found that finances, while having a direct effect on persistence decisions, moderated the effects of goal commitments. In short, students satisfied with their ability to pay for college had higher aspirations and higher chances to persist in college than their less-satisfied and lower-motivated counterparts.

Then Cabrera et al. (1992) postulated that finances could have a dual role in the persistence of college students, as a refinement to the ability-to-pay model. Finances were believed to increase the chances of persistence to graduation because of their role in increasing cost-related benefits while at the same time facilitating the social and academic integration of the student on campus. The researchers also argued that finances were comprised of two dimensions: an objective component, reflecting a student's availability of resources; and a subjective or intangible component that underscored a student's self-perceptions of ability to finance college-related expenses. They considered that the reception of financial aid could be a more reliable indicator of a student's ability to pay than his/her socioeconomic status. Cabrera et al. (1992) approached persistence as a complex process linking experiences with the institution, cognitive and affective changes resulting from collegiate experiences, a student's commitments to the institution and to the goal of college completion, his/her intent to persist at the institution, perceptions of finances, and the extent to which the student felt encouraged and supported by friends and family.

As a whole, results supported the proposition that persistence decisions underscore a process among cognitive and affective variables as well as financial-related factors. While financial aid was found to exert only indirect effects on persistence decisions, the total effect of this variable ranked third among all the constructs in the model. The results, however, emphasized the indirect nature of the role of finances on the adjustment of students to college. Receiving some form of financial aid facilitated a student's interactions with peers. Financial aid was also found to enhance the student's academic performance in college while increasing intent to persist. Being satisfied with one's ability to pay for college, on the other hand, facilitated the student's academic and intellectual development in college. While highlighting the indirect nature of finances, the study also emphasized that decisions to persist are the result of a complex process in which finances, however important, were but one of the many factors that played a role.

The College Choice–Persistence Nexus Model

Similar to other recent models (e.g., Cabrera et al. 1992; St. John et al. 1994), the nexus model (St. John, Paulsen, and Starkey 1996) reflected the need to merge the economic perspective with the student-institution fit perspective.* However, St. John, Paulsen, and Starkey (1996) noted that efforts at integrating both perspectives had failed to incorporate a major component in the enrollment-persistence process: namely, the decision-making process in selecting a college (i.e., a student's college-choice phase) (Hossler, Braxton, and Coopersmith 1989). The omission of this component led to creating an "artificial" and isolated endeavor rather than being part of a continuous and interconnected student decision process. To compensate for this deficiency in earlier models, St. John and colleagues formulated a model that articulated a nexus between college choice and persistence, while at the same time clarifying the role that financial aid–related factors exert in student matriculation to and persistence in college.

The nexus model hypothesized that persistence was shaped through a three-stage process. In the first stage socioeconomic factors as well as academic ability were believed to affect a student's predisposition to pursue a college education and perceptions of financial circumstances. During the second stage the student estimated the benefits and costs associated with a particular institution that would induce the student to develop an initial commitment to enroll in college and further affect the decision to remain in college. Within this context, financial aid would not only positively influence thoughts of matriculation but would also predispose the student to select a particular institution. Once the student entered college (the third stage), college characteristics (e.g., the type of college attended), collegiate experiences, and academic performance in college helped modify or reinforce educational aspirations. Positive social and academic experiences in college and an adequate academic performance reinforced or even enhanced the student's perceptions of economic and noneconomic benefits associated with enrollment in and graduation from the institution. Financial aid was believed to positively affect persistence decisions by maintaining an equilibrium between the cost of attending college and the benefits to be derived from the attainment of an educational degree. Negative college experiences, such as increases in tuition, affected the benefits/cost equilibrium and pushed the student toward withdrawal.

---

* St. John et al. (1994) merged the two perspectives by treating aspirations as an indicator of initial commitment and incorporating detailed information on college characteristics and experiences as being logically related to integration processes. The nexus model further adapted this approach.

St. John, Paulsen, and Starkey (1996) established support for the proposition that there existed a nexus between a student's college-choice stage and that student's subsequent persistence in college. They also reported that by incorporating college choice, along with college-experience variables included in the base model (St. John et al. 1994), the new choice-related variables modestly increased the proportion of variance explained. The nexus model revealed that financial factors were found to exert effects on both college choice and persistence in college. However, about half the total variance in this persistence process was explained by tuition, student financial aid, food and travel, housing, and other living costs. In addition, a follow-up study using the nexus model found that the direct effect of financial variables explained about half of the variance in persistence by students in both public and private colleges (Paulsen and St. John 1997).

New Understandings

Though differing in conceptualizations, unit of analysis (national cohorts vs. institutional cohorts), methodologies (logistic regression vs. linear structural equation modeling), and databases used, the integrative efforts by the nexus and the ability-to-pay models converge in reaching two major conclusions regarding finances. We state these as new understandings that can inform future research efforts.

First, both models substantiate the fact that a student's finances are comprised of tangible and intangible factors. The tangible element includes indicators of a student's ability to afford college-related costs—e.g., personal savings, reception of financial aid, financial-aid packaging (Cabrera, Stampen, and Hansen 1990; Cabrera, Nora, and Castañeda 1992, 1993; St. John 1994; St. John, Paulsen, and Starkey 1996). The second component of a student's finances is more psychological in nature; it embodies the student's perceptions regarding her/his financial circumstances. Integrative efforts also concur in depicting these perceptions as being cognitive and affective in nature. The cognitive strand represents calculations by which the student ponders the value of attending college against its costs. Satisfaction with cost of attendance, the affective component, is the outcome of this cognitive process. To be satisfied with the cost of attending means the student believes that the benefits of attending a particular institution outweigh its costs (Cabrera, Stampen, and Hansen 1990; Cabrera, Nora, and Castañeda 1992, 1993; St. John 1994; St. John, Paulsen, and Starkey 1996). Integrative efforts also concur in viewing satisfaction with finances as a dynamic process. Since satisfaction is closely associated with a delicate balance between perceived costs and benefits, it then follows that any factor affecting any component of the cost/benefit equation can trigger major changes in the correlated attitude. In the nexus model (St. John, Paulsen, and Starkey 1996), for instance, changes in the composition of the original student-aid package or unexpected increases in tuition and fees are seen to lead to dissatisfaction by the effect these changes have on the original cost/benefit computations. In the ability to pay model, another major source of change is played by those individuals who exert a significant role in the life of the student (Nora 1990; Cabrera, Stampen, and Hansen 1990; Cabrera, Nora, and Castañeda 1992, 1993). Both approaches support the proposition that the student can modify her/his original cost/benefit estimates as new significant people enter her/his life or when the original significant others revalue the benefits attached to a particular institution.

Second, these efforts concluded that finances exert both direct and indirect effects on persistence. While both the nexus and the ability-to-pay models have substantiated this connection empirically, they have provided little grounded discussion for this interconnection. Such a frame of reference, however, can be found in Maslow's (1954) motivation theory. Maslow argues that individuals evolve when they are driven to satisfy such higher-order needs as self-esteem and self-actualization. The pursuit of a college degree and a concurrent intellectual development clearly fit within Maslow's higher-order taxonomy. For Maslow, the desire to satisfy higher-order needs can only take place once basic needs are satisfied. With regard to the student-institution fit model, the meeting of tangible and intangible financial needs provides the freedom to engage in and establish relationships with faculty and peers, to actively participate in classroom activities, and to commit enough time to all those endeavors that promote intellectual development. According to Maslow, dissatisfaction of basic needs can lead to stagnation and even regression to earlier developmental stages. For Maslow, these basic needs become prepotent; that is, they dominate an individual's life, diverting all efforts and thoughts to the satisfaction of those primary needs. Extending the Maslow concept of prepotency to integrative efforts portrays a situation where a student's pursuit of cognitive and affective development can be redirected when financial needs are no longer met. Financial need then becomes a psychological stressor compelling the student to divert his/her attention from academic endeavors to monetary concerns. If financial circumstances remain as such, the student is pulled away from the academic and social domains of the institution to pursue alternative activities (e.g., working, obsessing over financial problems).

Integrating Financial Variables into Student-Institution Fit Models

In their review of the research that has tested Tinto's student integration model, Braxton, Sullivan, and Johnson (1997) not only document the validity of the relationship among college-related variables but also stress that incorporation of financial variables in the student integration model is wanting. Our review of those efforts that integrate finances into models of student departure (Cabrera, Stampen, and Hansen 1990; Cabrera, Nora, and Castañeda 1992, 1993; St. John, Paulsen, and Starkey 1996) provides empirical evidence that this emerging approach offers the means to conceptualize the role of finances both in the adjustment to college and in persistence decisions. Below we explore ways the new understandings reached from these integrative studies can inform future efforts to refine and reconceptualize persistence models.

The Influence of Perceptions of Finances to Institutional Commitment

Research that focuses on the interactions between financial variables and the social and academic integration processes essentially treats perceptions of aid as integral to the formation of commitments. Cabrera et al. (1992) conducted a survey that asked students about the adequacy of their aid, receiving perceptual responses. Further, these perceptions of the ability to pay represented an aspect of the initial commitment students made to their college. In their nexus model St. John, Paulsen, and Starkey (1996) distinguished between the financial reasons for choosing a college and the actual prices and price subsidies students received. They treated these initial calculations about college affordability (e.g., choosing a college because of low tuition, high aid, proximity to home, or opportunity to work) as an integral part of the initial commitment process. Both these lines of inquiry clearly indicate that the early judgments students make about their financial circumstances influence the initial commitments they make to their institutions.

This research illustrates two ways of constructing variables related to perceptions about aid by considering: (1) whether students' decisions to enroll in the fall were influenced by high aid, low tuition, or other cost-related factors (the nexus approach); or (2) whether students thought their financial support was adequate, given the costs of attending (the integrated approach). Both of these approaches to constructing variables relate to perceptions of finance and provide insights that relate to, or take place at the same time as, the initial institutional commitments that are made to attend. There is a slightly different logic related to entering both types of variables into an integrated model.

The nexus model also offers a way of reconceptualizing the conceptual underpinning of initial commitment variables typically included in persistence research. Rather than treating initial commitment as a single variable with a scale, the model suggests identifying three sets of variables related to initial commitments that are integral to the college choice process and that, by extension, can have an influence on subsequent experiences in the persistence process. In other words, the college choice–persistence nexus provides an alternative way of conceptualizing how students make their initial commitments. The research clearly demonstrates that financial commitments are based on an understanding of the financial circumstances—including the ability to pay for college, as well as the ability to earn money for this purpose—and are not only part of this initial cost/benefit decision but also integral to the formation of initial institutional commitments.

The Influence of Perceptions on Social and Academic Integration

The initial financial commitments students make—in the form of finance-related reasons for choosing to attend a college as well as their perceptions of their ability to pay—have an influence on subsequent integration processes. The logic of the integrated model (Cabrera, Nora, and Castañeda 1993) argues that financial attitudes can directly influence the social and academic integration processes. In their research Cabrera, Nora, and Castañeda (1992, 1993) have documented that their question about finances had a direct influence on academic integration and college grades. Their study suggests that if students do not have sufficient resources, their academic work suffers. The underlying question addressed when this approach is used differs fundamentally from the questions that most economic analysts have been concerned with when they investigate the adequacy of student aid. Economic analyses assess whether subsidies are adequate to support students through the academic year (St. John et al. 1994; St. John 1999). However, students' perceptions of adequacy are also important because their perceptions influence commitments and integration processes. If students feel their aid is inadequate, then they may take fewer courses or find work off campus, behaviors that could limit opportunities for social and academic integration.

Thus, the integrated model (Cabrera, Nora, and Castañeda 1993) provides a complete approach for systematically examining the relationship between perceptions of financial circumstance on social and academic integration processes. By focusing on this set of interactions, researchers can discern how perceptions of the adequacy of student aid influence ways students interact in their academic environments, e.g., whether the time they have for informal interactions with faculty is influenced. However, this line of research does not incorporate information on the types and amounts of aid students actually were awarded or on actual family resources, data elements necessary to assess the direct effects of student aid.

The logic of the nexus approach argues that the initial commitments students make are of a specific nature: students reconsider the specific academic, social, and financial reasons they selected their colleges when they make their eventual persistence decisions. Paulsen and St. John (1997) and St. John, Paulsen, and Starkey (1996) identify three possible linkage structures: (1) from the financial reasons for choosing a college to the eventual experience of college affordability; (2) from the academic reasons for choosing a college to the eventual academic integration process; and (3) from the social reasons for choosing a college to the social integration process. Research to date verifies the financial nexus. These studies have found that the financial reasons for choosing to attend did interact with variables related to the college experience, including achievement in college (Paulsen and St. John 1997; St. John, Paulsen, and Starkey 1996). However, the logic of the other two approaches to examining the college choice–persistence nexus has not been explicitly examined and merits examination.

Thus, the nexus approach provides a second proven approach to integrating perceptions of finances into a complete persistence model. Further, the nexus model provides a way of examining how students' perceptions of affordability—including perceptions of tuition, work, and living costs, as well as perceptions of student aid—influence their integration processes and their subsequent cost/benefit calculations about persistence (i.e., commitments at the time the departure decision is made). The model also reveals that changes over time in financial-aid packages can influence students' academic and social integration processes, as well as their subsequent persistence decisions.

The Crucial Direct Effects of Aid and Tuition

There has long been a debate within the community of persistence researchers about whether finances actually influence persistence. Initially

Tinto (1987) argued that if students said they were leaving college for financial reasons, it could be an excuse for other reasons, possibly a change in commitments. Such a claim could be true if a student truly had adequate resources to complete college. If students received adequate student aid, a condition that existed in many colleges in the 1970s because of generous federal financial aid, then such a statement could have valid logic. However, research that tested this proposition on students enrolled in the 1980s consistently found that aid was not adequate (Paulsen and St. John 1997; St. John, Oescher, and Andrieu 1992; St. John et al. 1994; St. John, Paulsen, and Starkey 1996; St. John and Starkey 1995a, 1995b). Indeed, in national studies finance-related factors (student aid, tuition, and other costs, including living) explained about half of the total variance in the persistence process (Paulsen and St. John 1997; St. John, Paulsen, and Starkey 1996). Therefore it seems naive to overlook the direct effects of financial variables based on a self-sealing assumption such as: *if* students say they withdraw because of finances, *then* they are making polite excuses for changes in commitment.

If researchers who have access to information on family income and aid awards actually build appropriate controls for these factors into their persistence models, then they can assess the direct effects of aid. If they control for family income in a multi-institution study or in a study of a campus with differentiated tuition charges, then it is also possible to assess the effects of the tuition charges as well as aid subsidies. However, it is not logical to assume that influences on academic or social integration processes will influence the amount or type of aid awarded. Rather, aid awards are made based on certain criteria, which is why high school achievement and family income should be included in models that assess the effects of amounts of aid. Therefore, it is appropriate to treat student costs and subsidies as variables that directly influence withdrawal.

It is especially important to include income from aid applications because students do not accurately report parental income in response to surveys (Byce and Schmitt 1993). Recent research that includes this type of control has proven empirically that significant and negative coefficients for an aid variable indicate aid is inadequate and that a neutral and/or positive coefficient indicates aid is adequate (St. John forthcoming; St. John, Paulsen, and Starkey 1996). Thus, there are logical and empirical reasons to examine the direct effects of student aid, especially when researchers can attain accurate information on family finances and student aid awards.

Future Research

The review of the evolution of efforts to integrate economic variables into the student-institutional fit models frequently used to investigate student departure has illuminated three ways of integrating financial variables into persistence models. More important, it has been revealed that students' perceptions of their ability to pay are integral to the commitments students make to their institutions and, thus, need to be included for multiple logical reasons.

First, persistence researchers who work within the boundaries of the student-institutional fit model should consider the influence of the ability to pay (Bean 1982; Cabrera, Nora, and Castañeda 1992, 1993). Clearly students' perceptions of their ability to pay can influence their academic performance and the extent and nature of their academic integration (Cabrera, Nora, and Castañeda 1992, 1993). Further, it is relatively easy to modify the data-collection instruments used in these integration models to include questions about perceptions of affordability. Thus, such refinements to the student-institutional fit models are both desirable conceptually and feasible.

Second, the nexus approach merits consideration by researchers who are interested in reconceptualizing the initial commitment process and the ways this process influences the college experience (inclusive of variables typically treated as social- and academic-integration processes). The initial commitments students make to colleges and universities are really comprised of a set of judgments about affordability, academic opportunities, and potential social interactions. Research that has explored the financial aspect of this early commitment has found that student perceptions about affordability interact with their college experiences (St. John, Paulsen, and Starkey 1996) and their integration processes (Cabrera, Nora, and Castañeda 1993). More researchers should begin to explore the role of the financial nexus in the persistence process because it is linked to the basic financial commitments colleges and students make to each other in the recruitment process (Paulsen and St. John 1997).

However, more research is needed to assess the influence of choosing colleges for academic and social reasons on the college experiences and (social and academic) integration processes. The need for research on the nexus between college choice and persistence can be illustrated by several examples. First, consider the student who chose a private college for a middle-class-earning major (e.g., education) but is confronted by larger-than-expected debt. She may feel it is necessary to change to a higher-earning major or transfer to a less expensive college in order to complete the major she intended. Second, consider the student in the same college who had hopes of getting into a preferred major as an upper-division student but was unable to do so. She would be confronted by a decision to persist with another major or to change colleges to follow her interest. Financial perceptions are part of the choice process in the first instance; but they are not in the second case. Clearly, in order to untangle these types of interactions in persistence research it is necessary to include, along with finance-related reasons for choosing certain institutions, a variable related to choosing colleges based on specific majors.

Third, including variables related to actual family resources, tuition, and student aid awards is necessary in comprehensive persistence models. Research on the college choice–persistence nexus indicates no interaction between current postsecondary aspirations and finance-related variables (St. John et al. 1994; St. John, Paulsen, and Starkey 1996). In other words, students who leave college often still aspire to complete their college degrees, but their institutional commitments have changed by virtue of their decision to drop out. Thus, while affordability does influence institutional commitments through student perceptions, prices and financial aid also exert a large direct effect.

Research on the direct effects of student aid on persistence is especially important in colleges and universities with large percentages of low-income and adult students, since they are more price sensitive than traditional undergraduates (St. John and Starkey 1995a, 1995b). However, it is necessary to control for income to measure the direct effects of student aid. Therefore, if appropriate controls are included, it is possible to assess the adequacy of student aid. This means that researchers will need to integrate information from student aid applications. A workable approach for this type of analysis has been proposed (St. John 1992) and tested (St. John forthcoming; Somers 1992). Given the decline in federal grants, it is increasingly important for financial planners to know when aid is not adequate. Therefore, the economic impact approach should not be abandoned in efforts to build more complete models.

References

Alexander, K., and B. Eckland. 1978. Basic attainment processes: A recapitalization and expansion. *Sociology of Education* 48: 457–495.

Andrieu, S. C., and E. P. St. John. 1993. The influence of prices on graduate student persistence. *Research in Higher Education* 34 (4): 399–419.

Astin, A. W. 1975. *Preventing students from dropping out.* San Francisco: Jossey-Bass.

Average cost of tuition is up 5 percent for 1997–98: Study by the College Board finds increases at 4–year colleges than at 2–year institutions. 1997. *The Chronicle of Higher Education,* October 3, pp. A49–A54.

Bean, J. 1982. Student attrition, intentions and confidence: Interaction effects in a path model. *Research in Higher Education* 14: 425–429.

Bean, J. 1980. Dropouts and turnover: The synthesis and test of a causal model of student attrition. *Research in Higher Education* 55: 485–540.

Becker, G. S. 1964. *Human capital: A theoretical and empirical analysis with special reference to education.* New York: National Bureau of Economic Research.

Bowen, H. R. 1977. *Investing in learning: The individual and social value of American higher education.* San Francisco: Jossey-Bass.

Braxton, J. M., A. V. S. Sullivan, and R. M. Johnson. 1997. Appraising Tinto's theory of college student departure. In J. C. Smart (ed.), *Higher Education: A handbook of theory and research,* vol. 12, pp. 107–164. New York: Agathon Press.

Byce, C., and C. Schmitt. 1993. *Quality of responses in the 1987 National Postsecondary Student Aid Study.* NCES-93–446. Washington, D.C.: Office of Educational Research and Improvement, U.S. Department of Education.

Cabrera, A. F., A. Nora, and M. B. Castañeda. 1992. The role of finances in the persistence process: A structural model. *Research in Higher Education* 33 (5): 571–593.

Cabrera, A. F., A. Nora, and M. B. Castañeda. 1993. College persistence: Structural equations modeling test of an integrated model of student retention. *Journal of Higher Education* 64 (2): 123–139.

Cabrera, A. F., J. O. Stampen, and W. L. Hansen. 1990. Exploring the effects of ability to pay on persistence in college. *Review of Higher Education* 13 (3): 303–336.

Cabrera, A. F., M. B. Castañeda, A. Nora, and D. Hengstler. 1992. The convergence between two theories of college persistence. *Journal of Higher Education* 63 (2): 143–164.

Clagett, C. 1992. Enrollment management. In M. A. Whiteley, J. D. Porter, and R. A. Fenske (eds.), *The primer for institutional research,* pp. 12–24. Washington, D.C.: Association for Institutional Research.

Hossler, D., J. Braxton, and G. Coopersmith. 1989. Understanding student choice. In J. C. Smart (ed.), *Higher education: A handbook of theory and research,* vol. 5, pp. 231–288. New York: Agathon Press.

Lewis, G. L. 1989. Trends in student aid. 1963–64 to 1988–89. *Research in Higher Education* 30: 547–562.

Manski, C. F., and D. A. Wise. 1983. *College choice in America.* Cambridge, Mass.: Harvard University Press.

Maslow, A. H. 1954. *Motivation and personality.* New York: Harper & Row.

Moline, A. E. 1987. Financial aid and student persistence: An application of causal modeling. *Research in Higher Education* 26 (2): 130–147.

Murdock, T. A. 1987. It isn't just money: The effects of financial aid on student persistence. *Review of Higher Education* 11 (1): 75–101.

Nora, A. 1990. Campus-based programs as determinants of retention among Chicano college students. *Journal of Higher Education* 61 (3): 312–331.

Nora, A., and F. Horvath. 1989. Financial assistance: Minority enrollments and persistence. *Education and Urban Society* 21 (3): 299–309.

Olivas, M. A. 1985. Financial aid packaging policies: Access and ideology. *Journal of Higher Education* 56: 462–475.

Pascarella, E. T., and P. T. Terenzini. 1991. *How college affects students: Findings and insights from twenty years of research.* San Francisco: Jossey-Bass.

Paulsen, M. B., and E. P. St. John. 1997. The financial nexus between college choice and persistence. In R. A. Vorhees (ed.), *Researching student aid: Creating an action agenda,* pp. 65–82. New Directions in Institutional Research, no. 95. San Francisco: Jossey-Bass.

St. John, E. P. 1989. The influence of student aid on persistence. *Journal of Student Financial Aid* 19 (3): 52–68.

St. John, E. P. 1990. Price response in enrollment divisions: An analysis of the high school and beyond sophomore cohort. *Research in Higher Education* 31: 161–176.

St. John, E. P. 1992. Workable models for institutional research on the impact of student financial aid. *Journal of Student Financial Aid* 22 (3): 13–26.

St. John, E. P. 1994. *Prices, productivity, and investment: Assessing financial strategies in higher education.* ASHE-ERIC Higher Education Reports (1994 Report Three). Washington, D.C.: George Washington University.

St. John, E. P. 1999. Evaluating state grant programs: A case study. *Research in Higher Education* 40: 149–170.

St. John, E. P., and S. Andrieu. 1995. The influence of price subsidies on within-year persistence by graduate students. *Higher Education* 29: 143–168.

St. John , E. P., and J. B. Starkey. 1995a. An alternative to net price: Assessing the influence of prices and subsidies on within-year persistence. *Journal of Higher Education* 66 (2): 156–186.

St. John, E. P., and J. B. Starkey. 1995b. The influence of prices on the persistence of adult undergraduates. *Journal of Student Financial Aid* 25 (2): 7–17.

St. John, E. P., R. Kirshstein, and J. Noell. 1991. The effects of student aid on persistence: A sequential analysis of the High School and Beyond Senior Cohort. *Review of Higher Education* 14 (3): 383–406.

St. John, E. P., J. Oescher, and S. C. Andrieu. 1992. The influence of prices on within-year persistence by traditional college-age students in four-year colleges. *Journal of Student Financial Aid* 22 (1): 27–38.

St. John, E. P., M. B. Paulsen, and J. B. Starkey. 1996. The nexus between college choice and persistence. *Research in Higher Education* 37 (2): 175–220.

St. John, E. P., S. C. Andrieu, J. Oescher, and J. B. Starkey. 1994. The influence of student aid on persistence by traditional college-age students in four-year colleges. *Research in Higher Education* 35 (4): 455–480.

Somers, P. 1992. A dynamic analysis of student matriculation decisions in urban public universities. Ph.D. diss., University of New Orleans.

Spady, W. 1970. Dropouts from higher education: An interdisciplinary review and synthesis. *Interchange* 1: 64–85.

Spady, W. 1971. Dropouts from higher education: Toward an empirical model. *Interchange* 2: 38–62.

Stage, F. K., and D. Hossler. 1989. Differences in family influences on college attendance plans for male and female ninth graders. *Research in Higher Education* 30 (3): 301–315.

Stampen, J. O., and A. F. Cabrera. 1986. Exploring the effects of student aid on attrition. *Journal of Student Financial Aid* 16: 28–37.

Stampen, J. O., and A. F. Cabrera. 1988. Is the student aid system achieving its objectives? Evidence on targeting and attrition. *Economics of Education Review* 7: 29–46.

Terkla, D. G. 1985. Does financial aid enhance undergraduate persistence? *Journal of Student Financial Aid* 15 (3): 11–18.

Tinto, V. 1975. Dropout from higher education: A theoretical synthesis of recent research. *Review of Educational Research* 45: 89–125.

Tinto, V. 1987. *Leaving College: Rethinking the Causes and Cures of Student Attrition.* Chicago, Ill. University of Chicago Press.

Tinto, V. 1993. *Leaving college: Rethinking the causes and cures of student attrition.* 2d ed. Chicago: University of Chicago Press. (1st ed., 1987).

Voorhees, R. A. 1985. Financial aid and persistence: Do the federal campus-based aid programs make a difference? *Journal of Student Aid* 15: 21–30.

Wilcox, L. 1991. Evaluating the impact of financial aid on student recruitment and retention. In D. Hossler (ed.), *Evaluating student recruitment and retention programs,* pp. 47–60. New Directions for Institutional Research, no. 70. San Francisco: Jossey-Bass.

A Psychological Model of College Student Retention

John P. Bean and Shevawn Bogdan Eaton

Perhaps because William Spady (1970) and Vincent Tinto (1975, 1987) were sociologists and their work was widely influential, readers and researchers have relied on sociological theories to explain why students leave college. The decision to depart from college can also be understood in terms of psychological theories and processes. We hope to show in this chapter how researchers can shift the basis of their research from sociological to psychological explanations of withdrawal decisions.

Pascarella and Terenzini (1991) state, "Developmental theories and the research based on them suggest that other important student traits may be overlooked if the perspective is strictly sociological" (p. 58). Psychological theories have only played a tangential role in research influenced by Tinto's model. For example, while guided by Tinto, several authors expanded the model: Stage (1989) added motivation; Peterson (1993) added self-efficacy; and Brower (1992) added life task constructions from cognitive psychology. Bean's (1982a) synthetic model and Eaton and Bean's (1995) approach/avoidance model are two attempts to integrate psychological theory into retention modeling.

Psychological approaches to the study of student retention have been proffered, but a consistent psychological approach to retention has not been developed. In this chapter we have two main objectives. First, we present four psychological theories that help explain student departure from college. Second, we hope to synthesize these theories into a heuristic psychological model of student retention.

Psychological Theories That Can Inform Retention/ Departure Model Development

Our assumption in developing this model is that the factor in question, leaving college, is a behavior and that behavior is psychologically motivated. The purpose of our model is to describe the factors associated with leaving (the content of the model) and the psychological activities associated with leaving (the processes that explain why a student leaves).

Here we are making a distinction between the actual variables included in a study (the content) and why those variables should be in the given configuration (the process). For example, institutional fit is part of the content of the model. The fact that institutional fit leads to intent to leave, which in turn leads to persistence reflects a theoretical process linking variables. When estimating the model statistically, a content concern is to find variables that best explain the variance in persistence, or the R-squared. A process concern is to discover if the variables in the model are associated with others according to theoretical expectations that are reflected in the regression coefficients. The process of the model (theory) can remain stable while the particular variables included in a study (content) can vary. In the psychological model of student retention developed here, our primary purpose is to provide theoretical explanations for why certain factors affect others.

Explaining behavior is an enormously complex enterprise, and no single theory of motivation has dominance in the field. The model we develop here borrows from and integrates several psychological theories. To begin with, action precedes outcomes (Bandura 1998). Actions prior to matriculation result in matriculation, and students' interactions with institutions precede departure decisions. Second, cognitive processes such as expecting, evaluating, choosing, desiring, and intending precede behavior. In this case, as indicated by Fishbein and Ajzen (1975), attitudes such as institutional fit or commitment precede intentions, which precede persistence behavior. Students who adopt the attitude that they fit in certain academic environments are likely to become more academically integrated. Third, psychological processes result in attitudes about one's self. The theories examined here include self-efficacy theory, coping theory (specifically approach/ avoidance behavioral theory), and attribution theory.

A symbolic retention model contains constructs (variables, factors, ideas) that are linked to other constructs by lines or arrows. In a theoretical model the lines or arrows represent a theoretical explanation of the process that connects one construct to another. Some of the most important links in sociological retention models can be explained through psychological theories. In this section we present four psychological theories that are useful to retention research. They are attitude-behavior theory, coping behavioral (approach/avoidance) theory, self-efficacy theory, and attribution (locus of control) theory.

Attitude-Behavior Theory

Fishbein and Ajzen (1975) proposed a theory linking beliefs, attitudes, intentions, and behavior. An attitude is defined as "a person's favorable or unfavorable evaluation of an object" (p. 12). A belief represents a link between an object and some attribute. The following sentence provides an example: My college (the object) is great (the attribute). A normative belief "corresponds to the individual's beliefs regarding whether those referents who are important to him or her think that he or she should perform a given behavior" (Bentler and Speckart 1979, p. 453). Referents for college students include parents, siblings, close friends, and mentors. An example of a normative belief is: I believe my parents think I should attend this college. Influential normative beliefs include such things as others' beliefs about the quality of the institution, the capabilities of the student, the usefulness of an education for getting a job, and the importance of attending this school as opposed to some other.

The model posits that behavior is the result of the intention to perform the behavior. Intention has two antecedents. First, intention is linked to an attitude toward the behavior, where attitude is based on beliefs about the consequences of the behavior. Second, intention is based on subjective norms that come from normative beliefs about the behavior. A feedback loop from the behavior to beliefs completes the model. Over time, beliefs lead to attitudes, which lead to intentions, which lead to behavior. Bentler and Speckart (1979) added the variable of past behavior to this process, showing that past behavior, attitudes, and norms all influence intention. All four of these variables, then, have direct effects on future behavior.

Bean (1982a, 1982b, 1985, 1990) has used this theory to guide empirical studies and develop conceptual models of retention. Empirical investigations show expected relationships among attitudes, intentions, and behaviors. In the empirical studies above, as well as in at least eight other unpublished studies conducted by one of the authors (Bean) or his doctoral students, intention to leave college was the best predictor of actual departure. This finding was also true for Cabrera, Castañeda, Nora, and Hengstler (1992), who found further empirical evidence to support the other relationships that links intent to behavioral choice in Bean's model.

Coping Behavioral Theory

Based on psychological theory, self-assessment in a given environment, the assessment of the environment, and adaptation to that environment are important ways to adjust to a life situation. Adjustment can be viewed as the process by which an individual acquires "goodness of fit" (French, Rodgers, and Cobb 1974, p. 316) in a new environment, whereas adaptation can be defined as the process by which an individual chooses to cope with a particular situation (Lazarus, Averill, and Opton 1974). Adjustment may be most similar to what Tinto's model terms integration. Within that context, then, adaptation may be considered the process by which an individual achieves integration in a new environment. Coping is the collection of behaviors an individual uses in order to adapt.

Fit has long been considered an important part of retention research and had a prominent role in Bean's 1990 model as "institutional fit" (Bean 1990). Institutional fit differs from social or academic integration in that it is possible for students to feel that they fit in the environment of an institution socially or academically while they still may feel inadequate in the other area. For example, a loner with high grades and a social leader in academic difficulty may both view themselves as fitting in but still lack some of the qualities necessary to be fully integrated. In terms of retention theory, academic and social integration may be construed as attitudinal outcomes of adaptive (coping) behaviors toward the institutional environment.

Stress has been defined as the emotional and physiological response to perceived threats from the environment (Appley and Trumbull 1986). Stress increases when an individual feels that he/she is responding to a situation ineffectively. Coping is a wide-ranging form of adaptive behavior used to deal with all stressful situations. Lazarus (1966) describes coping as the behavioral process that can improve an existing situation or defuse a potentially dangerous one. In either case the goal in a given situation is to reduce stress. Students who cope well with the difficulties of college are those who successfully reduce stress with positive outcomes. Such students are more likely to gain the attitudinal perspectives of successful academic and social integration. As a result, they are less likely to leave college before graduating.

Eaton and Bean (1995) found the approach/avoidance model of coping helpful in examining the ways students become integrated into a university environment. Approach behaviors are those practices individuals use to focus attention on and respond aggressively to a stressor in order to reduce stress. Avoidance behaviors are passive practices an individual may use to avert the stressor. In an empirical study based on their model, Eaton and Bean found evidence of the association between coping behaviors and academic and social integration. Academic avoidance behaviors, such as avoiding courses or avoiding studying, had a negative relationship with academic integration, while academic approach behaviors, such as asking questions in class or pursuing tutoring, were positively related to academic integration.

We also found similar relationships between social behaviors and social integration. Social approach behaviors, such as attending parties, holding an office in a campus organization, or involvement in a Greek organization, were positively related to social integration. Socially avoidant behaviors, activities drawing a student away from the social environment on campus, such as hours worked on a job off campus or the frequence of weekends at home, were negatively related to social integration.

Several other studies have found a relationship between positive social behaviors and perceptions of feeling comfortable on campus (for example, Nora et al. 1996; Cooper, Mahler, and Whitt 1994; Chapman and Pascarella 1983). Collectively this research supports the idea that coping behavioral choice theories have a place in attrition research.

Motivational determinants are also strongly associated with academic and social adaptation. Two motivational theories, self-efficacy and attribution theory, will be discussed in the next two sections.

Self-efficacy Theory

Bandura's (1986, 1998) model of self-efficacy has received growing attention in higher education research. Bandura states that individuals acquire a perception of their ability to perform a particular task or deal with a particular situation based on past experience and observation. Bandura defines self-efficacy as an individual's own perception of his or her ability to carry out the necessary actions to reach a certain outcome. As the individual recognizes his/her competence and gains self-confidence, that individual will demonstrate higher aspirations for persistence, task achievement, and personal goals. For example, students who are academically at risk and who, despite past difficulties, watch others succeed and begin to believe that they can succeed in academic tasks are more likely to invest the emotional energy necessary to achieve academic goals.

Self-efficacy is a task-specific self-assessment, and research has shown that the more specific the task, the better the individual is able to assess his/her self-efficacy for that task (Mone, Baker, and Jeffries 1995). Bean (1982b) also found that self-confidence interacted with other factors in affecting retention in a positive way.

Several studies have shown self-efficacy to provide insight into the motivational and behavioral components of academic and social integration and persistence. Solberg et al. (1993) found that academic and social measures of efficacy showed a positive relationship with college persistence in Hispanic students. In that study they suggest that some social efficacy factors may actually serve as measures of social integration. Lent, Brown, and Larkin (1987) found that self-efficacy for academic performance was a predictor of both academic performance and persistence. For underprepared students in particular they found that high levels of self-efficacy were exceedingly important to success. Peterson (1993) demonstrated that there was a link between career decision making skill self-efficacy and social and academic integration for students at risk. She recommended that career decision making self-efficacy should be included as a variable in further studies of integration. Finally, Chartrand, Camp, and McFadden (1992) also found that along with commitment, self-efficacy was significant in its relationship with academic adjustment. Through these studies and others self-efficacy theory has been shown to contribute to theories of student retention by providing insight into the motivational components of integration. Becoming integrated requires attitudinal and behavioral energy from the student that moves her/him in a positive direction. Such motivation can even supercede skill in allowing the student to persist academically (Solberg et al. 1993).

A strong sense of self-efficacy with regard to the particular events and situations that compose campus life enables a student to gain confidence in his or her ability to survive and adapt. The reciprocity of these processes is clarified in psychological literature in a way that has not been as evident in past retention theory. Here reciprocal and iterative processes build a foundation from which the student gains confidence and motivation to persist to graduation.

Attribution Theory

Weiner's (1986) causal model of attribution is useful in examining academic performance and academic integration. Weiner's theory provides three categories of attribution. The most frequently studied of these is locus of control.

Locus of control, previously described by Rotter (1966), indicates an individual's ability to provide an internal or external causal perspective for past outcomes and experiences. An individual with an internal locus of control recognizes that personal, internal attributes, such as aptitude or skill, are responsible for an outcome. An individual with an external locus of control attributes outcomes to factors outside of the person's control, such as fate or luck (Weiner 1986). A student who believes she can receive an A on an exam because she worked hard has an internal locus of control, while a student who thinks he cannot get an A because the book is stupid, the professor is boring, and only the smartest students can get A's has an external locus of control.

A student with external locus is less likely to be motivated to produce the effort to perform well academically, since he perceives that the situation is not within his control. Successful adaptation to the external social environment, though not well studied, is most likely equally a function of internal locus of control. Locus is based on an attributional perception of the external environment, as opposed to some "objective" assessment. Thus, one's social integration, in a psychological model, is a function of one's attribution toward how one comes to have friends, how accepting a club or Greek organization may be, who wins elections, and so on.

Weiner theorized that if individuals believed that they had control over the outcomes of given situations, they were more likely to be motivated to respond to them. Individuals who believed that the outcomes were beyond their control would be less motivated to take action toward improving their situations.

In recent years Weiner's model has often been used to study academic performance in college. Van Overwalle, Mervielde, and De Schuyer (1995) found that along with other emotional contributors, internal locus had a strong positive association with academic success. Yan and Gaier (1994) also found that the internal attributes of effort and ability were significantly related to academic success in both American and Asian students. In another study Wilhite (1990) found that internal locus of control was positively related to academic achievement.

More support for this supposition can be found in other studies that pertain to attributional retraining (Perry et al. 1993; Wilson and Linville 1982). Attributional retraining provides activities designed to reorient individuals so they perceive that future situations are controllable. These studies show that students can reorient their perceptions of causal attribution, such as locus of control, and can become more successful academically. These findings also support the theory of causal attribution and locus of control as processes that contribute to students' success in achieving academic integration.

Academic performance in college involves student attributions and the interplay between these attributions and the educational environment (Perry et al. 1993). These relationships seem analogous to Tinto's conception of academic integration as the interplay between the student and the environment. In any case, attribution as locus of control explains some of the process dynamics of how a student becomes integrated in the academic environment and, by analogy, the social environment of the institution.

A Psychological Model of Student Retention

Some authors (e.g., Tinto 1993) emphasize the distinction between voluntary withdrawal and involuntary withdrawal from college. Involuntary withdrawal occurs when a student might wish to remain in school but is dismissed for violations of academic or social conduct. Our assumption is that the model presented here will work for both voluntary and involuntary leaving. The model would work least well for students who lack the abilities or skills required for college academic work. But we believe that many students have low GPAs because they lack motivation, have low expectancies that they could achieve better GPAs even if they tried, feel their GPAs are beyond their control, and so on. We would include this subpopulation in estimations of the model because while these students may leave involuntarily, their leaving would be explained by factors in the model that apply to voluntary departure.

We propose this model as a heuristic device in order to visualize how individual psychological processes can be understood in the retention process. Each of the psychological theories is complicated in its own right, and with limited space and limited empirical evidence for the various components, we recognize that the model is a simplification. We have explained the linkages in the model in terms of the psychological processes just described. While a thorough explanation of how each factor is related to each other factor in the model is not possible in this brief presentation, scholars are encouraged to read further in the psychological theory literature to better understand how these processes work. It is our intention to render the complex simple, recognizing that we give up accuracy. We hope others might find it useful to assess certain sections of the model, gathering evidence that can refine and clarify how it is specified. The model, which integrates the four psychological theories discussed, appears in figure 1.

The model falls into the general category of psychological models that are intended to explain behavior, that indicate that a given behavior is a choice, and that assume people are motivated to make choices that lead to or away from any given behavior. The overall structure of the model is based on Bentler and Speckart's (1979) adaptation of Fishbein and Ajzen's (1975) model. Past behavior, beliefs, and normative beliefs affect the way a student interacts with the institutional environment. Based on the psychological theories presented here, these beliefs arise from initial perceptions and assessments of personal characteristics—that is, from the entry characteristics of a student. For example, the individual's efficacy for various tasks within the institutional environment will be based on an assessment of skills and abilities from the past. An initial attributional perspective, also developed from past similar experiences, will provide a belief in how the institution will work. Past experience with stressful situations similar to those anticipated to exist in the new environment will establish a foundation for the development of a repertoire of coping strategies that can be used in the new environment.

All of these initial characteristics will then be affected by the filter of the institutional environment. Students will react to new academic and social interactions. These reactions will be based partly on their past experiences and partly on how successful they are in choosing strategies to negotiate in their new environment. They will meet bureaucratic obstacles and have to deal with forces from outside the institution, such as parents' or spouses' approval of their enrollment. At that point students will make new psychological assessments by which to interpret and respond to future situations. From Bandura (1997), self-efficacy assessments are ongoing. From Lazarus (1966), coping behavioral choices will shift as the result of the increase or decrease in stress that results from past choices. Finally, from Weiner (1986), attributions are reassessed as students evaluate the ways in which their actions have improved given academic or social situations.

These psychological processes result in students' development of a revised perspective of their universe. If all goes well, students will gain in perceptions of their self-efficacy in academic and social situations. Coping

Figure 1
A Psychological Model of College Student Retention

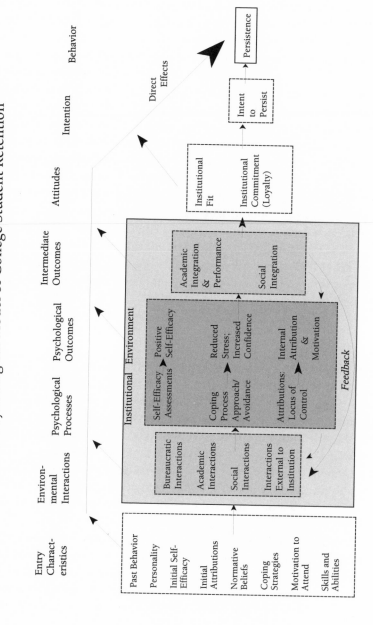

strategies will result in a reduction of stress and increased confidence in the new environment. Students will begin to perceive that they are in control of their academic and social destiny and be motivated to take action consistent with that perception. The result of these intermediate attitudes and behavioral choices are the intermediate outcomes of social and academic integration and, hopefully, academic success.

Feelings of integration feed back into the students' psychological assessments and affect future attitudes and behaviors. Thus, a student with a positive assessment of self-efficacy feels a sense of integration in the environment and returns to the environment to reinvest in her/his success in the academic and social milieu of the higher-education environment.

Let us summarize the model. Students enter college with a complex array of personal characteristics. As they interact within the institutional environment several psychological processes take place that, for the successful student, result in positive self-efficacy, reduced stress, increased efficacy, and internal locus of control. Each of these processes increases a student's scholarly motivation. These internal processes are reciprocal and iterative with continuous feedback and adjustment. Following Bentler and Speckart (1979), these processes in turn lead to academic and social integration, institutional fit and loyalty, intent to persist, and to the behavior in question, persistence itself.

Conclusion

In this chapter we examined the ways in which psychological theories can be used to explain the relationships proposed in Tinto's model. How might this strategy be useful in guiding future research? The model posits relationships between variables and provides psychological theories to explain why those relationships exist. The first task for a quantitative researcher would be to find or develop measures of the concepts in the model. Other tasks would be to find evidence for the relationships between those concepts, to measure the strength of the relationships, and to see if these behaviors and beliefs are involved in reshaping attribution, self efficacy, and coping behavior.

This model indicates that students are psychological beings and that collective issues of sociology play a secondary role. The social environment is important only as it is perceived by the individual. Therefore, the model should work equally well in any social context consistent with the expectations from the model. Qualitative researchers could investigate how these psychological processes operate at the community college, urban university, research university, or elite college. They could also involve themselves in discovering new factors at play in these psychological processes in these different milieus.

It is almost certain that individuals from different cultures or of different genders perceive the world differently. This situation should lead future researchers in two directions. First, they should examine which of these psychological processes seems most important for any demographic group being studied. Next, they should identify the particular factors that lead, say, to approaching homework, to a sense of self-efficacy as a student, or to thinking that the grades they receive are due to their own efforts. The psychology of staying in or leaving schools should provide a new set of insights into the processes that lead to student success and ultimately to programs that help students succeed.

References

Appley, M. H., and R. Trumbull. 1986. Development of the stress concept. In M. H. Appley and R. Trumbull (eds.), *Dynamics of stress,* pp. 3–18. New York: Plenum.

Bandura, A. 1986. *Social foundations of thought and action: A social cognitive theory.* Englewood Cliffs, N.J.: Prentice-Hall.

Bandura, A. 1997. *Self efficacy: The exercise of control.* New York: W. H. Freeman & Co.

Bean, J. P. 1982a. Conceptual models of college dropout: How theory can help the institutional researcher. In E. Pascarella (ed.), *Studying student attrition,* pp. 17–33. San Francisco: Jossey-Bass.

Bean, J. P. 1982b. Student attrition, intentions, and confidence: Interaction effects in a path model. *Research in Higher Education* 4: 291–320.

Bean, J. P. 1985. Interaction effects based on class level in an explanatory model of college student dropout syndrome. *American Educational Research Journal* 22: 35–64.

Bean, J. P. 1990. Why students leave: Insights from research. In D. Hossler and J. P. Bean, *The strategic management of college enrollments,* pp.147–169. San Francisco: Jossey-Bass.

Bentler, P. M., and G. Speckart. 1979. Models of attitude-behavior relations. *Psychological Review* 86 (5): 452–464.

Brower, A. 1992. The "second half" of student integration. *Journal of Higher Education* 63 (4): 441–462.

Cabrera, A. F., M. B. Castañeda, A. Nora, and D. Hengstler. 1992. The convergence between two theories of college persistence. *Journal of Higher Education* 63 (2):143–164.

Chapman, W. D., and Pascarella, E. T. 1983. Predictors of academic and social integration of college students. *Research in Higher Education* 19: 295–322.

Chartrand, J. M., C. C. Camp, and K. L. McFadden. 1992. Predicting academic adjustment and career indecision: A comparison of self-efficacy, interest congruence, and commitment. *Journal of College Student Development* 33: 293–300.

Cooper, S., M. Mahler, and R. Whitt. 1994. A survival kit for black students: Coping response mechanisms to stresses. *Negro Educational Review* 45 (1): 16–21.

Fishbein, M., and I. Ajzen. 1975. *Belief, attitude, intention and behavior: An introduction to theory and research.* Reading, Mass.: Addison-Wesley.

French, J. R., W. Rodgers, and S. Cobb. 1974. Adjustment as person-environmental fit. In G. V. Cochlo, D. A. Hamburg, and J. E. Adams (eds.), *Coping and adaptation,* pp. 316–333. New York: Basic Books.

Lazarus, R. S. 1966. *Psychological stress and the coping process.* New York: McGraw-Hill.

Lazarus, R. S., J. Averill, and E. Opton. 1974. The psychology of coping: Issues of research and assessment. In G. V. Coehlo, D. A. Hamburg, and J. E. Adams (eds.), *Coping and adaptation,* pp. 249–315. New York: Basic Books.

Lent, R. W., S. D. Brown, and K. C. Larkin. 1987. Comparison of three theoretically derived variables in predicting career and academic behavior: Self-efficacy, interest congruence, and consequence thinking. *Journal of Counseling Psychology* 34: 293–298.

Mone, M. A., D. D. Baker, and F. Jeffries. 1995. Predictive validity and time dependency of self-efficacy, self-esteem, personal goals, and academic performance. *Educational and Psychological Measurement* 55 (5): 716–727.

Nora, A., A. Cabrera, L. S. Hagedorn, and E. Pascarella. 1996. Differential impacts of academic and social experiences on college-related behavioral outcomes across different ethnic and gender groups at four-year institutions. *Research in Higher Education* 37 (4): 427–451.

Pascarella, E. T., and P. T. Terenzini. 1991. *How college affects students: Findings and insights from twenty years of research.* San Francisco: Jossey-Bass.

Perry, R. P., F. J. Hechter, H. M. Verena, and L. E. Weinberg. 1993. Enhancing achievement motivation and performance in college students: An attributional retraining perspective. *Research in Higher Education* 34 (6): 687–723.

Peterson, S. L. 1993. Career decision-making self-efficacy and institutional integration of underprepared college students. *Research in Higher Education* 34 (6): 659–685.

Rotter, J. B. 1966. Generalized expectancies for internal versus external control of reinforcement. *Psychological Monographs* 80 (1, Whole No. 609).

Solberg, V. S., K. O'Brien, P. Villareal, R. Kennel, and B. Davis. 1993. Self-efficacy and Hispanic college students: Validation of the college self-efficacy instrument. *Hispanic Journal of Behavioral Sciences* 15 (1): 80–95.

Spady, W. G. 1970. Dropouts from higher education: An interdisciplinary review and synthesis. *Interchange* 1 (1): 64–85.

Stage, F. K. 1989. Motivation, academic and social integration, and the early dropout. *American Educational Research Journal* 26 (3): 385–402.

Tinto, V. 1975. Dropout from higher education: A theoretical synthesis of recent research. *Review of Educational Research* 45: 89–125.

Tinto, V. 1987. *Leaving college.* Chicago: University of Chicago Press.

Van Overwalle, F., I. Mervielde, and J. De Schuyer. 1995. Structural modelling of the relationships between attributional dimensions, emotions, and performance of college freshmen. *Cognition and Emotion* 9 (1): 59–85.

Weiner, B. 1986. *An attributional theory of motivation and emotion.* New York: Springer-Verlag.

Wilhite, S. 1990. Self-efficacy, locus of control, self-assessment of memory ability, and student activities as predictors of college course achievement. *Journal of Educational Psychology* 82 (4): 696–700.

Wilson, T. D., and P. W. Linville. 1982. Improving the academic performance of college freshmen: Attribution therapy revisited. *Journal of Personality and Social Psychology* 42: 367–376.

Yan, W., and E. Gaier. 1994. Causal attributions for college success and failure: An Asian-American comparison. *Journal of Cross Cultural Psychology* 25 (1): 146–158.

College Climate and the Tinto Model

Leonard L. Baird

Vincent Tinto's model (1993) of student departure is one of the most studied in the field of higher education, and it may be one of the most studied in social science. However, as the review by Braxton, Sullivan, and Johnson (1997) indicates, empirical support for the propositions of the model is mixed. This relatively meager support may be due to several possibilities: weaknesses in the model itself, limitations in the operational measures of the constructs, and/or ambiguity about the locus of the model's operation. Critics and other researchers have suggested that the first possibility is important. For example, such researchers as Bean and Metzner (1985) and Cabrera, Stampen, and Hansen (1990) have suggested that the Tinto model does not include all the variables needed to understand departure behavior. Tierney (1992) has criticized the model on the grounds that it misapplies anthropological concepts, and Hurtado and Carter (1997) have pointed out the ambiguities in some of the concepts, notably social integration.

The second possibility is suggested by an examination of the operational definitions used to study the model empirically, which reveals an extraordinary range. As Hurtado and Carter (1997) point out, just the measures of academic and social integration include " the effort or time spent in activities; students' perceptions, reported behaviors, and participation in specific activities; students' satisfaction with aspects of the social or academic environments; students' interpersonal relations; objective performance criteria; or a combination of these measures" (p. 376). Such diversity undoubtedly reflects the fact that the model is often tested in secondary analyses of data sets that were developed for other purposes. Thus the researchers often looked for items that might in some way be related to Tinto's concepts rather than constructing items and scales designed to measure the constructs carefully. The result, however, is a rather confusing empirical and theoretical understanding of the meaning of the variables in the model.

The third possibility is suggested by Hurtado and Carter's (1997) observation that Spady's (1971) original empirical definition of perceived social integration was primarily a psychological rather than a behavioral measure. This distinction emphasizes the subjective interpretations and judgments of the individual student. We can extend this line of reasoning to argue that many of the variables in the Tinto model can be seen to operate intrapsychically. Goal and institutional commitments are personal statements of intent; social and academic integration can be viewed as the psychological consequence of interactions with the institutions' systems. In the more recent versions of the model the significance of external commitments would lie in students' perceptions of the degree to which they help or hinder their educational progress. This view is consistent with Stage's (1989b) psychological orientation to college outcomes. By focusing on the internal perceptions as the locus of the model, we are also reflecting the unit of analysis usually used in empirical studies of the model, the individual student. This chapter proposes a more psychological approach to Tinto's model, and to departure decisions in general, and emphasizes the role of psychological climates.

Specifically, this chapter discusses (1) reconceptualizing departure decisions as part of more general psychological models; (2) analyzing the processes by which the psychological climate is formed, using a scheme developed by Naylor, Pritchard, and Ilgen (1980) as an example; (3) describing the major dimensions of psychological climate as they are found in research studies; (4) examining evidence for the importance of perceptions of the environment in departure decisions; (5) considering the consequences of climate research for theory; (6) considering the consequences for measurement and research design; and (7) considering the consequences for policy.

Reconceptualizing Departure Decisions in General Psychological Terms

Given these theoretical and empirical issues, it would seem that some reconceptualization of the model emphasizing a psychological approach is warranted. Once we adopt this approach we can also see the importance of

Figure 1

A Comprehensive Social/Eecological Model

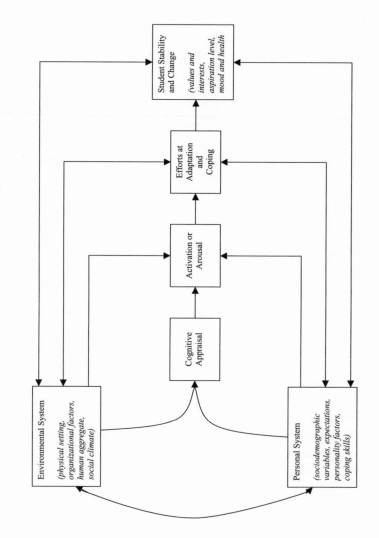

other psychological constructs, notably the campus climate or environment. That is, students' personal interpretations of their institutions' opportunities and challenges shape their decisions and behaviors. Although there are many theories that describe these processes (Walsh, Craik, and Price 1992), perhaps the most relevant for higher education is that developed by Rudolf Moos (1979). As shown in figure 1, Moos's model is a comprehensive social/ecological model that considers a number of variables. The environmental system includes four major domains: the physical setting, organizational factors, the human aggregate, and social climate. The physical setting has been shown to influence student behavior in terms of academic performance, satisfaction, and retention (Holahan 1982). Organizational factors, although somewhat distal from students' experiences (Baird 1988), have still been shown to influence students. For example, Astin (1993) reported that the simplest organizational factor, size, has a wide range of effects on student outcomes, many of them negative. The idea behind the human aggregate is that the character of an environment depends on the most common characteristic of its members. The work of Holland (1997) has shown these effects, especially on vocational choice. Research on the social climate has a long history (see Baird 1988 and 1993 for reviews). The social climate includes normative structures, reward and sanctioning systems, and in general the things that are emphasized and style of life that is valued on campus.

The personal system includes students' demographic characteristics, expectations, plans, roles, personalities, and coping skills. Many studies have found that these variables, often described as student input, have major influences on student outcomes. For example, Astin (1993, resource A) reported that for most student outcomes after four years of college freshman input was the dominant predictor. This trend held for achievement of a bachelor's degree.

Cognitive appraisal is a mediating factor by which students perceive their environments as being potentially threatening, beneficent, or irrelevant (primary appraisal) and their perceptions of their available coping responses. Activation or arousal is the result of appraising the environment as requiring a response. This, in turn, leads to efforts at coping and adaptation, which may involve attempts to change the environmental system or the personal system. An example of the former would be changing to another section of a course, and an example of the latter would be willingness to seek help when needed. (A set of these kinds of coping or adaptation strategies, labeled "cognitive mapping," was found by Hurtado and Carter [1997]

Figure 2

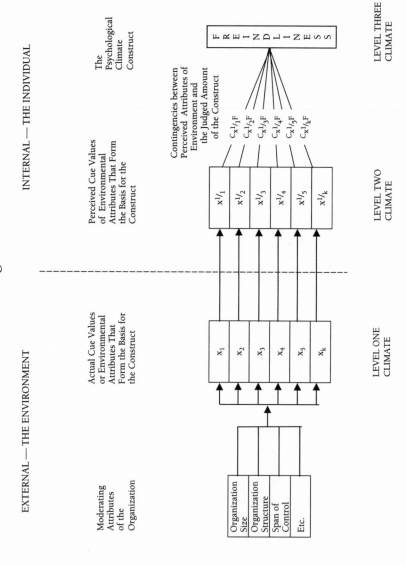

to be a major factor in Hispanic students' sense of belonging on their campuses.) These coping and adaptation behaviors will have varied successes and consequences for students' stability and change.

The most important aspect of this model for understanding the influence of the climate of the institution is that it emphasizes the central role of students' appraisals of their environments. These appraisals represent students' personal understandings of the structures of the environments and their opportunities and constraints upon behavior. Applying this point to the Tinto model suggests that it is students' perceptions of the opportunities and constraints within the academic and social systems that would lead them to various behaviors, which in turn would affect their levels of social and academic integration. Further, if we conceive of social and academic integration ("membership" in Tinto's most recent approach) as a personal psychological judgment, then the relations between the perceived environment and the sense of integration are much closer, as will be elaborated later in this chapter.

The Formation of Perceptions of Climate

If perceptions of the environment or climate play a central role in students' coping and adaptation efforts, it is important to understand the nature of these perceptions. How are they formed and what are the common elements or dimensions of the perceptions? One of the most important contributions of organizational research to the study of college environments is its general analysis of the components of organizational climate. One example is the schema developed by Naylor, Pritchard, and Ilgen (1980), who consider the individual's perceptions of the climate as a judgmental process "involved in attributing a class of humanlike traits to an entity outside the individual where this entity may be a work-group or even an entire organization" (p. 254). This schema is shown in figure 2. Although the actual flow of influence is from left to right, Naylor, Pritchard, and Ilgen find it advantageous to consider the schema from right to left, that is, to begin with the individual's psychological climate construct, in this case "Friendliness," a variable likely to influence behaviors in the social system.

These general constructs represent anthropomorphic characteristics that the individual attributes to the organization and are the most fundamental aspects of "climate." In the schema they are at "Level Three Climate." It is important to emphasize that these perceptions are affect-free; that is, it is important to keep the distinctions between perceptions of the degree to which an attribute is present in an organization and the positive or negative affect that the individual has due to that perception. For example, an individual might perceive his or her organization as having middling friendliness but could be quite happy or sad about that perception. These global constructs are based on contingencies or weights that the individual gives to various categories of cues, or on the relationships that the individual sees between a construct and the cues shown in the figure as $Cx^{1/1}F$, $Cx^{1/2}F$, and so on. For example, one person might consider "friendliness" to be based on the number of times each day people say hello, another person might consider being greeted with a smile *and* a verbal greeting to be required, and another might consider the number of parties important. The point is that each person may have his or her own *set* of contingencies or types of cues that represent a construct. (This suggests that one approach to the college environment is to examine the referents or types of cues that individuals use to define difficult constructs such as "scholarship" and "sense of community." If most people use the same cues, then one would have good evidence that the bases for their judgments of environments—that is, the ways they define environments—are the same.) The contingencies are related to the individual's perception that the required cues actually exist— that is, that they perceive that people say hello to them a certain number of times a day, or that there are so many parties each week. This is the "Level Two Climate" described in the figure as "Perceived Cue Values of Environmental Attributes Which Form the Basis for the Construct." (Studying the extent of variability in people's reports of the rate or incidence of the various behaviors or cues that define their constructs would provide additional evidence of a "shared" environment.) Up to this point the figure has referred to the internal, psychological perceptions of environment.

Moving across the boundary separating the internal world from the external world, we move to the "Level One Climate," which is the "Actual Cue Values or Environmental Attributes Which Form the Basis for the Construct" in the figure. These are the *actual* cue values associated with the cue values that are *perceived* by the individual—for example, the *actual* number of times people say hello in a day. It would be theoretically possible for external observers to provide measures of these various cues or behaviors, although it would be almost impossible in practice.

Finally, on the far left of the figure are the "Moderating Attributes of the Organization," such as organization size and organization structure, that influence the incidence of the cues that influence the individuals' perceptions.

For example, at a small college there is a high probability that many times a day a student will meet many other students whom he or she knows and who will therefore say hello frequently. At a large college, given the physical space and the numbers of other students and classes, it is less probable that a student would encounter many people he or she knows, and therefore that student may report a lower frequency of hellos. It is a mistake, in this view, to regard such moderating attributes as forms of climate, as has sometimes been done; rather, they should be regarded as important influences *on* climate. It is also important to distinguish between Level Two and Level Three climates. Although studies of the Tinto model have sometimes mixed these two levels, Moos's approach would suggest that the summative perceptions of Level Three have a more powerful effect on behavior, including departure.

Given this rather elaborate process of formulating perceptions of the climate, does the process result in highly idiosyncratic perceptions, or are there commonalties across students? The answer to this question has important consequences for theory and empirical research.

Lessons from Attempts to Assess Campus Climates

The long history of attempts to assess the climates of colleges and universities, outlined in Baird (1988), suggests a good deal of commonalty. It is useful to understand this history, not only because it includes so much work devoted to understanding and assessing campus climates but also because much of the logic of the approaches used applies today.

Although there were many implicit theoretical approaches to the campus climate, with attendant assessment procedures, the first formal proposal for measuring college climate was the work of Pace and Stern (1958), who developed an instrument to assess students' perceptions of campus climate or its "press," the College Characteristics Index (CCI). A press is a property or attribute of an institution that encourages or discourages the individual to behave in particular ways. Presses are of two types: first, as they exist in reality or are described by an objective inquiry; and second, as they are perceived or interpreted by the individual (an approach similar to that of Naylor, Pritchard, and Ilgen [1980]). The individual press is further composed of a "private press" based on the unique and personal view each person holds about his or her experience, and a "consensual press," which is the common or mutual interpretation of experiences shared by people participating in events. Thus, an individual's perception of the climate is based partly on his or her own interpretation of experience and partly on the interpretations of important reference groups.

The distinction between individual perceptions of the climate and group and consensual perceptions of the climate is still critical. Any study of campus climate must deal with this question. This distinction led Pace (1969) to adapt the CCI to reflect consensus and consensual differences among campus climates using the college rather than the individual as the unit of analysis. An item would be counted toward a score in a scale only if two-thirds of the respondents agreed (or disagreed) in the scored direction. For example, if 69 percent agreed that "students are encouraged to take an active part in social reforms or political programs," it would count for one point for a college scale; if only 62 percent agreed, it would not count.

The outcome of Pace's analyses was the College and University Environment Scales (CUES), which eventually included scales on seven dimensions: pragmatism; community; awareness, reflecting an active cultural and intellectual life; propriety; scholarship or academic rigor; campus morale; and quality of teaching (faculty-student relationships). Pace (1969, 1974) showed how these scores were related to a wide array of factual, student, and alumni variables. CUES has been used in many studies, reviewed in Feldman and Newcomb (1969) and in Baird (1988). The interest in the mid 1960s to the late 1970s in the environment per se and student characteristics led to a variety of additional measures that attempted to assess the overall campus climate, including the College Student Questionnaire, the Institutional Functioning Inventory, the Institutional Goals Inventory, and the University Residential Environment Scales. These are reviewed in Baird (1988, 1993).

Despite being based on rather different concepts of the college environment, a close examination of these measures reveals considerable consensus. Frequently analyses find the following dimensions of climate: friendliness or cohesiveness of the student culture, warmth or quality of faculty-student relations, flexibility and freedom versus rigidity and control of academic and other programs, overall rigor of academic standards, emphasis on personal expression and creativity, emphasis on research versus concern for undergraduate learning, importance of fun and big-time sports, and sense of a shared identity or mission. These are all important aspects of the psychological climate as perceived by respondents in many studies, and many have relevance for Tinto's model, if we accept the general logic of Moos's approach. The sense of friendliness or cohesiveness and the sense of shared identity certainly are related to seeing opportunities that would lead to social integration. Warmth or quality of faculty-student relations, flexibility of academic programs, and emphasis on undergraduate learning should be related to exercising choices that would lead to social integration. These are, of course, general relations among general perceptions of the climate. More specific measures of the climate that are more closely related to Tinto's model by reflecting opportunities and barriers show clearer relationships in empirical studies.

Evidence for the Importance of Climate

There is evidence for the influence of climate on variables related to Tinto's model, notably among minority students. These latter studies have focused on the climate of hostility for minority students and have shown a negative climate to be related to minority students' alienation (Oliver, Rodriguez, and Mickelson 1985), the opposite of the sense of integration; poor academic performance, a sign of low levels of academic integration; and social, academic, personal, and emotional adjustment, all of which can be seen as related to social and academic integration (Smedley, Myers, and Harrell 1993). It is interesting that Hurtado and Carter (1997) have reconsidered the meaning of social integration from a variety of perspectives and for theoretical and empirical reasons reconceptualized it as the sense of belonging. In their study of Hispanic students a measure of hostile climate was significantly related to the sense of belonging in a structural equation model. Hurtado and Carter call for additional studies to validate this link among the racial-ethnic groups.

Direct examination of the influence of perceptions of climate on constructs in the Tinto model was conducted by Nora and Cabrera (1996). They developed a measure of perceptions of prejudice and discrimination on campus, and for minority students they found it to have significant negative effects on academic experiences with faculty and academic staff, social integration, academic and intellectual development, GPA, and institutional commitment. Perceptions of prejudice had significant negative indirect effects on persistence among minority students but no direct effects. It is interesting that perceptions of discrimination had negative effects on all subsequent variables in the model among nonminority students. Nora and Cabrera offer the explanation that "perhaps minorities have become more accustomed to discriminatory acts on campuses and . . . have subsequently become more hardened to pressures that would otherwise push students away from persisting in college. For whites, these experiences may be so new that their exposure to them has a stronger effect on their persistence decisions" (p. 141). This explanation suggests the importance of analyzing student adaptations and coping mechanisms, as is consistent with Moos's model. Milem and Berger (1997) conducted a study that included measures of perceptions in an approach similar to the one proposed here. They proposed a modified Tinto model that included a "Behavior-Perception-Behavior Cycle." In this cycle students entering colleges begin to engage in a variety of behaviors representing different levels of involvement. This involvement influences their perceptions of their institutions' and peers' support for their academic and social experiences. These perceptions then lead to different subsequent levels of involvement. This cycle then affects academic and social integration, which then affects institutional commitment, which finally affects retention (intent to reenroll in their courses of study). Milem and Berger found that perceptions of institutional and peer support had few effects on their behavioral measures of involvement but that perceptions of institutional support had the second highest Beta coefficients in predicting academic integration, and perceptions of peer support had the highest Beta coefficient in predicting social integration. Social integration, in turn, was a predictor of final institutional commitment and intent to reenroll.

More general evidence for the influence of perceptions of climate can be found in Astin's (1993) large-scale study of student outcomes over four years of college in a large sample. Astin reported that what are defined as climate measures here were related to many of the eighty-four outcomes studied. Particularly strong relations were reported for several measures of satisfaction with college. Perhaps most germane, retention was positively affected by the perception of the student orientation of the faculty and negatively affected by the lack of student community. Less direct but relevant evidence can be found in Pace's (1984) study of the quality of college student experiences. Pace developed a measure of satisfaction with college that consisted of two items: "How well do you like college?" and "If you could start over again, would you go to the same college you are now attending?" Pace used all the measures from the College Student Experiences Questionnaire, which included students' background, status in college, quality-of-effort scales, ratings of gains toward objectives, and ratings of the environment to predict satisfaction. These analyses were conducted in five different kinds of institutions: doctoral, public comprehensive, private comprehensive, liberal arts type 1, and liberal arts type 2. Pace reports: "In all types of colleges, the single most important contributor to

students' satisfaction was an environment described as friendly, supportive, helpful etc.—most commonly the supportive relations among students, but also in some cases the helpful, encouraging relationships with
faculty members, or the flexible, considerate style of the college's opera-
tions. Also contributing to satisfaction was an environment strong in its
emphasis on intellectual qualities— whether academic, scholarly, or critical, analytical" (p. 53).

More general evidence for the influence of the environment came from
the prediction of students' sense of gain toward five general categories of
outcomes. Many relationships with environmental measures were significant, second in frequency only to the quality-of-effort scales. (It should be
noted that the quality-of-effort scales are carefully constructed ten-item
measures; the environment measures are single-item ratings of various
campus characteristics.) More recently Watson and Kuh (1996) reported
similar results among black and white students at predominantly black
and predominantly white institutions. They found a differential pattern of
results for the quality-of-effort scales at different institutions, and also that
"the college environment has a significant influence on virtually all outcome domains, from personal to cognitive. Activities and relationships
with faculty, administrators, and students greatly influenced Black students' gains at PBLAIs, which suggests that historically Black institutions
provide Black students with a developmentally powerful educational environment. For example, a college marked by supportive relationships
among peers, faculty, and administrators is almost as influential as student
development for all students. An environment that emphasizes development of academic, scholarly, and intellectual qualities appears to be the
most influential factor in Black-minority student educational gains" (p.
421).

Altogether these research results suggest the importance of students'
perceptions of the climates of their institutions for a variety of criteria,
many of which are related to the constructs in Tinto's model. However,
most measures of college climates were developed for other purposes,
many of them are atheoretical, and certainly they were not designed to
match the environmental conditions related to Tinto's constructs. These
environmental conditions would need to be identified based on concepts
related to theories of group membership, sense of cohesion, and commitment. That is, it would be profitable to concentrate on understanding how
students are attracted to one another, how informal groups form, how cohesiveness operates, how peers influence one another, how norms are

formed and enforced, how people become identified with their groups and colleges, how social judgments are formed, and how the social roles on campuses conflict with or reinforce each other. However, the resulting concepts and measures should focus on the end result of these processes on students' conceptions of their institutions and the coping or adaptation decisions they result in, rather than specific behaviors. For example, in the area of peer support for academic integration a student might base his/her ideas of the right number of hours to study on interactions with members of an informal math class study group but in the area of peer support for social integration might base his/her partying behavior on a group of friends in the residence hall. Different groups are salient for different behaviors for different students. In this sense it may be a mistake to concentrate on specific behaviors. What is important is the overall perception of support for commitment and integration. However, following Moos's approach, it would also be important to develop concepts and measures of students' adaptation and coping strategies. Overall, it is important to develop our conceptions of underlying processes carefully, rather than assuming that our constructs and measures work in a commonsense way.

Consequences of Climate Research for Theory

By reconceptualizing Tinto's variables in more clearly psychological terms, several things emerge. One is that theoretical analyses from other areas of research should be examined for their implications for the study of departure decisions. For example, Hurtado and Carter (1997) noted the importance of a sense of belonging to minority students found in many studies. However, from existing conceptual critiques, they felt that Tinto's integration concept did not adequately capture the meaning of "integration" among minority students. They turned to sociological conceptions of cohesion, which distinguished between perceptions of group cohesion held by individuals, and observed cohesion, which would be based upon researchers' assumptions of what cohesion represents. Hurtado and Carter profited from Bollen and Hoyle's (1990) review and study of cohesion, in which they examined concepts of cohesion from Durkheim through Festinger to current discussions in sociology. Bollen and Hoyle concluded that it was probable that cohesion was composed of an individual's sense of belonging in a group and his or her feelings of morale associated with membership in the group. They also speculated that perceived cohesion would be more closely related to other subjective phenomena than objective cohesion. They then reviewed existing indexes of cohesion, developed their own measure based on them, and demonstrated its psychometric stability. Hurtado and Carter then applied these ideas to Tinto's sense of integration, and on theoretical and empirical grounds they decided that sense of belonging was more appropriate to describe minority students' reactions to their institutions than "integration." They then found that certain academic and social organization activities were positively related to the sense of belonging measured in a sample of Latino students, while a scale of hostile climate was negatively related.

This example illustrates the importance of examining related literatures of theoretical and empirical relevance. When we consider other elements in the Tinto model we should look to this literature. For example, the idea of institutional commitment in Tinto's model is similar to the concept of organizational commitment in organizational and vocational psychology. The construct of organizational commitment has been developed, critiqued, and measured by many researchers (Brown 1996). Perhaps most important, it has been related to a criterion similar to college departure, attrition or turnover among employees. Organizational climate has also been related to organizational commitment and employee attrition. A related concept, organizational identification, is also relevant to Tinto's conception of institutional commitment (Wan-Huggins, Riordan, and Griffith 1998). The point is not that we should abandon Tinto's conceptions but that we should use the theoretical debates in these analogous areas to sharpen and reconsider the meanings we attach to the conceptions and develop more appropriate measures. The psychological literature is rich in ideas and careful analysis of related constructs, as well as empirical attempts to operationalize and study them. More particularly, studies of organizational climate have provided useful ideas (see Baird 1988 for a discussion of some of these). This work is too voluminous to review here, but it is clear that organizational climate has pervasive and sometimes powerful effects on a wide variety of criteria, including employees (or in some voluntary groups, members), attrition, and turnover. It also seems to be the case that the perceived climate at Naylor, Pritchard, and Ilgen's (1980) Level Three has the most consistent effects. That is, the perceived climate mediates much of the objective climate's effects. The implication is that the concept of perceived college climate should have analogous effects. The theoretical task is to identify the aspects of the environment that are most relevant to the criterion of concern.

Consequences of Climate Research for Measurement and Research Design

As the last section suggests, measures of climates need to be developed from theoretical conceptions related to the construct of concern. Thus, careful distinctions should be made between arenas of climate, such as the classroom, residence hall, and peer groups, and the aspects of those arenas that are relevant to the construct being studied. For example, a researcher may be concerned with the role of sexism in women's departure decisions. The climate in the classroom, the topic of many studies, is only one area of concern; the residence hall or peer group could have larger effects on women's departure decisions. Or it may be students' overall impressions of sexism on campus that affect departure decisions. Thus, in addition to measures of specific arenas for a sexist climate, an overall measure may be needed. As this example suggests, climate needs to be studied both in specific areas and globally.

Moos's model also suggests the importance of identifying and measuring students' adaptation efforts and coping mechanisms in reaction to the processes of the climate. These efforts mediate the climate, other variables in the Tinto model, and departure decisions. The measures of these efforts should also be based on existing research and theory in the area of concern. For example, the literature on how women deal with sexism should guide development of measures of coping with such pressures. A similar strategy was used by Hurtado and Carter (1997), who developed measures of what are called coping strategies here, based on the earlier work of Attinasi (1989). These included managing resources, maintenance of family ties, and cognitive mapping; the latter was directly related to the sense of belonging.

Another consequence of climate research derives from Naylor, Pritchard, and Ilgen's (1980) discussion of levels of climate. It is important to distinguish between organizational attributes and Levels One, Two, and Three of climate in studies. They are not the same thing, although they are related, and should be measured in appropriate ways. Naylor, Pritchard, and Ilgen's distinctions also have implications for the design of studies, in particular the unit of analysis. If we conceive of climate as primarily an individual construct, then the individual student should be the unit of analysis. If, however, we conceive of climate as an attribute of the institution, then the institution should be the unit of analysis. The more psychological approach promoted in this chapter argues for the former approach, using organizational attributes and Level One Climate primarily as stimuli. However, it may be profitable to use student aggregate perceptions of climate to study departure decisions, focusing on institutional effects. These studies can be supplemented with indicators of institutional policy in order to study their effects on the overall retention rate. Of course, recent statistical procedures allow for a mixed design that studies both institutional- and individual-level variables. However, to reiterate, care must be taken in the assessment and interpretation of climate and its effects.

Consequences of Climate Research for Policy

Climate, when compared to culture, is more malleable and can be changed by various direct or indirect means (Peterson and Spencer 1990). Thus, there are more potential levers for policy and action in approaching the climate rather than the culture of an institution. Organizational and industrial studies indicate that climate can be changed, particularly in specific well-defined areas. There is some evidence that climates in colleges and universities can be changed through a variety of means. For example, an assortment of programs is available for addressing and changing sexism, racism, and other prejudices in the classroom (Adams, Bell, and Griffin 1997). In addition to these efforts at changing the stimuli in various areas (Naylor, Pritchard, and Ilgen's [1980] Level One Climate), the programs can work on the interpretation of the perceived stimuli (contingencies in Naylor, Pritchard, and Ilgen). That is, the perceived climate can be changed both by altering the experiences presented and by helping students to reexamine their (largely) unconscious judgment processes. This suggests that efforts to change, for example, the climate for commuting students would involve changes in practice and policy, and working with students in considering their perceptions.

A related consequence derives from Moos's model. If the effects of experiences and climates are mediated by coping and adaptation efforts, then institutions can work directly with students on these efforts. For example, Milem and Berger (1997) found that early involvement with faculty appeared to have a positive influence on retention. Since some studies suggest that new students are reluctant to approach faculty, one strategy would be to provide students with experiences and specific strategies for approaching and interacting with faculty. Much of the reluctance to engage faculty may be based on the lack of knowledge of how to go about such engagement.

All of these efforts to use climate concepts for change can be undertaken at different levels. Much can be done at the departmental level, for example. Rather than attempting to change an entire institution, a department can make specific changes in specific areas (Pascarella and Terenzini 1991). The same is true in residential units (Schroeder, Mable, and Associates 1994). All of these efforts at change can be fairly direct and can have rapid effects on students. Of course, limited efforts will have limited effects. The goal for colleges should be to organize their many particular climates to be consistent in their effects so that greater retention may result from the overall effect of students' varied experiences. As Pace and Baird (1966) put it, "the more massive, the more cumulative, and the more congruent are the stimuli, the greater is the impact they have on the students" (p. 241). By carefully assessing and changing the climates on our campuses, we can have an impact on the departure decisions of our students.

References

Adams, M., L. A. Bell, and P. Griffin. 1997. *Teaching for diversity and social justice: A sourcebook.* New York: Rutledge.

Astin, A. W. 1993. *What matters in college?* San Francisco: Jossey-Bass.

Attinasi, L. C., Jr. 1989. Getting in: Mexican Americans' perceptions of university attendance and the implications for freshman year persistence. *Journal of Higher Education* 60: 247–277.

Baird, L. L. 1988. The college environment revisited: A review of research and theory. In J. C. Smart (ed.), *Higher education: Handbook of theory and research,* vol. 4, pp. 1–52. New York: Agathon Press.

Baird, L. L. 1993. Campus climate: Using surveys for policy making and understanding. In W. G. Tierney (ed.), *Assessing academic climates and cultures.* San Francisco: Jossey-Bass.

Bean, J. P., and B. S. Metzner. 1985. A conceptual model of nontraditional student attrition. *Review of Educational Research* 55: 485–540.

Bollen, K. A., and R. H. Hoyle. 1990. Perceived cohesion: A conceptual and empirical examination. *Social Forces* 69: 479–504.

Braxton, J. M., A. V. S. Sullivan, and R. M. Johnson, Jr. 1997. Appraising Tinto's theory of college student departure. In J. C. Smart (ed.), *Higher education: Handbook of theory and research,* vol. 12, pp. 107–164. New York: Agathon Press.

Brown, R. B. 1996. Organizational commitment: Clarifying the concept and simplifying the existing construct typology. *Journal of Vocational Behavior* 49: 230–251.

Cabrera, A. F., J. O. Stampen, and W. L. Hansen. 1990. Exploring the effects of ability to pay on persistence in college. *Review of Higher Education* 13 (3): 303–336.

Feldman, K. A., and T. M. Newcomb. 1969. *The impact of college on students.* San Francisco: Jossey-Bass.

Holahan, C. J. 1982. *Environmental psychology.* New York: Random House.

Holland, J. L. 1997. *Making vocational choices: A theory of vocational personalities and work environments*. Odessa, Fla.: Psychological Assessment Resources.

Hurtado, S., and D. F. Carter. 1997. Effects of college transition and perceptions of the campus racial climate on Latino college students' sense of belonging. *Sociology of Education* 70: 324–345.

Milem, J. F., and J. B. Berger. 1997. A modified model of college student persistence: Exploring the relationship between Astin's theory of involvement and Tinto's theory of student departure. *Journal of College Student Development* 38: 387–400.

Moos, R. H. 1979. *Evaluating educational environments*. San Francisco: Jossey-Bass.

Naylor, J. P., R. D. Pritchard, and D. R. Ilgen. 1980. *A theory of behavior in organizations*. New York: Academic Press.

Nora, A., and A. F. Cabrera. 1996. The role of perceptions of prejudice and discrimination on the adjustment of minority students to college. *Journal of Higher Education* 67: 119–148.

Oliver, M. L., C. J. Rodriguez, and R. A. Mickelson. 1985. Brown and black in white: The social adjustment and academic performance of Chicano and black students in a predominantly white university. *Urban Review* 17: 3–24.

Pace, C. R. 1969. *College and university environment scales: Technical manual*. 2d ed. Princeton, N.J.: Educational Testing Service.

Pace, C. R. 1974. *The demise of diversity? A comparative profile of eight types of institutions*. New York: McGraw-Hill.

Pace, C. R. 1984. *Measuring the quality of college student experiences*. Los Angeles: UCLA–Higher Education Research Institute.

Pace, C. R., and L. L. Baird. 1966. Attainment patterns in the environmental press of college subcultures. In T. M. Newcomb and E. K. Wilson (eds.), *College peer groups: Problems and prospects for research*, pp. 215–242. Chicago: Aldine.

Pace, C. R., and G. G. Stern. 1958. An approach to the measurement of psychological characteristics of college environments. *Journal of Educational Psychology* 49: 269–277.

Pascarella, E. T., and P. T. Terenzini. 1991. *How college affects students: Findings and insights from twenty years of research*. San Francisco: Jossey-Bass.

Peterson, M. W., and M. G. Spencer. 1990. Understanding academic culture and climate. In W. G. Tierney (ed.), *Assessing academic climates and cultures*, pp. 3–18. San Francisco: Jossey-Bass.

Schroeder, C. C., P. Mable, and Associates. 1994. *Realizing the educational potential of residence halls*. San Francisco: Jossey-Bass.

Smedley, B. D., H. F. Myers, and S. P. Harrell. 1993. Minority-status stresses and the college adjustment of ethnic minority freshmen. *Journal of Higher Education* 64: 434–452.

Spady, W. 1971. Dropouts from higher education: Toward an empirical model. *Interchange* 2: 38–62.

Stage, F. K. 1989a. Motivation, academic and social integration, and the early dropout. *American Educational Research Journal* 26 (3): 385–402.

Stage, F. K. 1989b. Reciprocal effects between the academic and social integration of college students. *Research in Higher Education* 30 (5): 517–530.

Tierney, W. G. 1992. An anthropological analysis of student participation in college. *Journal of Higher Education* 63: 603–617.

Tinto, V. *Leaving college: Rethinking the causes and cures of student attrition.* Chicago: University of Chicago Press.

Walsh, W. B., K. H. Craik, and R. H. Price. 1992. *Person-environment psychology: Models and perspectives.* Hillsdale, N.J.: L. Erlbaum Associates.

Wan-Huggins, V. N., C. M. Riordan, and R. W. Griffith. 1998. The development and longitudinal test of a model of organizational identification. *Journal of Applied Social Psychology* 28: 724–749.

Watson, L. W., and G. Kuh. 1996. The influence of dominant race environments on student involvement, perceptions, and educational gains: A look at historically black and predominantly white liberal arts institutions. *Journal of College Student Development* 37: 415–424.

Linking Learning and Leaving

*Exploring the Role of the College Classroom
in Student Departure*

Vincent Tinto

T he one experience that most college students share is that of the classroom. Indeed, for many students who commute to college, it may be the only educational experience they have in common, the only place where they meet each other and the faculty.* That being the case, it is striking that the experience of the classroom has been largely absent from studies of student persistence and virtually ignored in theories of student departure (e.g., Bean 1983, Cabrera, Castañeda, Nora, and Hengstler 1992; and Tinto 1987, 1993).

This chapter represents a first attempt to address this shortcoming. Specifically, it seeks to better understand how student experience of the classroom and persistence are linked and how current theories of student departure might be changed to include the classroom. It argues that we must reconstruct our theoretical models to include not only the classroom, but also the faculty and, in turn, pedagogy in our discussions of student persistence.

---

*This chapter is derived, in part, from an earlier article by this author entitled Classrooms as communities: Exploring the educational character of student persistence. *Journal of Higher Education* 68 (6): 599–623.

Classrooms as Communities

The beginning point of the discussion lies in the recognition that it is possible to speak of college classrooms as smaller communities located at the very heart of the college's broader academic and social communities. For most students classrooms serve as smaller academic and social meeting places or crossroads that intersect the diverse faculty and student communities marking the college generally. Membership in the community of the classroom can provide important linkages to membership in communities external to the classroom. For new students in particular, engagement in the community of the classroom can become a gateway for subsequent student involvement in the academic and social communities of the college generally. Thus it is easy to understand the frequent observation that if students, especially those who commute, do not get engaged within the classroom, they are unlikely to get engaged beyond the classroom.

At this point the informed observer might argue that there has been little research to support this claim. Indeed, she might note that measures of academic integration have not always been found to be associated with persistence. But issues of specification aside—that is, of the ways we have measured or perhaps mismeasured the concept academic integration—it is likely the case that what we have measured reflects the fact that most classrooms are not involving and therefore are not a factor in student persistence. This does not mean that they *could not* play a role in persistence, but rather only that they have typically *not yet* played that role.

Reconstructing the Classroom

The fact is that most college classrooms, especially those in the first year of college, are not engaging. Unfortunately, classroom participation is still very much a "spectator sport" in which faculty talk dominates (Fischer and Grant 1983; Fassinger 1995) and where there are few active student participants (Smith 1983; Karp and Yoels 1976; Nunn 1996). Most students continue to experience college as isolated learners whose learning is disconnected from that of others, and they engage in solo performance and demonstration in what remains largely a show-and-tell learning environment. At the same time, students keep taking courses as detached, individual units. One course is separated from another in both content and peer group, one set of understandings unrelated in any intentional fashion to what is learned in other courses. Though there are majors, there is little academic or social coherence to student learning. It is not surprising, then, that students seem so uninvolved. Their learning experiences are not involving ones.

Fortunately, some changes have taken place. Partly in response to a series of reports in the 1980s by the National Institute of Education (1984) and the Association of American Colleges (1985), and studies in the late 1980s and early 1990s by scholars such as Astin (1987), Boyer (1987), and Tinto (1987), a growing number of institutions have begun to reform educational practice and restructure classrooms to more actively involve students in learning. One such effort that is gaining increased attention is that encompassed by learning communities and the collaborative pedagogy that underlies them. Unlike many programs that exist at the periphery of the academic experience of students, learning communities seek to restructure the very classrooms in which students find themselves and alter the ways students experience both the curriculum and learning within those classrooms.*

In their most basic form learning communities are a kind of coregistration or block scheduling that enables students to take courses together. The same students register for two or more courses, forming a sort of study team. In some cases, typically referred to as "linked courses," students will enroll together in two courses, most typically a course in writing or math with a course in selected literature or, in the case of math, a course in science. In the larger universities such as the University of Oregon and the University of Washington, students in a learning community may attend two or more lecture classes with two hundred to three hundred other students but stay together for a smaller discussion section (Freshman Interest Group) led by a graduate student or upperclassman. In other cases, such as the Federated Learning Communities of LaGuardia Community College, students take three or more courses in which they are the only members of the class. In this way they form a "community of learners" whose members are all studying the same material. In Seattle Central Community College, however, students in the Coordinated Studies Program take all their courses together in

---

*Learning communities are not new. In the United States they date back to the early work of the philosopher and educational theorist Alexander Meiklejohn and to the Experimental College at the University of Wisconsin, which he helped establish in 1927 (Meiklejohn 1932). However, like Joseph Tussman's experiment at the University of California at Berkeley (Tussman 1969), early learning communities were limited in scope and in the students they served. The current movement, led over the past twelve years by the Washington Center at The Evergreen State College, is different not only because it involves a greater range of institutions public and private, two- and four-year, but also because it is being adapted to the learning needs of a broad range of students.

one block of time so that the community meets two or three times a week for four to six hours at a time.

Typically, a learning community is organized around a central theme that links the courses—say, "Body and Mind," in which required courses in human biology, psychology, and sociology are linked in pursuit of a singular piece of knowledge: how and why humans behave as they do. The point of such organization is to ensure that the sharing of a curriculum provides students with a coherent interdisciplinary experience that promotes a deeper type of learning than is possible in stand-alone courses.

The themes, of course, can vary, as do the audiences to whom the learning community is directed. At New York's LaGuardia Community College, for instance, learning communities are designed for students studying for careers in business (the Enterprise Center). At Cerritos College in California they are designed for students in science and engineering. At Shoreline Community College in Washington they are directed toward the needs of "remedial" students. In other institutions, such as Iowa State University, learning communities serve the needs of new students. In those cases the learning communities frequently link the shared courses to freshmen seminars (e.g., University of Washington, Frostburg State University).

Though they may vary in structure and content, nearly all learning communities have three things in common. One is *shared knowledge*. By requiring students to take courses together and organizing those courses around themes, learning communities seek to construct shared, coherent curricular experiences that are not just unconnected arrays of courses in, say, composition, calculus, history, Spanish, and geology. In doing so, they seek to promote higher levels of cognitive complexity that cannot easily be obtained through participation in unrelated courses. The second characteristic common to learning communities is *shared knowing*. Learning communities enroll the same students in several classes so they get to know each other quickly and fairly intimately and in a way that is part and parcel of their academic experience. By asking students to construct knowledge together, learning communities seek to involve students both socially and intellectually in ways that promote cognitive development as well as an appreciation for the many ways in which one's own knowing is enhanced when other voices are part of that learning experience. The third common characteristic is *shared responsibility*. Learning communities ask students to become responsible to each other in the process of gaining knowledge. They participate in collaborative groups that require students to be mutually dependent on one another so that the learning of the group does not advance without each member doing her or his part.*

Recent research by this author on several first-year learning-community programs reveals that such restructuring can have a significant impact on student academic and social involvements and, in turn, on student persistence (Tinto, Goodsell, and Russo 1993). The results of this multiyear study that pertain to our current discussion can be summarized under three headings, each of which reveals something about the underlying forces that link classroom experiences to persistence. These are Building Supportive Peer Groups, Shared Learning: Bridging the Academic-Social Divide, and Increased Involvement, Effort, Learning, and Persistence.

Building Supportive Peer Groups

Participation in a first-year learning community enabled students to develop a network of supportive peers that helped students make the transition to college and integrate them into a community of peers. This community of peers, formed in their learning communities, provided students with a small, knowable group of fellow students with whom early friendships were formed. Some friendships lasted; others faded. But in all cases students saw those associations as an important and valued part of their first-year experience.

Meeting people and making friends during the first year of college is a major preoccupation of student life, especially among younger students who have yet to establish families or acquire significant work obligations. While making friends may be a relatively easy task in smaller, more intimate residential colleges, it is far more difficult in commuter institutions and in

---

* As a pedagogical strategy, learning communities are being adapted to the needs of a variety of students. Learning communities are designed for students studying for careers in business at New York's LaGuardia Community College, for engineering and science majors at the University of Texas—El Paso, and for students in law and journalism at the University of Hawaii at Manoa. At California State University at Los Angeles, the University of Hawaii at Manoa, and Gateway Community College in the Maricopa Community College District, learning communities have been adapted to the needs of students requiring developmental education assistance. At larger universities, such as Illinois State University, the University of Washington, the University of Oregon, and Arizona State University, they have been employed to address the needs of beginning students. In such cases a freshman seminar is typically one of the linked courses.

large institutions. It is not surprising, then, that many students talked of their learning communities as places to meet new people and make new friendships, ways to make remote colleges more knowable places. One student in the program put it this way: "That's why the cluster is really great, because right now I've made a lot of friends. In another school if I had different classmates, it would have been harder. I've made a lot of friends that I didn't know before, so that's good."

Not surprising, many students saw participation in a learning community as an important part of being able to manage the many struggles they faced in getting to and participating in class (see Russo 1995). Through seminars, group projects, class discussions, and self-evaluation reports the learning communities contributed not only to a high level of student participation in learning, but also to the development of supportive peer groups that helped students balance the many struggles they faced in attending college. The groups, which developed within the classroom, extended beyond the classroom, providing support which students saw as influencing their desire to continue college despite the many challenges they faced. One student, looking back on her experience in the prior autumn's learning community, put it this way: "In the cluster we knew each other, we were friends, we discussed and studied everything from all the classes. We knew things very, very well because we discussed it all so much. We had a discussion about everything. Now it's more difficult because there are different people in each class. There's not so much . . . togetherness. In the cluster if we needed help or if we had questions, we could help each other."

Shared Learning: Bridging the Academic-Social Divide

The shared learning experiences of learning communities did more than simply cement new friendships; they served to bridge the academic-social divide that typically plagues student life. Often social and academic concerns compete, causing students to feel torn between the two so that they have to choose one over the other. Learning communities helped students draw these two worlds together.

The development of interpersonal relationships was important because it was against this backdrop of a supportive network of peers that academic engagement arose both inside and outside the classroom. Groups that formed within the classroom often extended beyond the classroom in informal meetings and study groups. Once these were in operation, students were able to turn toward the material presented in class and their assignments. A common perception among program students was captured in the following comment: "You know, the more I talk to other people about our class stuff, the homework, the tests, the more I'm actually learning . . . and the more I learn not only about other people but also about the subject because my brain is getting more, because I'm getting more involved with the students. I'm getting more involved with the class even after class." In this and other ways participation in shared learning experiences enabled new college students to bridge the academic-social divide that typically confronts students in these settings. It allowed them to meet two needs, social and academic, without having to sacrifice one in order to meet the other. But more than simply allowing the social and academic worlds to exist side by side, learning communities provided a vehicle for each to enhance the other. Students spoke of learning experiences that were different and richer than those with which they were acquainted. As one student noted, "Not only do we learn more, we learn better."

Increased Involvement, Effort, Learning, and Persistence

It is hardly surprising, then, that students in the learning communities had higher peer and learning activity scores, as measured on Robert Pace's College Student Experience Questionnaire (CSEQ). Their engagement with their peers inside and outside the classroom served to involve them more fully in the academic matters of the classroom. They spent more time with their peers and more time on class matters. As a result, they spent more time studying. As one student noted, they "spent more time in class even after class." Equally important, learning-community students saw their peers and faculty as more supportive of their needs, their classroom experiences as more involving, and themselves as having gained more from participation in the learning communities.*

The results of such engagement and perceptions were, in each case, heightened quality of student effort on the CSEQ scale and increased

---

* The scores for learning-community students on each of the subscales that comprise the Quality of Student Effort Scale in the CSEQ were significantly higher than those for comparison-group students. This was particularly noticeable at Seattle Central Community College, where faculty also employed cooperative teaching methods in their classes. Learning-community students' scores on the multi-item scale used to measure students' sense of their own intellectual gain were also higher than comparison-group students' scores.

persistence to the following fall term. In the case of Seattle Central Com-smunity College, for instance, students in their learning-community program scored higher on each factor that comprises the Quality of Student Effort scales (see Pace 1984) and continued their studies into the next fall at a rate of 72.3 percent, as compared to 51.4 percent for comparison-group students. These higher scores were the results of a relatively simple restructuring of the classroom educational environment to actively engage students in ways that required them to share knowledge.

It should be noted that the impact of the learning communities on persistence remained even after taking account of a variety of individual and contextual data (Tinto 1997). That is to say, the impact of altered educational environments on student persistence was not simply the reflection of the students who participated in those environments. In this regard, it is noteworthy that findings were the same regardless of when students enrolled in the learning-community classes. Students who enrolled late in the learning community—that is to say, for whom it was the only available option, since some were not aware of the program prior to enrolling—showed similar outcomes and expressed similar views of their experiences. Clearly, one could not dismiss the outcome of program participation as merely the result of having allowed particular types of students to self-select themselves into a program that permitted them to engage in behaviors they would otherwise have carried out elsewhere.

Classrooms as Educational Communities

These results yield important insights into the ways classroom experiences shape student persistence and, by extension, how current theories of student persistence might be modified to better reflect the educational character of college life. Specifically, important relationships are suggested, on one hand, among the educational activity structure of the classroom, student involvement, and the quality of student effort, and on the other hand, among quality of student effort, learning, and persistence.

Student social involvement in the educational life of the college, in this instance via the educational activity structure of the curriculum and classroom, provides a mechanism through which both academic and social involvement arise and student effort is engaged. The more students are involved, academically and socially, in shared learning experiences that link them as learners with their peers, the more likely they are to become more involved in their own learning and invest the time and energy needed to learn (Tinto, Goodsell, and Russo 1993). The social affiliations those activities provide serve as vehicles through which academic involvement is engaged. Both lead to enhanced quality of effort. Students put more effort into educational activities that enable them to make friends and learn at the same time. That increased effort leads to enhanced learning in ways that heighten persistence (Endo and Harpel 1982; Tinto and Froh 1992).

It does not follow, however, that the linkages between involvement and learning, on one hand, and between learning and persistence, on the other, are simple or symmetrical. As to the impact of involvement upon learning, one has to ask about the specific nature of student involvement. Not all involvements lead to learning in the same fashion. Much depends on the degree to which student involvement is a meaningful and valued part of the classroom experience. Having a voice without being heard is often worse than having no voice at all. As to the linkage between learning and persistence, though learning is in general positively associated with persistence, it is not the case that learning guarantees persistence or that failure to learn, beyond the obvious case of academic failure, ensures departure. While it is the case for most, if not all, institutions that academic involvement matters more than social involvement, it is also true that social and academic involvement both influence persistence. For some students, even high levels of academic involvement and its consequent learning may not be enough to offset the effect of social isolation. For others, sufficient social integration or involvement may counterbalance the absence of academic involvement. They stay because of the friendships they have developed. Of course, the absence of any academic involvement typically leads to academic failure and thus forced departure.

Colleges, then, can be seen as consisting not merely of multiple communities, but of overlapping and sometimes nested academic and social communities, each influencing the other in important ways. By extension, the broader process of academic and social integration (involvement) can be understood as *emerging from* student involvement with faculty and student peers in the communities of the classrooms. It is a complex, multidimensional process that links classroom engagement with faculty and student peers to subsequent involvement in the larger academic and social communities of the college.

Bringing Faculty Back into Theories of Student Persistence

This view of the role of classrooms in student academic and social involvement underlines the importance of faculty to student persistence
(see Pascarella and Terenzini 1980, 1991). This is the case not only because contact with faculty inside and outside the classroom serves to
directly shape learning and persistence, but also because their actions,
framed by pedagogical assumptions and teaching skills, shape the nature
of classroom communities and influence the degree and manner in which
students become involved in learning in and beyond those communities.
Faculty do matter, and not only because of their out-of-classroom activities.

This is what Braxton, Milem, and Sullivan (forthcoming) found in their
recent study of the impact of active learning on student persistence. In a
study of 718 first-time, full-time students at a highly selective private research university, they found that active learning experiences had positive
direct and indirect effects on social integration and, in turn, on subsequent
institutional commitment and intent to return. As in research on learning
communities, involvement in learning becomes a vehicle through which
subsequent involvement or integration arises.

In this regard, it is noteworthy that both Fassinger (1995) and Nunn
(1996) found classroom traits, specifically the existence of a supportive
atmosphere for student learning, to be as important to student participation and learning as are student and faculty traits. The implication is
clear: namely that much of the impact of faculty upon student involvement and persistence is likely to arise indirectly via their impact on the
ethos and educational activity structure of the classroom and, in turn,
on the ways that those classroom attributes shape students' engagements
with each other, as well as with the faculty, in learning beyond the classroom.

It can therefore be argued that at least part of the often-observed relationship between persistence and student-faculty contact outside the classroom is a reflection of faculty actions. Among other things, this relationship
is likely to mirror how faculty actions shape student experiences within the
classroom and, in turn, student willingness to seek out faculty beyond the
classroom. In effect, faculty help create student-faculty contact. This is precisely what we observed in our study of learning communities. Students in
learning communities were not only more involved in learning within the

classroom, they were also more likely to seek out and make contact with faculty outside the classroom. Therefore, while it is undoubtedly true that many students find "validation" outside the classroom (Rendón 1994), it is also likely that validation is at least partially the result of events within the classroom.

Constructing Seamless Learning Environments

Kuh et al. (1991) have spoken eloquently of the need to construct "seamless learning environments" that bridge the gap between classroom and out-of-classroom experience. They argue that colleges must build learning environments outside the classroom, ones that merge seamlessly with those of the classroom. In this regard, Kuh (1993, 1995) has shown that out-of-class experiences are important to student learning and development.

In this chapter we have argued that the likelihood that students will take advantage of such environments is, for most students, a reflection of their experiences within the classroom. This is certainly the case for students who commute to college, in particular those who have numerous obligations outside college. In policy terms, it follows that if we are serious about building "seamless learning environments," we must begin by building those environments from the classroom out.

Closing Observations

What does all this mean for our existing models of student persistence? First, we need to be reminded that our current two-dimensional graphic representations of interaction that depict social and academic systems of colleges as two separate boxes mask the fuller relationship between these two spheres of activity. A more accurate representation would show academic and social systems as two nested spheres, with the academic system occurring *within* the broader social system that pervades the campus. Such a depiction would more accurately capture the ways, noted here, in which social and academic life are interwoven and social communities *emerge* out of academic activities that take place within the more limited academic sphere of the classroom, a sphere of activities that is necessarily also social in character.

As a methodological aside, this research reminds us that we would be well served by supplementing our use of path analysis to study the process of persistence with network analysis and/or social mapping of student interaction patterns. These analyses will better illuminate the complexity of student involvements and the linkages that arise over time between classroom and out-of-class experiences. More important, they will shed important light on how interactions across the academic and social geography of a campus shape the educational opportunity structure of campus life and, in turn, shape both student learning and persistence.*

The fact is that we have too long overlooked the essentially educational, developmental character of persistence as it occurs in most college settings. There is a rich line of inquiry into the linkage between learning and persistence that has yet to be pursued. We need to invest our time and energies in a fuller exploration of the complex ways in which the experience of the classroom comes to shape student learning and persistence. Among other things, we need to pursue Braxton, Bray, and Berger's lead (2000) and ask about the role of faculty teaching in persistence and more carefully consider the notion, as we have here, that choices of curriculum structure (e.g., learning communities) and pedagogy invariably shape both learning and persistence on campus (e.g., cooperative teaching). They do so because they serve to alter both the degree to which and manner in which students become involved in both the academic and social lives of institutions. Through further consideration of the topics presented here, we likely will discover what many educators have been trying to tell us for years—namely that at its core college is an educational experience and that discussions about persistence that ignore important questions of educational practice are at best shallow.

References

Association of American Colleges. 1985. *Integrity in the curriculum: Report to the academic community*. Washington, D.C.: Association of American Colleges.

Astin, A. 1987. *Achieving educational excellence*. San Francisco: Jossey-Bass.

Attinasi, L. 1989. Getting in: Mexican Americans' perceptions of university attendance and the implications for freshman year persistence. *Journal of Higher Education* 60: 247–277.

*Much like the concept "opportunity structure" that sociologists have employed to study the dynamic aspects of social stratification, the term "educational opportunity structure" can be seen as describing the interconnected chains of relationships and interactions out of which personal affiliations are wrought and contextual learning arises.

Bean, J. 1983. The application of a model of turnover in work organizations to the student attrition process. *Review of Higher Education* 6: 129–148.

Boyer, E. 1987. *College: The undergraduate experience in America.* New York: Harper & Row.

Braxton, J. M., N. J. Bray, and J. B. Berger. 2000. "Faculty Teaching Skills and Their Influence on the College Student Departure Process." *Journal of College Student Development,* 41(2): 215–227.

Braxton, J. M., J. F. Milem, and A. S. Sullivan. Forthcoming. "The Influence of Active Learning on the College Student Departure Process: Toward a Revision of Tinto's Theory." *Journal of Higher Education.*

Cabrera, A. F., M. Castañeda, A. Nora, and D. Hengstler. 1992. The convergence between two theories of college persistence. *Journal of Higher Education* 63: 143–164.

Endo, J. J., and R. L. Harpel. 1982. The effect of student-faculty interaction on students' educational outcomes. *Research in Higher Education* 16: 115–135.

Fassinger, P.A. 1995. Understanding classroom interaction: Students' and professors' contribution to students' silence. *Journal of Higher Education* 66: 82–96.

Fischer, C. G., and G. E. Grant. 1983. Intellectual levels in college classrooms. In C. L. Ellner and C. P. Barnes (eds.), *Studies of college teaching,* pp. 47–60. Lexington, Mass.: D. C. Heath.

Karp, D., and W. Yoels. 1976. The college classroom: Some observations on the meaning of student participation. *Sociology and Social Research* 60: 421–439.

Kuh, G. 1993. In their own words: What students learn outside the classroom. *American Educational Research Journal* 30: 277–304.

Kuh, G. 1995. The other curriculum: Out-of-class experiences associated with student learning and personal development. *Journal of Higher Education* 66: 123–155.

Kuh, G., J. Schuh, E. Whitt, and Associates. 1991. *Involving colleges.* San Francisco: Jossey-Bass.

Meiklejohn, A. 1932. *The experimental college.* New York: Harper & Row.

Nunn, C. E. 1996. Discussion in the college classroom. *Journal of Higher Education* 67: 243–266.

Pace, C. R. 1984. *Measuring the quality of college student experience.* Los Angeles: Higher Education Research Institute, University of California.

Pascarella, E. T., and P. Terenzini. 1980. Predicting persistence and voluntary dropout decisions from a theoretical model. *Journal of Higher Education* 51: 60–75.

Pascarella, E. T., and P. Terenzini. 1991. *How college affects students: Findings and insights from twenty years of research.* San Francisco: Jossey-Bass.

Rendón, L. 1994. Validating culturally diverse students: Toward a new model of learning and student development. *Innovative Higher Education* 19: 33–52.

Russo, P. 1995. Struggling for knowledge: Students, coordinated studies, and collaborative learning. Ph.D. diss., Syracuse University.

Smith, D. G. 1983. Instruction and outcomes in an undergraduate setting. In C. L. Ellner and C. P. Barnes (eds.), *Studies in college teaching,* pp. 83–116. Lexington, Mass.: D. C. Heath.

Tinto, V. 1993. Leaving college: Rethinking the causes and cures of student attrition. 2d ed. Chicago: University of Chicago Press.

Tinto, V. 1997. Classrooms as communities: Exploring the educational character of student persistence. *Journal of Higher Education* 68 (6): 599–624.

Tinto, V., and R. Froh. 1992. Translating research on student persistence into institutional policy. Paper presented at the annual meeting of the Association for the Study of Higher Education, Chicago.

Tinto, V., A. Goodsell, and P. Russo. 1993. Building learning communities for new college students. Final report of the learning communities project for the National Center on Postsecondary Teaching, Learning, and Assessment, Syracuse University.

Tussman, J. 1969. *Experiment at Berkeley*. London: Oxford University Press.

Optimizing Capital, Social Reproduction, and Undergraduate Persistence

A Sociological Perspective

Joseph B. Berger

B ourdieu's theory of social reproduction is gaining increasing popularity with American social scientists as a conceptual framework for explaining inequities in levels of educational (Lareau 1989; Mehan 1992; Persell, Catsambis, and Cookson 1992; McDonough 1994) and status attainment (DiMaggio and Mohr 1985) in America. Bourdieu's work is appealing to many social scientists because it provides a means for helping to explain social inequities, and it is the hope of some that Bourdieu's theory might help further inform the battle against social inequities (DiMaggio 1979; Brubaker 1985; Lareau 1989). Although several researchers have investigated the implications of Bourdieu's theory of social reproduction on primary and secondary education in the United States (e.g., Lareau 1990; Mehan 1992), there have been only a few attempts to apply his work to U.S. higher education. However, recently this has begun to change. For example, Bourdieu's concepts have been applied to the study of the college-choice process (McDonough 1994, 1997; Freeman 1997), postsecondary educational access (Rhoads and Valadez 1996), and postsecondary educational attainment (DiMaggio and Mohr 1985). Moreover, others advocate the use of Bourdieu's concepts as a valuable way to examine issues related to institutional selectivity (Hearn 1990).

Less directly, the issue of social class has been mentioned as a potentially important factor to consider when examining the undergraduate persistence process (e.g., Berger 1997b; Milem and Berger 1997; Berger and Milem 1999; Tinto 1993). Tinto (1993), in his seminal work on undergraduate persistence, mentions the importance that social class and race may play in student departure, although he observes that most studies have examined race more than social class.

Investigating the role that students' access to capital plays in the persistence process is not new. However, most existing studies have focused exclusively on economic capital resources (e.g., Cabrera, Nora, and Castañeda 1992; St. John, Paulsen, and Starkey 1996). Similarly, for years many studies of college choice focused primarily on the role of economic capital, yet recent work by McDonough (1994) has generated a great deal of interest in the ways that social and cultural capital affect college choice. Additionally, it has been suggested that financial reasons (or what might be called "economic capital resources") are the "nexus" between college choice and persistence (St. John, Paulsen, and Starkey 1996). Extending this logic to include other kinds of capital (such as cultural capital), it may be that the process of optimizing capital resources is an important influence on undergraduate persistence. Hence, a social reproduction perspective may help us better understand how student access to and manipulation of capital resources affects undergraduate retention.

It has also been suggested that organizations, as well as individuals, pursue the optimization of capital resources. Bourdieu (1973) argues that there are certain "laws of the educational market" that guide "the hierarchy of educational establishments" (p. 494). According to Bourdieu, the European educational systems he studied consist of different types of institutions arranged hierarchically in a manner that mirrors existing social classes. These institutions, through the perspectives and actions of administrative leaders who act as agents for the schools, have access to and attempt to optimize various forms of capital at the organizational level. Evidence of organizational social reproduction has been identified in American educational institutions as well. Schools at the elementary and secondary levels have been documented as pursuing their own efforts to optimize cultural and economic capital (McDonough 1997). In doing so, these institutions affect student progress through the educational pipeline.

Although the terminology is slightly different, the same type of phenomenon has been documented in the American system of education. For example, Riesman's (1956) description of higher education as a "snake-like procession" and Meyer's (1970) concept of "social charter" both speak to the differential levels upon which educational organizations are able to acquire and use various types of resources to enhance their places in the educational hierarchy. It has also been noted in a wide range of literature (e.g., Kamens 1971, 1974; Astin 1985) that different types of postsecondary institutions tend to produce different retention rates—for example, institutions at the top of the institutional hierarchy tend to have much higher retention rates than those located lower in the hierarchy. Hence, it seems that if we are to fully understand undergraduate persistence from a social reproduction perspective, then we must account for what is happening at both the individual and organizational levels in the persistence process. Attending to both the organizational and individual levels also provides a means for viewing the undergraduate persistence process from the interactional perspective promoted by Tinto (1975, 1993) in his seminal work on persistence.

Building upon the concepts originally introduced by Bourdieu and further developed by McDonough (1994, 1997), among others, the purpose of this chapter is to develop a conceptual framework for viewing undergraduate persistence through a social reproduction lens. More specifically, this chapter uses Bourdieu's notions regarding the optimization of cultural capital and other resources to guide the development of this conceptual framework. This framework will focus on how students' initial levels of capital resources and their use of various optimizing strategies affect persistence in different types of postsecondary institutions, which are themselves also attempting to optimize their own capital resources.

Summarizing Bourdieu's Theory of Social Reproduction

Given the tremendous impact Bourdieu's work has had on the ways in which we have come to define various forms of capital, it makes sense to begin with a brief review of the key concepts within his theoretical framework. Bourdieu (1973, 1977), in his theory of social reproduction, lays out several constructs that can be used to explain student attrition at institutions of higher education. Rather than using the Marxian emphasis on access to material production as the essential criterion of class, Bourdieu defines multiple class resource bases (Brubaker 1985). He does so by identifying multiple types of capital, including economic (money and material objects) and cultural (informal interpersonal skills, habits, manners, linguistics, educational credentials, and lifestyle preferences). As Bourdieu's writings developed over a period of years he identified an increasing number of types of capital. He continually refined his concepts and elaborated upon his original concept of cultural capital, first adding social capital, then symbolic, followed by many other types of capital, including artistic, intellectual, credentialed, cultural, and others. Bourdieu's inclination to progressively expand his repertoire of types of capital led DiMaggio (1979) to observe, "As the number of capital increases, the metaphorical currency undergoes inflation and its value declines accordingly" (p. 1469). Hence, it seems most practical, parsimonious, and efficient to focus on the constructs of cultural and economic capital in this chapter. This type of focus also remains true to Bourdieu's original conception in which he focused primarily on the roles of cultural capital and economic capital as the two *primary* types of commodities used in the social reproduction process.

Individuals with access to the most capital resources, in various combinations, constitute the upper class, and they use their resources to maintain and/or expand their capital resources and class standing. All forms of capital can be converted, to a limited extent, from one into another. Careful manipulation of existing capital resources allows individuals to increase their position and status in society through the accumulation of greater sums of capital. Capital has a cumulative effect; the greater the early accumulation, the easier it becomes to expand one's personal holdings (DiMaggio and Mohr 1985).

Understanding cultural capital is the key to comprehending Bourdieu's work. It was originally conceptualized as a means for explaining why access to economic capital alone failed to adequately explain social stratification. Cultural capital is a symbolic, rather than material, resource. It has no intrinsic value, other than the ways in which it can be converted, manipulated, and invested in order to secure other highly valued and scarce resources, including economic capital (McDonough 1997). Moreover, it is a type of knowledge that members of the upper class value but is not taught in schools (McDonough 1997).

In keeping with much of the existing literature, the terms "high" and "low" will be used throughout this chapter to describe individual and organizational levels of cultural capital. This is not intended to indicate that the symbolic resources of some individuals and groups are inherently better or superior to the symbolic resources of others. Rather the terms "high" and 'low" are used to refer to the value that is typically attached in American society to certain kinds of symbolic resources, such as cultural capital. It is important to recognize that there are existing inequities in the ways in which value is ascribed to different patterns of cultural behavior. This type of distinction is important because such recognition provides the means for understanding how symbolic resources, in addition to material resources, play an important role in reproducing existing patterns of inequality.

Individuals with access to similar types and amounts of capital share a common habitus, according to Bourdieu (1971). He further elaborates that habitus is a "system of lasting, transposable dispositions which, integrating past experiences, functions at every moment as *a matrix of perceptions, appreciations, and actions*" (p. 83). In other words, people who live similar lifestyles because of their common level of access to capital develop a shared worldview as a result of common experiences and interaction. This habitus fosters a common representation of the world in a class-specific manner at a cognitive, taken-for-granted level. Thus, certain preferences and tendencies become routinized as part of an individual's worldview. People unconsciously classify themselves with others based on common preferences and expectations. This also serves as a mechanism for marginalizing others who have access to different amounts and types of capital.

Bourdieu also discusses the existence of fields or competitive arenas, each with its own logic and stakes (e.g., education, religion), where capital is employed so that agents, individual (e.g., students) or collective (e.g., educational institutions), can protect or enhance their existing resources (DiMaggio 1979). Capital and habitus come into play within a specific field because that field and its specific logic dictate in what ways different amounts and types of capital can be used for competitive advantage. Education is generally the locus of much competitive activity in modern society (DiMaggio 1979). Bourdieu (1973) argues that schools reproduce and legitimate existing class structure by transforming class distinctions into distinctions of merit. Given that cultural capital tends to be cumulative, students with higher initial levels of cultural capital (acquired from primary socialization in the family) tend to be able to use the initial familial investments of cultural capital to gain further cultural wealth through the secondary socialization process in the schools (Bourdieu 1973; Mehan 1992).

Bourdieu's theory clearly has implications for the study of American higher education. Indeed, the work of several scholars, particularly McDonough (1994, 1997), demonstrates that the American educational system does serve as an arena in which students and institutions strive to optimize capital resources. McDonough (1994, 1997) applies Bourdieu's concepts to the study of the college choice and admission process. She explores "the inter-institutional transition of an individual from high school to college" (1994, p. 428) and asserts that colleges and universities are becoming increasingly competitive for the best students, while at the same time it is harder for students to get "into the 'right' college because of increased competition and standards" (1994, p. 427).

Class, McDonough (1994) argues, is a major shaping force of ways in which students perceive and pursue college attendance. Choosing the "right" college is important because it provides opportunities for individuals to maximize their previous education, skills, and abilities in socially legitimate ways. Students from higher socioeconomic classes have a narrow range of legitimately appropriate collegiate institutions from which to choose if they want to maintain or improve the social and economic status that has been provided by their parents and families. For many students, going to college is not a matter of conscious choice. Rather, it is taken for granted as part of their cognitive schemes that have been shaped by their home and community environments. As a result, the goals of these students often have less to do with going to or graduating from college and instead focus on matriculating into and graduating from the "right" or "elite" colleges. A student's habitus dictates what she/he considers to be the right kind of college and how that student personally defines ultimate educational aspirations.

Students' beliefs about their postsecondary educational choices and outcomes are called "entitlements" by McDonough (1997). In other words, students, based on their class backgrounds and subsequently the nature of each's habitus, have different perceived higher education entitlements to which they should have access. Students from "higher" social classes are more likely to believe that they are entitled to attend a highly selective institution (DiMaggio 1982), whereas students from a "lower" social class are less likely to believe that they are entitled to a college education. Student beliefs about college choices and entitlements are limited by the "bounded rationality" (March and Simon 1958) that is defined by their habitus (McDonough 1997). Indeed, student decisions and behaviors are less the results of intentional, autonomous choices than they are the enactments of predetermined scripts (McDonough 1997).

Recent work by St. John, Paulsen, and Starkey (1996) indicates that student finances affect both college choice and persistence. In fact, they suggest that finances are the "nexus" for studying choice and persistence as one longitudinal process, rather than as two discrete components within the educational pipeline. Rephrasing these findings in terminology consistent with Bourdieu's theory, one might say that the optimization of economic capital affects educational attainment at the levels of both college choice and persistence. If we consider the work by St. John, Paulsen, and Starkey (1996) in conjunction with the work of McDonough (1997), it makes sense to examine how the optimization of capital resources, cultural in addition to economic, affects undergraduate retention. For example, students with greater cultural capital may believe not only that they are entitled to college education at a particular type of institution but that they are entitled to a degree from that institution as well, while students with less access to cultural capital may feel less entitled to earn a degree.

The remainder of this chapter is devoted to developing a new theoretical perspective on retention that is based on Bourdieu's theory of social reproduction. The role of cultural capital at the individual level is considered first, followed by a discussion of the role played by cultural capital at the institutional level in higher education and then an explanation of how these two levels might interact to affect persistence. The chapter concludes with discussions of implications for research and policy.

Individual Student Social Reproduction in American Higher Education

Bourdieu's emphasis on educational systems as one of the primary venues through which families and individuals seek to optimize capital resources has led to a number of educational studies that use his work as a guiding conceptual framework. There is evidence that education at all levels, from the beginning of elementary school through postsecondary educational attainment, serves as an important arena in which individuals strive, consciously and unconsciously, to optimize economic and cultural capital.

Several studies have examined the role that cultural capital plays in educational access and equity at various points in the educational process— including elementary, secondary, and the transition to college. Throughout his extensive body of work, Bourdieu emphasizes the important role that educational institutions serve in acting as intermediary agents through which individuals optimize existing capital in order to accumulate greater shares of economic and cultural capital later in life. Hence, choosing whether or not to go to college is one important decision that is largely guided by previous accumulations of economic and cultural capital. While the economic capital resources of students are accumulated almost exclusively within the home environment, the school environment contributes to students' acquisition of cultural capital resources above and beyond family contributions (Bourdieu 1973).

For example, observation of elementary-school children and teachers has demonstrated that even young children are already engaged in the process of optimizing the capital they possess as a result of their families' resources (Lareau 1989; Mehan 1992). It has also been noted that schoolchildren who already possess higher levels of cultural capital from home are often rewarded in the classroom with greater recognition and reinforcement from teachers (Lareau 1989; Mehan 1992). Hence, students, even at the elementary-school level, are able to use existing capital resources to further accumulate cultural capital from within the school environment. Studies of secondary-school attendance and achievement have also noted the important role played by access to and optimal use of capital resources in both public (Mehan 1992) and private school settings (Persell, Catsambis, and Cookson 1992). Cultural capital, gained through both primary (the home) and secondary (school and peers) socialization, has also been found to be advantageous for students who seek to attend more prestigious postsecondary educational institutions (Persell, Catsambis, and Cookson 1992). It has also been noted that once students have acquired certain levels of capital resources, school teachers and administrators begin to "channel" these students into college prep and advanced placement tracts and courses (Freeman 1997).

Although this chapter focuses on undergraduate persistence, it is important to mention the role that earlier educational experiences play in educational attainment. Understanding the role that earlier educational experiences play in shaping future chances of persistence is a key part of understanding retention from a social reproduction perspective. Undergraduate persistence is only one portion of a longer educational attainment process. Bourdieu emphasizes that the accumulation of capital resources is cumulative in nature. The earlier one begins to accumulate capital in various forms, and the earlier one is able to begin optimizing those same resources, the greater advantage one will have later in the educational process. Hence, the elementary- and secondary-school experiences contribute to the individual accumulation of cultural capital of students. These earlier experiences, by affecting the accumulation of cultural capital for students, seem to have an effect on whether or not students are likely to attend college and if so, an effect on where students choose to go to college and how likely they are to persist.

Student choices regarding whether or not to attend college, which college to attend, whether to go full-time or part-time, what to study, whether to drop out, stop out, transfer, or complete their studies are all examples of important choices that individuals make regarding postsecondary educational attendance. These are examples of what St. John, Paulsen, and Starkey (1996) identify as patterns of decision-making behavior. These patterns might also be defined in terms of an individual's habitus, and it stands to reason that students with similar habitus would be likely to continue to make similar choices once they enter college. Hence, we expect students with similar levels of capital resources to make similar types of decisions and act in similar ways while in college.

Existing literature on postsecondary educational attainment suggests that access to capital resources plays a pivotal role in helping determine the chances for success that different types of students have with regard to the completion of a college degree. Astin (1993) studied a large and longitudinal national sample of college and university student peer groups. The findings from Astin's study indicate that completion of college is more likely for students from the upper socioeconomic stratum. DiMaggio and Mohr (1985) found that high levels of cultural capital increase opportunities for help from teachers and gatekeepers. They also found that cultural capital has a strong positive impact on college completion, graduate education, and educational attainment. Evidence clearly exists that suggests that cultural, in addition to economic, capital plays an important role in the undergraduate persistence process for individual students.

Postsecondary Educational Organizations as Optimizers of Capital

Because most American scholars have focused on individual social reproduction, we have little direct empirical evidence about organizational social reproduction, at least in terms that Bourdieu might use to describe these processes. However, there is indirect evidence that organizations, postsecondary educational organizations in particular, strive to optimize both economic and cultural capital as part of the social reproduction process. An examination of a number of organizational studies of postsecondary institutions in America reveals how institutional attempts to maximize capital resources affect student enrollment, experiences, and outcomes in American higher education.

Paying attention to social reproduction processes at both the individual and organizational levels in higher education has important ramifications for the study of undergraduate persistence. McDonough (1997) suggests that educational organizations are themselves involved in the process of social reproduction. Building upon the ideas originally conceptualized by Bourdieu, she suggests that student perceptions of what they are "entitled" to in life, educationally and otherwise, are shaped by a combination of the ways in which students access capital resources and the social organizations they interact with (educational in particular). Examination of such processes may help account for different persistence rates at the individual level and may also help explain how and why retention rates vary by institutional type. Hence, it is the interaction of individual and organizational social reproduction processes that best explains undergraduate persistence from a Bourdieuian perspective.

The idea that educational organizations are competing for resources (economic and cultural) is not a new idea in the study of American higher education. This concept was first introduced in the 1950s when Riesman (1956) described the "snakelike procession" of the American academic community. Just as the tail of a snake eventually follows the head, institutions at the bottom and middle of the higher education institutional hierarchy (those institutions with less access to capital resources) are trying to catch up with the institutions at the top of the hierarchy. However, institutions higher in the hierarchy continually watch and protect their positions. Hence, in a serpentine manner institutions lower in the hierarchy pass where those institutions had been previously without ever catching up. Thus, the basic hierarchical institutional order remains preserved, and the status quo is "socially reproduced." This pattern of organizational behavior provides some initial indications that postsecondary institutions, like individuals, can use their greater access to economic and cultural resources to protect their positions of status and socially reproduce the existing order. The most compelling pieces of evidence come from work done in the 1970s (e.g., Meyer 1970; Kamens 1971, 1974, 1978; Clark et al. 1972). Meyer (1970) defines the existence of institutional "charters" and describes them as socially constructed and legitimized definitions of the product of a socializing organization. In the case of a college or university, this product is a graduate with specific attributes. These attributes are believed to represent the kind of education provided by the institution and the quality of that education. Meyer suggests that social charters are more important than the internal conditions at a college or university. Social charters can be thought of as socially agreed upon and legitimated assessments of the cultural capital of an institution.

Kamens (1971, 1974) further develops the concept of social charter in higher education and the effects of an institution's charter on students. Highly selective and/or large universities (that have traditionally held access to large sums of economic and cultural capital) hold charters as a result of widespread and important societal constituencies believing that these institutions are more likely to graduate their students and more likely to graduate them into high-status careers. The charter also defines and legitimates the different hierarchical levels of status of various institutions within higher education.

In a later work Kamens (1978) takes a slightly different approach and explores the different types of myths used by elite institutions to legitimize their socially defined roles as the producers of a particular kind of individual in society. In the case of elite institutions, individuals are transformed to a higher status level because of their experiences in a particular educational organization. Their transformation occurs as a result of their immersion in an environment that espouses a particular educational ideology, which may be viewed as a manifestation of the organizational habitus. This provides Kamens (1978) with an excellent mechanism, socially legitimated myths, for explaining ways in which elite universities are able to construct and reproduce distinctive charters. This in turn makes individuals more likely to believe that these universities promise a more successful graduate better chances of individual success in American society. Kamens's (1978) ideas focus on organizations. However, he also provides a mechanism for linking broader societal forces into the retention puzzle. He does so by explaining how organizational myths are transmitted and reproduced in ways that compel individuals from the upper class to see institutions as means for reproducing and increasing their cultural capital. Subsequently the charters of elite universities become institutionalized as part of the upper-class habitus, and graduation from these universities becomes an expected part of the cognitive schema for upper-class students. There may also be other types of expectations about other types of colleges and universities ingrained in the habitus for students from other places in the social strata.

The information presented in this section demonstrates that there are real and perceived societal benefits that result from attendance at and graduation from institutions with well-developed capital resources. These benefits, real or perceived, play a crucial role in perpetuating the institutional charters of these universities. The charter, in turn, enables these institutions to attract individuals who bring certain levels of cultural and economic capital. The high influx of capital ensures the continuation of dominant upper-class habitus within these institutions. This leads to better chances of future success for students. They can convert the capital they have brought with them or that they have accumulated into occupational and status opportunities. The charter of the institution is part of a circle in which real and perceived success of graduates from elite research universities reinforces existing societal beliefs about the student product of these institutions, and this ultimately perpetuates the same benefits that led to the charter in the first place. Hence, behavior at such institutions is generally limited to preestablished routines that represent the accepted patterns of the established charter and that are part of preexisting cognitive schemes within the dominant habitus.

Schools with stronger social charters, or greater amounts of institutional cultural capital, are able to more effectively retain students for two reasons. First, they attract students who possess habitus in which graduation from college is most often an inevitable, foregone conclusion. Second, the power these institutions have to allocate graduates to high status roles provides a compelling reason for students to persist at these institutions. Even if students are not satisfied with their collegiate experiences, they are apt to realize that leaving such an institution is a less than optimal use of capital resources. Conversely, as the social charters of institutions become increasingly weaker, they are less likely to attract students with such strong graduation commitments or to have the ability to help retain students. This inability occurs because the degree at that institution offers a less optimal utilization of capital. In other words, the stronger the social charter of an institution, the better the odds that students will see a larger return on their initial economic and cultural investments.

The Interaction of Individual and Organizational Social Reproduction in the Persistence Process

The previous two sections of this chapter focused on different levels of social phenomena—individual and organizational. Yet there has been ample evidence presented to demonstrate that social reproduction, through the use of capital resources (cultural in particular), operates at both the individual and organizational levels throughout the American education system, including higher education. The interaction between the levels seems to occur via the sorting, choosing, and selecting processes as students choose which college to attend and colleges decide which students to admit. The result is well known to observers of American higher education: students are not randomly assigned across the many and diverse college and university campuses that dot the American landscape. Instead, each campus is composed of students who generally share a common habitus that is to some extent congruent with the organizational habitus of that institution.

The fact that student bodies may be primarily composed of students from certain socioeconomic classes is not a trivial matter. Extensive research on peer referent groups (Newcomb 1966; Feldman and Newcomb 1969; Clark et al. 1972; Weidman 1989; Astin 1993; Milem 1998) demonstrates how influential the dominant student attitudes and characteristics can be on a college or university campus. Peer group research on college campuses has shown that dominant groups tend to have conforming influences on most students within the same campus environment (Clark et al. 1972; Weidman 1989; Milem 1998). Hence, students who already share routinized behavior preferences, or those particularly adept at reading normative cues, are more likely to easily make the adjustments necessary to fit in with the dominant peer group(s). The similarity of shared backgrounds, aspirations, and attitudes among students who constitute the dominant majority on campus probably makes it easier for these students to adapt to campus life, and adaptation is likely more difficult for those who come from very different backgrounds. The importance of student congruence with their educational environments is well documented by a number of theories that focus on person-environment interaction (Chickering and Reisser 1993; Strange 1994). A number of studies have documented how students who are less congruent with their environments are less apt to be successful, while those who are more congruent are more likely to experience success (e.g., Pervin 1967; Stern 1970; Holland 1985; Banning 1989). This makes an argument for viewing the habitus as a powerful analytical construct. Students who already share or have exposure to the dominant habitus have the least amount of attitudinal and behavioral adjustment to make as they become integrated on campus.

Clark et al. (1972) also identify the educational institution's reputation or image as a powerful influence on students. Students choose colleges and universities based on image and tend to start adjusting their attitudes and behaviors to fit their perceptions of what it takes to be successful there. This is roughly akin to anticipatory socialization. Clark et al. (1972) warn that these same environments can also marginalize students. They note that students leave as a result of a "mismatch, usually more with the student body than with the educational program" (p. 316). The importance of access to cultural capital and the dominant habitus may highlight social integration, more than academic integration, as a key agent in student attrition. Clark et al. (1972) suggest that the public reputation of an institution ultimately influences the selection of students, colors their experiences on campus, and fosters perceptions about the value of a degree from that institution.

Peer group influence is particularly important in light of Feldman and Newcomb's (1969) observation that universities are and should be agents of socialization for society. Newcomb and Wilson (1966) argue that peer groups impact students as a result of selection and peer influence. Selection refers to the characteristics possessed by students as they enter college. The information in the immediately preceding paragraphs shows that students enter elite universities with a distinct set of characteristics, generally possess access to large amounts of capital, and share a certain habitus. These selection characteristics facilitate powerful peer influences.

This could be particularly insightful when socioeconomic class is considered as a major demographic factor. Bourdieu (1973, 1977) provides a compelling argument that people from a similar class background share a common conscious or unconscious understanding about the world. This allows them to communicate among themselves with a greater degree of clarity and understanding than they have in communications with people from dissimilar classes. This theoretical perspective suggests that individuals from different classes could experience the same organizational environment in very different ways. Hence, the social subsystem of a campus is an important mechanism for explaining how social reproduction plays out on the college or university campus.

Much of this discussion is reminiscent of Tinto's (1975, 1993) seminal theory. Indeed, the entitlements that McDonough (1997) speaks of are roughly analogous to Tinto's formulations about goal and institutional commitment. Moreover, those students who are fully congruent with the organizational habitus might be thought of as fully integrated into the academic and social subsystems of a campus. However, those students who lack the requisite cultural capital may have a hard time or be unable to fully integrate because their frame of reference is just too different from the organizational habitus and the habitus of the dominant peer group on campus. While clearly there are parallels to Tinto's work, it would be misleading to simply recast Tinto's theory in social reproduction language or vice versa. Bourdieu's theory is what Tinto might call a "societal level" theory and as such has been dismissed by Tinto (1993) as impractical for the study of retention at the campus level. Additionally, Tinto's model builds upon the assumption that students need to successfully integrate into the life of the campus and that on doing so they relinquish some norms, values, and beliefs from their home lives. A social reproduction perspective suggests that there are built-in organizational mechanisms that result when an institution pursues its own agenda for social reproduction. These mechanisms preclude students without the right cultural capital or habitus from integrating. Moreover, students who do successfully integrate from a social reproduction perspective do so not at the expense of their home backgrounds but because of them.

If the social subsystem is important, so too is the academic subsystem. Tinto (1975, 1993) stresses the importance of academic integration as a key construct in his model. However, a review of empirical tests of the Tinto model does not provide support for this construct as a precursor for persistence (Braxton, Sullivan, and Johnson 1997). However, more recent work by Tinto (1997) demonstrates the importance of the classroom in retention. It may be that academic integration, as conceptualized by Tinto (1975, 1993), is not important for all students. The academic subsystem may be more important in terms of how well students' habitus and entitlement beliefs match with academic expectations manifested as a reflection of the organizational habitus. For example, the ways in which faculty view and interact with students with different levels of cultural capital may be an important consideration. Given the different ways that teachers, counselors, and administrators treat elementary and secondary students who have different levels of cultural capital, it may be that the same phenomenon is occurring at college and university campuses. Indeed, Astin (1993) suggests that faculty tend to have different expectations for and perceptions of students at campuses where high socioeconomic backgrounds permeate the student body. Additionally, Astin (1993) contends that students from wealthier backgrounds are more prepared or trained for the type of academic environment typically found in higher education.

Rhoads and Valadez (1996) document some of the ways that courses, curricula, educational programs, and pedagogical practices often serve to protect the social reproduction process and, in doing so, privilege some students (those with high levels of cultural capital) while marginalizing others (those with less access to cultural capital). Hence, it may be that students' academic behaviors are shaped by their own personal habitus and by the expectations of the organizational habitus as manifested in academic programs and faculty interaction with students. Peer interaction may also be a component of the academic subsystem in terms of study habits, classroom behaviors, and other peer-oriented academic behaviors.

The previously mentioned built-in organizational mechanisms are also key to understanding how forces of individual and organizational reproduction interact as an influence on undergraduate persistence. These organizational mechanisms begin with the admissions process but include financial aid, student services, and other administrative offices that deal directly with students. The people who deal with students out of class in terms of determining what is and is not appropriate behavior and/or types of activities, formal and informal, that students can or cannot be involved in, have an important influence on the type of collegiate experience students encounter on campus. It is also likely that administrative institutional agents are prone to the same patterns of interaction with students from different backgrounds as are faculty members.

There is a growing body of work that suggests that organizational, or administrative, behavior at colleges affects a number of student outcomes (Astin and Scherrei 1980; Berger 1997a; Berger and Milem 2000). Such work indicates not only that student experiences and outcomes are affected by how administrative agents interact directly with students, but also that various patterns of administrative decision making and functioning impact student experiences and outcomes. Moreover, existing studies that focus specifically on retention suggest that how students perceive the organizational functioning on a campus has direct and indirect effects on persistence (Bean 1980, 1983; Braxton and Brier 1989; Berger and Braxton 1998). In fact, such perceptions were found to have a bigger effect on persistence at a highly selective institution (Berger and Braxton 1998) than had been found at a less selective, commuter institution (Braxton and Brier 1989). This discrepancy in findings between two different types of institutions, each of which is likely to have a distinct type of organizational habitus, suggests that the organizational subsystem does affect different types of students in different ways at different types of institutions.

The three campus subsystems—academic, social, and organizational—could be thought of as sources of both challenge and support for students. The more congruent a student's habitus is with the organizational habitus as it is manifested through these subsystems, the more apt the student is to perceive them as a source of support. In contrast, less congruence might lead to a perception of the subsystems as too challenging. Hence, the literature discussed in this section demonstrates how the organizational, social, and academic subsystems of a campus interact with students to affect persistence. Obviously, students who do a good job of matching their individual access to capital with a school having congruent amounts has the best chance for success.

Putting It All Together: Undergraduate Retention from a Social Reproduction Perspective

The previous sections of this chapter provide ample evidence that a social reproduction perspective provides one possible theoretical contribution to the development of our growing understanding of the undergraduate persistence process. In a social reproduction model of student persistence, a student makes college choice decisions and enters college with a variety of background characteristics. Typically, researchers interested in retention have looked at background characteristics such as race, gender, academic achievement (high school grade point average and standardized test scores), family income, and other basic sociodemographic characteristics. However, in order to fully understand persistence from a social reproduction perspective, we must also consider the issue of access to various capital resources. While previous research has used measures of socioeconomic status or family income as a proxy for economic capital, there has been no research on the effects of students' initial levels of cultural capital on retention.

Students' backgrounds, particularly their accumulations of cultural capital, shape their habitus, which in turn are major determinants of students' expected entitlements regarding postsecondary education—all of which affect their choices of educational institutions. At the same time colleges also have certain characteristics, including their own access to capital resources, that lead to their organizational habitus. The organizational habitus influences admissions processes and decisions. Hence, the combination of individual student college choice and organizational student selection determines which types of students in certain concentrations attend each institution.

As students encounter the subenvironments of an institution—academic, social, and organizational—their chances of persistence are affected by the extent to which their habitus and related beliefs of entitlement are congruent with the dominant organizational habitus. The dominant organizational habitus permeates the campus subenvironments. The academic subsystem reflects the extent to which academic expectations of the institution reflect the organizational habitus. For example, the nature and design of the curriculum, the role of developmental classes, pedagogical strategies, expected classroom behaviors, types of academic support, studying norms, and nature of faculty contact are shaped by the more general habitus of the college or university. In a similar fashion, the social subsystem reflects the organizational habitus through the type (or types) of dominant peer groups on campus and the way social opportunities and activities are structured on campus. The organizational subsystem mirrors the institution's habitus in the way decisions are made and how administrators interact with students.

The financial subsystem of an educational institution may also be important in terms of how well the financial package (including considerations of tuition and financial aid) meets student expectations regarding the amount of material resources they are willing to invest for a degree from that institution. Although this chapter focuses on the use of symbolic resources as the primary conceptual keys to understanding persistence from a social reproduction perspective, it is important to remember that economic capital often plays an important role in the persistence process (St. John, Paulsen, and Starkey 1996; Paulsen and St. John 1997).

Collectively, the ways in which these subsystems represent the organizational habitus directly affect students' chances for persistence. The more congruent a student's habitus and expectations in terms of entitlements are with the way in which an organization manifests its habitus through these subsystems, the more likely that student is to persist. Although most literature on retention has used Tinto's (1975, 1993) description of a "departure decision," often there may not be a decision involved in the persistence process. Those students who are truly congruent with their environments, or are fully "integrated," to use Tinto's (1975, 1993) term, are apt to take their collegiate experiences for granted as part of their habitus. As such, the college experience is routinized such that persistence and graduation occur as a natural progression for these students. In other words, not graduating is not an option in the bounded rationality used by these students as they move through the collegiate experience. Students who feel that their entitlements have been shortchanged by their experiences with campus environments may leave. Upper-class students are less likely to leave higher education altogether and more likely to transfer to other colleges as a resource optimization strategy.

In contrast, students who have relatively lower levels of either economic or cultural capital may leave for either voluntary or involuntary reasons. The bounded rationality that occurs as a result of their backgrounds and habitus is more likely to include a range of choices that lead to dropout or stop-out. Students from lower socioeconomic classes are also less likely to feel that they have a wide range of options in terms of colleges to attend—because they feel geographically constrained, they believe that they cannot make the admissions standards, or they cannot afford other colleges (McDonough 1997). As a result, they may simply leave college for good if their first experiences are not satisfactory and/or successful. They may also leave voluntarily to find environments where they fit in better or can be more successful. This may happen as a result of needing to find a better economic or cultural match. This type of student may also leave involuntarily. From an economic perspective this may be due to the inability to pay the bills. However, from a cultural capital point of view, departure may be due to failure to meet either social or academic expectations that are congruent with the organizational habitus or because of the difficulty of understanding the cues from the organizational subsystem.

It is important to note that students with relatively lower levels of cultural capital may still persist and graduate, but this will be more difficult in an environment that has developed an organizational habitus around attracting, educating, and graduating students with access to higher levels of cultural capital. Indeed, in order for schools to maintain or improve upon their social charters, they must continue to produce a specific type of social product in terms of the students they graduate. Viewing this phenomenon from another perspective, an institution needs to protect its campus potency in order to preserve its image potency (Clark et al. 1972).

The preceding discussion provides a conceptual foundation for developing some specific propositions that could be used to test a social reproduction perspective on undergraduate persistence. Two of these propositions are focused at the level of higher education as a system, and two are focused at the level of the individual student. All of the propositions build on the assumption that colleges and universities serve as organizational junctions in which individual students are transmitters and receivers of broader societal expectations and influences. The propositions concerning the system of higher education follow.

Proposition 1—Institutions with higher levels of cultural capital will have the highest retention rates.

It is much more likely that students from upper-class, high cultural capital backgrounds will invest a great deal of time and energy in the college search and choice process than will students from lower socioeconomic strata (McDonough 1997); this is part of the bounded rationality that is generally associated with the upper-class habitus. Additionally, institutions with high organizational cultural capital tend to be extremely selective. The result is that such institutions tend to attract students with high levels of cultural capital, and the congruence between students' expected entitlements and the social, academic, and organizational campus subsystems tends to be high. Conversely, postsecondary educational organizations with lower levels of cultural capital will have less ability to retain students because neither the students nor the institutions are as selective in the choice and admissions processes. Hence, the bounded rationality for this group of students inhibits them from having access to as much information about the college and its subsystems. This lack of knowledge, coupled with a habitus that is less likely to include a commitment to finishing college, leads to student bodies at these campuses that have higher attrition rates than do the student bodies at high cultural capital institutions.

In order to test this proposition it is necessary to identify institutions with high and low levels of organizational cultural capital. Highly selective institutions (primarily private), large public institutions, and major research universities would tend to have the highest levels of organizational cultural capital, along with organizational habitus that appropriately reflect the levels of institutional access to symbolic resources. This is consistent with previous findings that these types of institutions have the strongest social chartérs (Kamens 1971, 1974). Conversely, community colleges and less selective, small private colleges, termed "invisible colleges" by Astin and Lee (1971), would tend to have lower levels of organizational cultural capital. Other types of institutions, including most public and private comprehensive institutions, would tend to fall in the middle range with regard to levels of organizational cultural capital. These broad, general groupings of institutions are quite consistent with previous descriptions of the perceived institutional hierarchy that exists in American higher education (Astin and Lee 1971; Astin 1985).

Proposition 2—Students with higher levels of cultural capital are more likely to persist, across all types of institutions, than are students with less access to cultural capital.

The literature reviewed in this chapter clearly indicates that students with access to higher levels of cultural capital have advantages throughout the educational pipeline in attaining educational goals. This is particularly true given the fact that the social, academic, and organizational subsystems of college and university campuses have become institutionalized across the field of postsecondary education to be more congruent with the habitus and entitlement expectations of students with access to higher levels of cultural capital. Indeed, students from backgrounds that have afforded them the opportunity to access high levels of cultural capital are much more likely to operate out of a bounded rationality in which going to and graduating from college is taken for granted as a basic educational entitlement (McDonough 1997). The student-level propositions follow.

Proposition 3—Students with higher levels of cultural capital are most likely to persist at institutions with correspondingly high levels of organizational cultural capital.

The more congruent the fit between individual and organizational levels of cultural capital, the greater the chance for persistence. This is particularly true for individuals and institutions with higher levels of access to cultural capital, because the attainment of a bachelor's degree becomes an assumed, taken-for-granted part of the bounded rationality that is determined by the habitus at both the individual and organizational levels. Moreover, this proposition is supported by the work of McDonough (1997), who has demonstrated through her work the ways in which students with high cultural capital backgrounds and institutions that operate as high cultural capital educational organizations both invest a great deal of time, effort, and economic resources into the college choice process. Hence, both students and postsecondary institutions use the initial investments in the choice and admission processes to increase the likelihood of a high degree of congruence between student habitus and organizational habitus. Not surprising, the initial investment frequently pays off for students in the form of seamless transition into the campus environment, which affords them a greater chance of graduating with degrees that will enhance their cultural and social capital (and often opportunities for additional economic capital). Colleges and universities benefit from their initial investments because they are able to develop higher or maintain high retention rates and allocate students to desirable occupational and advanced educational roles, both (high retention rates and role allocation) of which enhance the cultural capital of the institution.

Students with high access to cultural capital are less likely to persist at institutions with lower levels of cultural capital because their expected entitlements are less likely to be met by the social, academic, and organizational subsystems of the campuses. However, it should be noted that these students with access to high levels of cultural capital are likely to transfer to institutions that they believe will be better investments of capital resources, rather than just dropping out of college altogether.

More specifically, the congruence between cultural capital levels of students and those of campus subsystems (academic, social, and organizational) enhances the likelihood of persistence. Three subpropositions related to proposition 3 are:

Proposition 3a—Students with higher levels of cultural capital are more likely to become integrated into the academic systems of institutions with correspondingly high levels of organizational cultural capital.

Proposition 3b—Students with higher levels of cultural capital are more likely to become integrated into the social systems of institutions with correspondingly high levels of organizational cultural capital.

Proposition 3c—Students with higher levels of cultural capital are more likely to become integrated into the organizational systems of institutions with correspondingly high levels of organizational cultural capital.

Proposition 4—Students with access to lower levels of cultural capital are most likely to persist at institutions with correspondingly low levels of organizational cultural capital.

While higher education, at any level, generally tends to cater to students from higher cultural capital backgrounds, students are still more likely to persist as the differences between the organizational levels of cultural capital and the individual levels of cultural capital are minimized. Hence, building on the logic developed in propositions 1 and 2, it makes sense that institutions with lower levels of organizational cultural resources are less likely to regulate students with access to lower levels of cultural capital out of the institution than are colleges and universities with higher levels of organizational cultural capital.

As was the case for proposition 3, the academic, social, and organizational campus subsystems play important roles in the persistence process for individual students. Three subpropositions related to proposition 4 are:

Proposition 4a—Students with lower levels of cultural capital are more likely to become integrated into the academic systems of institutions with correspondingly low levels of organizational cultural capital.

Proposition 4b—Students with lower levels of cultural capital are more likely to become integrated into the social systems of institutions with correspondingly low levels of organizational cultural capital.

Proposition 4c—Students with lower levels of cultural capital are more likely to become integrated into the organizational systems of institutions with correspondingly low levels of organizational cultural capital.

Implications for Future Research

The conceptual framework developed in this chapter suggests several directions for future research on the undergraduate persistence process. First, it suggests that the propositions laid out in this chapter should be empirically tested across a number of institutional types. This is particularly true given the fact that institutions are engaged in capital optimization activities and because students are not randomly assigned to these institutions. One of the important features of this perspective is that the persistence process is viewed such that it varies from campus to campus, depending on the organizational habitus of the institution.

One of the hallmarks of any good theory is its ability to be operationalized, and clearly, one of the biggest challenges is operationalizing this model. DiMaggio and Mohr (1985) noted over a decade ago that we have yet to find good measures of cultural capital, with most existing literature depending on the use of proxy measures. There has been little or no progress made in this area during the intervening years. The same problem also holds true for the concept of habitus, at the individual and organizational levels. Perhaps it is best to use a mixed quantitative-qualitative approach to begin operationally defining some of these constructs. Inductive qualitative approaches could be used to help better define these constructs, and the results of such investigations could be used to help construct items that might be used in deductive quantitative tests of the model.

In the interim, it is necessary to properly identify operational definitions of key terms used throughout this chapter. First, *cultural capital* is a symbolic, not material, resource. Hence, it should be measured in terms of students' knowledge about and manifestation of manners, styles, and norms that generally are believed to be found in the social interactions of the upper socioeconomic stratum. At the organizational level, cultural capital is probably best approximated by Meyer's (1970) concept of social charter. Those institutions that graduate students into social roles that members of society have generally agreed are appropriate for high socioeconomic class members can be thought of as having high organizational cultural capital. Measures of this construct should include information on students' beliefs about the status of degrees awarded by their institutions and their beliefs about the ability of those degrees to help them realize advanced educational degrees and high-status occupational positions.

Habitus is the bounded rationality of specific class groups and includes a matrix of preferences, attitudes, and behaviors. It might best be thought of as the manifestation of cultural capital. Habitus is both the product of one's access to cultural capital and the medium through which members of a specific social class are able to demonstrate their level of access to cultural capital. Measures of this construct should be multidimensional. Because habitus is a matrix of preferences, attitudes, and behaviors (Bourdieu 1977), all three types should be targeted for data collection. These preferential, attitudinal, and behavioral subconstructs should closely mirror the indicators of cultural capital since habitus is the product of cultural capital. In fact, given the direct, linear relationship between cultural capital and habitus (and the fact that Bourdieu was not always consistent in differentiating between the two constructs), finding a good measure of one provides an indicator of the other. Hence, future studies might find that providing only a measure of habitus or cultural capital, but not both, provides a more parsimonious model without sacrificing much in the way of comprehensiveness.

One of the challenges in attempting to measure organizational habitus is to avoid the problem of ecological fallacy in which something is measured at the individual level and that measurement is then ascribed to a group or organization. One way to avoid this problem is to focus on measures of organizational cultural capital, such as patterns of organizational behavior, presence of specific institutional symbols, and the rates at which graduates of an institution are able to move directly into high-status educational and occupational roles. Additionally, scholars may want to consider the existence of organizational habitus as the result of a "structuration" process (Giddens 1979). Structuration theory focuses on the reciprocal interaction between human actors and the features of an organization, which might include the organizational habitus. Individual human behavior and perception are enabled and constrained by such structures, but these structures are nothing more than the results of previous human actions. Structures become manifested in rules, resources, and patterns of behavior that are used in daily behavior. These structures mediate human action, perception, and interaction while becoming reaffirmed through continued use. Hence, an organization's habitus is reinforced or created by individuals, but the consequences of such actions continue to bound the possibilities for future actions. This process creates certain patterns of organizational thought and action that tend to persist within a given organization.

Entitlements are specific manifestations of habitus. For example, educational entitlements are beliefs about appropriate educational aspirations for someone who operates out of a specific level of bounded rationality that is in turn determined by a specific type of habitus determined primarily by one's access to cultural capital. Examples of educational entitlements include beliefs about the type of postsecondary institution to attend, the strength of one's commitment to graduate from college, and the attitudes one has toward obtaining advanced degrees.

The ideas formulated in this chapter suggest that we might start looking at a wide range of student outcomes and experiences using social class and its related concepts as the conceptual framework for such investigations. The conceptual evidence in this chapter has been applied to the issue of student persistence but could easily and appropriately be applied to other student outcomes as well.

This perspective also suggests that we may want to start examining the educational pathways for students from different social classes. Patterns of dropout, stop-out, and transfer activities are likely to differ for students with different levels and configurations of capital. Examining which institutions certain types of students transfer to and from might serve as an informative way of viewing the capital optimization process in higher education.

Taken together, the organizational studies conducted by Reisman (1956), Meyer (1970), Kamens (1971, 1974), Brint and Karabel (1991), and others indicate that colleges and universities do have an organizational habitus that guides much activity on campus. Hence, the idea of "organizational habitus" also requires future exploration. While McDonough (1997) provides illustrations of how this operates in secondary-school settings, we only have indirect conceptual evidence that this does in fact occur in higher education.

There are some interesting possibilities with regard to how issues such as race and gender are impacted by this model. Bourdieu does note that age, sex, and ethnicity partially define class divisions (Brubaker 1985), and this could prove to be a useful way to further develop the concepts presented in this chapter. This is particularly true in light of the work done by DiMaggio and Mohr (1985) and Persell, Catsambis, and Cookson (1992) showing that women may not accrue as many benefits from an elite education as do men. Bourdieu's original conceptions were developed in Europe where the role of race is not as large as it is in the United States. While a fair number of studies have been done evaluating race as a retention factor in institutions of higher education, social class has yet to receive proper attention, especially, as Tinto (1993) notes, with regard to white students from lower socioeconomic classes.

In a similar vein, recent work by Hurtado et al. (1999) suggests that many institutions provide "embedded benefits" for the white students who compose the majority of the campus population at most colleges and universities. This may be another manifestation of the organizational habitus that exists on college campuses. Such embedded benefits may also exist for students from higher social classes as well, particularly in light of Astin's (1993) observations about the role of socioeconomic status in student experiences and outcomes. Although examination of these topics is beyond the scope of this chapter, the interaction of race, gender, and class may have interesting implications for the constructs of capital and habitus.

Recognition of the existence of an organizational habitus also has ramifications for investigating the marginalization of certain types of students. It has been suggested that colleges, because of their own organizational habitus, often fail to recognize valuable skills, abilities, attitudes, perceptions, and knowledge possessed by students from traditionally underrepresented groups in higher education. This includes students from nonwhite racial/ethnic groups, women, gays and lesbians, older students, and students from lower socioeconomic classes (Rhoads and Valadez 1996). This knowledge has been identified as "border knowledge" or "knowledge that resides outside of the canon, outside the cultural mainstream . . . is essentially a form of cultural capital deemed unworthy of exchange in mainstream educational settings" (Rhoads and Valadez 1996, p. 7). In other words, the organizational habitus of most colleges and universities tend not to recognize certain forms of cultural capital as legitimate. Thus, colleges and universities marginalize certain students and inhibit their ability to optimize capital resources, which in turn might negatively affect their chances for educational success, including the attainment of a bachelor's degree.

Conclusion

This chapter suggests that the undergraduate persistence process is part of the larger social process of social reproduction. The educational arena, including higher education, is one of the primary forums where individuals strive to optimize their access to levels of economic and cultural capital. At the same time leaders of educational organizations are working to optimize the capital resources for their schools, colleges, and universities. Subsequently, undergraduate persistence is the result of an interaction between individuals and institutions as optimizers of capital resources. This chapter provides the embryonic beginnings of how we might investigate persistence as part of a larger societal social reproduction process. Viewing persistence, and other education-related phenomena, from this perspective has powerful implications for both future research and policy.

References

Astin, A. W. 1985. *Achieving educational excellence.* San Francisco: Jossey-Bass.

Astin, A. W. 1993. *What matters in college: Four critical years revisited.* San Francisco: Jossey-Bass.

Astin, A. W., and R. Scherrei. 1980. *Maximizing leadership effectiveness.* San Francisco: Jossey-Bass.

Banning, J. 1989. Creating a climate for successful student development: The campus ecology manager role. In U. Delworth, G. R. Hanson, and Associates, *Student services: A handbook for the profession.* 2d ed. San Francisco: Jossey-Bass.

Bean, J. 1980. Dropouts and turnover: The synthesis and test of a causal model of student attrition. *Research in Higher Education* 12: 155–187.

Bean, J. 1983. The application of a model of turnover in work organizations to the student attrition process. *Review of Higher Education* 6: 129–148.

Berger, J. B. 1997a. The relationship between organizational behavior at colleges and student outcomes: Generating a quantitatively grounded theory. Ph.D. diss. Vanderbilt University.

Berger, J. B. 1997b. Students' sense of community in residence halls, social integration, and first-year persistence. *Journal of College Student Development* 38 (5): 441–452.

Berger, J. B., and J. M. Braxton. 1998. Revising Tinto's interactionalist theory of student departure through theory elaboration: Examining the role of organizational attributes in the persistence process. *Research in Higher Education* 39 (2): 103–120.

Berger, J. B. and Milem, J. F. (1999). The Role of Student Involvement and Perceptions of Integration in a Causal Model of Student Persistence. *Research in Higher Education,* 40(6): 641–664.

Berger, J. B., and J. F. Milem. 2000. Organizational behavior in higher education and student outcomes. In J. C. Smart (ed.), *Higher education: A handbook of theory and research,* vol. 15, pp. 268–338. New York: Agathon Press.

Bourdieu, P. 1971. Systems of education and systems of thought. In M. K. D. Young (ed.), *Knowledge and control: New directions for the sociology of education,* pp.189–207. London: Collier Macmillan.

Bourdieu, P. 1973. Cultural reproduction and social reproduction. In R. Brown (ed.), *Knowledge, education and cultural change,* pp. 487–510. London: Tavistock.

Bourdieu, P. 1977. *Outline of a theory of practice.* Translated by Richard Nice. Cambridge, U.K.: Cambridge University Press.

Braxton, J. M., and E. M. Brier. 1989. Melding organizational and interactional theories of student attrition: A path analytic study. *Review of Higher Education* 13 (1): 47–61.

Braxton, J. M., A. V. S. Sullivan, and R. M. Johnson. 1997. Appraising Tinto's theory of college student departure. In J. C. Smart (ed.), *Higher education: A handbook of theory and research,* vol. 12, pp. 107–164. New York: Agathon Press.

Brint, S., and J. Karabel. 1991. Institutional origins and transformations: The case of American community colleges. In W. W. Powell and P. J. DiMaggio (eds.), *The new institutionalism in organizational analysis,* pp. 337–360. Chicago: University of Chicago Press.

Brubaker, R. 1985. Rethinking classical theory: The sociological vision of Pierre Bourdieu. *Theory and Society* 14: 745–772.

Cabrera, A. F., A. Nora, and M. B. Castañeda. 1992. The role of finances in the persistence process: A structural model. *Research in Higher Education* 33 (5): 571–593.

Chickering, A. W., and L. Reisser. 1993. *Education and identity.* 2d ed. San Francisco: Jossey-Bass.

Clark, B., P. Heist, T. R. McConnell, M. A. Trow, and G. Yonge. 1972. *Students and colleges: Interaction and change.* Berkeley, Calif.: Center for Research and Development in Higher Education.

DiMaggio, P. 1979. Review essay: On Pierre Bourdieu. *American Journal of Sociology* 84 (6): 1460–1474.

DiMaggio, P. (1982). Cultural Capital and School Success: The Impact of Status Culture Participation on the Grades of U.S. High School Students. *American Sociological Review* 47 (2):189–201.

DiMaggio, P., and J. Mohr. 1985. Cultural capital, educational attainment, and marital selection. *American Journal of Sociology* 90 (6): 1231–1261.

Feldman K. A., and T. M. Newcomb. 1969. *The impact of college on students,* vol. 1. San Francisco: Jossey-Bass.

Freeman, K. 1997. Increasing African Americans' participation in higher education. *Journal of Higher Education* 68 (5): 523–550.

Giddens, A. (1979). *Central problems in social theory Action, structure, and contradiction in social analysis.* Berkeley: University of California Press.

Hearn, J. C. 1990. Pathways to attendance at the elite colleges. In P. Kingston and J. Smart (eds.), *Elite undergraduate institutions.* New York: Agathon Press.

Holland, J. L. 1985. *Making vocational choices: A theory of vocational personalities and work environments.* Englewood Cliffs, N.J.: Prentice-Hall.

Hurtado, S., J. F. Milem, A. Clayton-Pederson, and W. Allen. 1999. *Enacting diverse learning environments: Improving the climate for racial/ethnic diversity in higher education.* ASHE-ERIC Report 26–8. Washington, D.C.: School of Education and Development, George Washington University.

Kamens, D. H. 1971. The college "charter" and college size: Effects on occupational choice and college attrition. *Sociology of Education* 44 (summer): 270–296.

Kamens, D. H. 1974. Colleges and elite formation: The case of prestigious American colleges. *Sociology of Education* 47 (summer): 354–378.

Kamens, D. H. 1978. Legitimating myths and educational organization: The relationship between organizational ideology and formal structure. *American Sociological Review* 42 (April): 208–219.

March, J., and H. Simon. 1958. *Organizations.* New York: Wiley.

McDonough, P. 1994. Buying and selling higher education: The social construction of the college applicant. *Journal of Higher Education* 65: 427–446.

McDonough, P. 1997. *Choosing colleges: How social class and schools structure opportunity.* Albany: State University of New York Press.

Mehan, H. 1992. Understanding inequality in schools: The contribution of interpretive studies. *Sociology of Education* 65: 1–20.

Meyer, J. W. 1970. The charter: Conditions of diffuse socialization in schools. In W. R. Scott (ed.), *Social processes and social structures: An introduction to sociology.* New York: Henry Holt.

Milem, J. F. 1998. Attitude change in college students: Examining the effects of college peer groups and faculty reference groups. *Journal of Higher Education* 69 (2): 117–140.

Milem, J. F., and J. B. Berger. 1997. A modified model of college student persistence: The relationship between Astin's theory of involvement and Tinto's theory of student departure. *Journal of College Student Development* 38 (4): 387–400.

Newcomb, T. M. 1966. The general nature of peer group influence. In T. M. Newcomb and E. K. Wilson (eds.), *College peer groups.* Chicago: Aldine.

Newcomb, T. M., and E. K. Wilson. 1966. *College peer groups.* Chicago: Aldine.

Paulsen, M. B., and E. P. St. John. 1997. The financial nexus between college choice and persistence. In R. A. Voorhees (ed.), *Researching student aid: Creating an action agenda.* New Directions for Institutional Research, no. 95, pp. 65–82. San Francisco: Jossey-Bass.

Persell, C. H., S. Catsambis, and P. Cookson. 1992. Differential asset conversion: Class and gendered pathways to selective colleges. *Sociology of Education* 65: 208–225.

Pervin, L. 1967. A twenty-college study of student x college interaction using TAPE (Transactional Analysis of Personality and Environment): Rational, reliability, and validity. *Journal of Educational Psychology* 58: 290–302.

Rhoads, R. A., and J. R. Valadez. 1996. *Democracy, multiculturalism, and the community college: A critical perspective.* Critical Education Practice, vol. 5. Garland Reference Library of Social Science. New York: Garland.

Riesman, D. 1956. *The academic procession: Constraint and variety in American higher education.* Lincoln: University of Nebraska Press.

St. John, E. P., M. B. Paulsen, and J. B. Starkey. 1996. The nexus between college choice and persistence. *Research in Higher Education* 37 (2): 175–220.

Stern, G. 1970. *People in context: Measuring person-environment congruence in education and industry.* New York: Wiley.

Strange, C. 1994. Student development: The evolution and status of an essential idea. *Journal of College Student Development* 35: 399–412.

Tinto, V. 1975. Dropout from higher education: A theoretical synthesis of recent research. *Review of Educational Research* 45: 89–125.

Tinto, V. 1993. *Leaving college: Rethinking the causes and cures of student attrition.* 2d ed. Chicago: University of Chicago Press.

Tinto, V. (1997). Classrooms as Communities: Exploring the Educational Character of Persistence. *Journal of Higher Education* 68 (6): 599–623.

Weidman, J. C. 1989. Undergraduate socialization: A conceptual approach. In J. C. Smart (ed.), *Higher education: A handbook of theory and research,* vol. 5, pp. 289–322. New York: Agathon Press.

Part II

New Theoretical Directions

Theoretical Considerations in the Study of Minority Student Retention in Higher Education

Laura I. Rendón, Romero E. Jalomo, and Amaury Nora

Research on college student persistence is by now voluminous. Much of this research is based on testing and validating Vincent Tinto's (1975, 1987, 1993) highly acclaimed model of student departure. The basic premise of Tinto's model is that social and academic integration are essential to student retention. Tinto's model (especially the 1975 and 1987 versions) has certainly provided a workable and testable foundation for analyzing the multiple factors involved with student departure, particularly employing quantitative methods. Quantitative researchers such as Nora and Cabrera (1996) note that there is sufficient empirical evidence establishing the validity of Tinto's (1975, 1987) model of student persistence. Others have modified and improved the model utilizing diverse study populations at different higher education institutions (Nora 1987; Nora, Attinasi, and Matonak 1990; Rendón 1982; Nora and Rendón 1990; Cabrera, Nora, and Castañeda 1992; Nora and Cabrera 1993, 1996; Cabrera et al. 1992; Pavel 1992; Cabrera and Nora 1994; Pascarella and Terenzini 1991; Pascarella 1980; Terenzini, Lorang, and Pascarella 1981). Yet, more remains to be done.

Braxton, Sullivan, and Johnson's (1997) assessment of Tinto's theory (based on the 1975 version) found that, in the aggregate, assessment of empirical evidence regarding thirteen of Tinto's primary propositions indicated only partial support for the theory. The researchers cited problems with empirical internal consistency in multi-institutional or single-institutional assessments, in both residential and commuter universities, and across female and male college students. Further, Tierney (1992), Attinasi (1989, 1994), and Kraemer (1997) have questioned the validity of the model to fully and appropriately capture the experiences of nonwhite students, given that the model is based on an assimilation/acculturation framework.

It is worthy at this point to note the linkage between Tinto's interactionalist theory and the assimilation/acculturation perspective. Interactionalist theory is concerned with the impact of person- and institution-related characteristics on a particular phenomenon (Caplan and Nelson 1973; Braxton, Sullivan, and Johnson 1997). Tinto (1993) notes that his persistence model is an "interactional system" (p. 136) in which both students and institutions (through social and educational communities) are, over time, continually interacting with one another in a variety of formal and informal situations. Key to the interactionalist view is that persistence is contingent on the extent to which students have become incorporated (integrated) into the social and academic communities of the college.

Interactionalist theory may be linked to the acculturation/assimilation perspective that was prevalent during the 1960s when social scientists from various fields studied how members of minority groups became integrated into the dominant white society. It was believed that minority individuals were engaged in a self-perpetuating cycle of poverty and deprivation and that they could avoid societal alienation by becoming fully absorbed (assimilated) or adapted (acculturated) into the dominant culture (Hurtado 1997). Assimilation required a process of separation, a cultural adaptation that required minority individuals to break away from their traditions, customs, values, language, etc., in order to find full membership in the predominantly white American society. However, during the 1970s and 1980s critics contested this perspective, citing problems such as the use of mainstream cultural norms as evaluative criteria, as well as the problematic assumption that minority group norms and cultural patterns were inferior, deviant, and self-destructive when compared to those of the majority culture (de Anda 1984).

Along these lines, Caplan and Nelson (1973) provided important distinctions between person-centered and situation-centered problems, noting that the way a problem was identified gave way to specific solutions. For example, researchers focusing on person-centered problems would focus on individual characteristics as the root of the issue and the target of the solution, while ignoring situationally relevant factors. In the case of studying why minority cultures experience alienation, a person-centered definition would identify the pathology as residing with minority group characteristics.

Conversely, Caplan and Nelson noted that situation-centered problems have a system change orientation. Here, the context in which individuals operate is examined and remedies are proposed to change the system.

Once in effect and legitimated, irrespective of their validity, these definitions resist replacement by other definitions or perspectives. For example, the idea that minority students are not motivated to learn or have low expectations has been around for decades and ignores how systemic inequities, racism, and discrimination have worked against minority populations. Within the past twenty years there has been greater emphasis on examining the interactions among individuals and systems. Yet Caplan and Nelson's (1973) view that to the extent that problem definitions conform to and reinforce dominant cultural myths and clichés, as indeed most definitions must in order to become widely accepted, their change or replacement will be stubbornly resisted. People tend to conform to public definitions and expectations, even when there are doubts regarding their accuracy.

Because interactionalist retention theory adheres to some of the basic premises of the acculturation/assimilation framework, such as separation and incorporation, several researchers have challenged the way these processes have been conceptualized in relation to explaining minority student retention in college. In particular, the assumption that minority students must separate from their cultural realities and take the responsibility to become incorporated into colleges' academic and social fabric in order to succeed (with little or no concern to address systemic problems within institutions or to the notion that minority students are often able to operate in multiple contexts) becomes central to the critique of Tinto's student departure model.

At the same time, emerging scholarship that is beginning to take root not only in education but in fields such as psychology, anthropology, and sociology is revolutionizing the way we conceptualize different phenomena and the selection of empirical tools to guide this understanding (Hurtado 1997; Rosaldo 1989). For example, Hurtado (1997) explains that much feminist research advocates a multidisciplinary and multimethod approach that is non-hierarchical (i.e., one dominant group is not favored over another) and reflexive (i.e., invites critique and further analysis). Given these developments, we believe that revisionist models and theory refinements are needed. Also needed are new models that consider the key theoretical issues associated with the experiences of minority students in higher education.

It is important to note that researchers (primarily white) began studying student retention prior to the time that minorities had become a critical mass on college campuses. Few minority students resulted in small sample sizes or total exclusion from the samples. Consequently, much of the most widely acclaimed research guiding theories of students' transitions to college, departure, involvement, and learning was often based on white male students (Tierney 1992; Belenky et al. 1986). This research produced a monolithic view of students devoid of issues of race/ethnicity, culture, gender, politics, and identity (Hurtado 1997).

The research on minority college students is relatively young, and the majority focuses on African American and Hispanic (primarily Mexican American) students. Especially fertile territory is research on American Indians, Asians, Pacific Islanders, Filipinos, Puerto Ricans, Cubans, and immigrant students from Asia and Central and South America. As our society becomes more multicultural and complex, the experiences of multiracial students will merit careful investigation. In the 1970s only a few studies, such as Gurin and Epps (1975) and Olivas (1979), focused on minority students. Only within the past fifteen years have researchers, many of them nonwhite, begun to study minority students (Nora and Cabrera 1994; Nora and Rendón 1988, 1990; Rendón 1982, 1994; Jalomo 1995; Tierney 1992, 1993; Wright 1988; Allen 1984; Ogbu 1978, 1987; Thomas 1984; Harvey and Williams 1989; Attinasi 1989; Fleming 1984; Nettles et al. 1985; London 1978, 1989; Weis 1985; Hurtado and Garcia 1994; Kraemer 1997; Nora, Attinasi, and Matonak 1990; Cabrera, Nora, and Castañeda 1993; Lowe 1989; Melchior-Walsh 1994; Galindo and Escamilla 1995; Gandara 1993; Wycoff 1996; Valadez 1996; Mow and Nettles 1990). This relatively new research not only lifts the knowledge base of student retention and development theories, it advances policy and practice and calls to question the predominant ways of structuring student development services employing research that included few, if any, minority students.

Much of the research that provides important modifications to the problem definition, introduces new variables to the retention equation, and attempts to refine traditional paradigms of student retention is scattered and unconnected. Consequently, a new, coherent vision of minority student persistence has failed to evolve. Researchers and practitioners alike tend to view issues related to the retention of minority students as similar, if not identical, to those of majority students. What transpires is an almost universally entrenched view that Tinto's (1975, 1987) departure model, with all of its assumptions, is complete, appropriate, and valid for all students regardless of their varied ethnic, racial, economic, and social backgrounds. To his credit, Tinto (1993) elaborates on the importance of supportive student communities for students of color and adult students who may experience difficulties making the transition to college and becoming incorporated. Tinto (1993) also notes the need to build inclusive campuses, explaining that "to be fully effective, college communities, academic and social, must be inclusive of all students who enter" (p. 187). Yet researchers such as Hurtado (1997) would argue that linear models based on an assimilation/acculturation framework leave many questions unanswered, especially with regard to multiple group identifications and how both minority and majority groups change when they come into contact with each other.

Purpose

The purpose of this chapter is to (1) provide a critical analysis of Tinto's student departure theory (1975, 1987, 1993) with a specific focus on the separation and transition stage, (2) critique Tinto's concepts of academic and social integration, and (3) present future directions designed to take retention theory to a higher level. The main concern is not whether the Tinto theory works for minority students. Rather, the emphasis is on the kind of theoretical foundation and methodological approaches that are needed to more fully understand and facilitate the retention process for minority students in an increasingly complex and multiracial institutional environment. Our critique is not meant to assault or discredit the work of researchers who have devoted their careers to studying how students become engaged in college. Rather, we offer alternative perspectives that seek a similar aim: to more fully understand student retention in college. We believe scholars ought to periodically reassess their work and how they apply their empirically based perspectives to new contexts in order to advance knowledge. Indeed, even the ideas advanced here should be taken further, and we encourage researchers to do so.

Theoretical Considerations in Tinto's Student Departure Model

Tinto's (1975, 1987, 1993) model of student departure has been extensively employed to study how majority and minority students become academically and socially integrated into institutional life. To help develop his theory on student departure, Tinto employed the rites-of-passage framework of Dutch anthropologist Arnold Van Gennep (1960). Van Gennep was concerned with the movement of individuals and societies over time and the rituals designed to move individuals from youth to adulthood in order to ensure social stability. To facilitate a discussion of theoretical issues on the concepts of separation, as well as academic and social integration, a brief summary of Van Gennep's theory is presented.

Conceptual Issues in Van Gennep's Rites of Passage

The rites of passage as described by Van Gennep (1960) included a three-phase process of separation, transition, and incorporation. In stage one, separation, the individual became separated from past associations and a decline occurred in interactions with members of the group from which the individual originated. Specific ceremonies marked outmoded views and norms of the old group. In stage two, transition, the individual began to interact in new ways with members of the new group in which membership was being sought. Rituals such as isolation, training, and ordeals were used to facilitate separation, which ensured that the individual acquired the knowledge and skills of the new group. In the third stage, incorporation, the individual took on new patterns of interaction with members of the new group and established competent membership. Though able to interact with members of the old group, individuals now did so only as members of the new group. In this stage individuals became fully integrated into the culture of the new group (Tinto 1987). Tinto stressed that it was "possible to envision the process of student persistence as functionally similar to that of becoming incorporated in the life of human communities" (p. 94).

How generalizable are Van Gennep's perspectives and assumptions when studying minority college students? First, let us consider the concept of separation and the ways some scholars have interpreted the theory. One of the assumptions scholars have made is that individuals should disassociate themselves from their native cultural realities in order to assimilate into college life. The assumption made is that an individual's values and beliefs rooted in his or her cultural background must be abandoned to successfully incorporate the values and beliefs not only of the institution but of the majority population upon which they are based. Only in this way can an individual student become integrated into the new environment. According to this assumption, minority students must reconcile the fact that they must leave the old world behind in order to find full membership in the new college world, since the two are distinctly different. A second assumption is that there is one "dominant" culture and that in order to succeed, members of minority cultures should become more similar to this dominant culture. A third assumption is that it will be relatively easy to find membership and acceptance in the new college world and that individuals who become integrated will have little or no contact with members of their old groups. Indeed, the hallmark of Tinto's (1993) revised model is that students should find social and intellectual communities to attain membership and receive support. Even students who initially resist separation will later determine that leaving their groups to succeed in college is appropriate and necessary. These assumptions are not entirely correct. Alternative views that challenge the three aforementioned assumptions are presented next.

A Critical Analysis of the Assumption of Separation

Scholars investigating how minority students make the transition to college should be familiar with the concepts of biculturalism and dual socialization, which challenge the assumption of separation. In addition, scholars should note the problematic issues in relation to the assumption of a dominant culture and the membership assumption.

The Concept of Biculturalism

While conducting an ethnographic study of poverty and Afro-Americans in a large northern city, Charles A. Valentine (1971) found that accepted cultural deficit and difference models of the time neglected and obscured important elements of the Afro-American culture. Referring to cultural deficit models as an alternative to analyze nonmainstream cultures, the researcher argued that "any theory of class or racial deficits of biological origin is quite undemonstrable, indeed scientifically untestable, in an ethically plural and structurally discriminatory society" (p. 138). While not negating cultural distinctions between black and mainstream cultures, Valentine (1971) observed: "The central theoretical weakness of the 'difference model' is an implicit assumption that different cultures are necessarily competitive alternatives, that distinct cultural systems can enter human experience only as mutually exclusive alternatives, never as intertwined or simultaneously available repertoires" (p. 141). Valentine cited cultural difference models as incorrect and harmful when employed for establishing new educational policies and programs.

As an alternative to predominant cultural difference models, Valentine (1971) proposed the employment of a bicultural educational model. The researcher argued that since many blacks were simultaneously committed to both black and mainstream cultures, the two were not mutually exclusive of each other. Rather, blacks could be simultaneously socialized in two different cultures. He relied on the findings of Steven Polgar (1960), who had earlier found that individuals living on an Indian reservation regularly went through a process he termed "biculturation." Biculturation occurred when individuals were simultaneously enculturated and socialized in two different ways of life. In Polgar's example teenage Mesquakie boys experienced a contemporary form of their traditional Amerindian lifeways and mainstream Euro-American culture.

Figure 1

Two Separate Cultures

A = Majority Culture

B = Minority Culture

Source: de Anda, 1984

Valentine (1971) used Polgar's (1960) research to expand the concept of biculturation, the ability of a minority individual to step in and out of the repertoires of two cultures that were seen as distinct and separate (de Anda 1984; see figure 1). For Valentine, biculturation helps explain how people learn and practice both the mainstream culture and ethnic cultures at the same time. He indicates: "the Black community is bicultural in the sense that each Afro-American ethnic segment draws upon a distinctive repertoire of standardized Afro-American group behavior and, simultaneously, patterns derived from the mainstream cultural system of Euro-American deviation. Socialization into both systems begins at an early age, continues throughout life, and is generally of equal importance in most individual lives" (Valentine 1971, p. 143). The concept of bilculturalism seriously challenges the first two assumptions (noted earlier) of the separation stage.

The Concept of Dual Socialization

Diane de Anda (1984) elaborates on Valentine's (1971) concept of biculturation, citing six factors that affect biculturalism: (1) the degree of overlap of commonalty between the two cultures with regard to norms, values, beliefs, perceptions, and the like; (2) the availability of cultural translators, mediators, and models; (3) the amount and type (positive or negative) of corrective feedback provided by each culture regarding attempts to produce normative behavior; (4) the conceptual style and problem-solving approach of the minority individual and their mesh with the prevalent or valued styles of the majority culture; (5) the individual's degree of bilingualism; and (6) the degree of dissimilarity in physical appearance from the majority culture, such as skin color and facial features (p. 102). Unlike Valentine, she indicates that the bicultural experience was possible not because the two cultures were totally disparate, but because there was some overlap between the two cultures (see figure 2). For de Anda, "dual socialization is made possible and facilitated by the amount of overlap between two cultures. That is, the extent to which an individual finds it possible to understand and predict successfully two cultural environments and adjust his or her behavior according to the norms of each culture depends on the

Figure 2
Biculturation

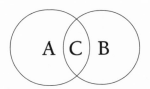

A = Majority Culture

B = Minority Culture

C = Shared Values and Norms

Source: de Anda, 1984

extent to which these two cultures share common values, beliefs, perceptions, and norms for prescribed behaviors" (p. 102). In short, de Anda's model is not about individual separation from an old world in search of membership in a new one. Instead, de Anda argues that converging the two worlds could allow individuals to function more effectively and less stressfully in both worlds. This requires changing, indeed transforming, the academic and social culture of institutions of higher education to accommodate culturally diverse students.

Kuh and Whitt (1988) suggest that culture, in the context of higher education, could be described as a "social or normative glue" that is defined by the shared values and beliefs that exist within a college or university while serving four general purposes: (1) conveying a sense of identity; (2) facilitating commitment to an entity, such as the college or peer group, other than self; (3) enhancing the stability of a group's social system; and (4) providing a sense-making device that guides and shapes behavior (p. 10). In addition, the researchers propose that the culture of a college or university defines, identifies, and legitimates authority in educational settings. However, they caution that institutions may, perhaps even unwittingly, have "properties deeply embedded in their cultures that make it difficult for members of historically underrepresented groups to prosper socially and environmentally" (p. 15). In cases such as this, students already potentially at risk often find themselves decidedly at odds with prevailing social and cultural norms on campus.

Dual socialization does not occur naturally in a college environment that contains values, conventions, and traditions that are alien to first-generation students, many of whom are minority. Jalomo (1995) substantiates de Anda's dual socialization model in a study of Latino community college students who had completed their first semester. For these students the transition was not linear. Rather, Latino students were found to operate in multiple contexts: the Latino culture, comprised of four subcultures (family, work, barrio, and gang); and the prevailing culture of the community colleges they attended. In the study, students who conveyed difficulty in their transition to college spoke of the growing incongruence between their native environment and the newly encountered college arena. These students indicated that they had maneuvered a number of social domains in their native environment while attempting to meet the growing demands associated with college life. Upon transiting to college, Latinos experienced the downside and upside of college attendance. They expressed some tension and loss associated with separation, although at the same time they experienced excitement at learning new things and making new college friends. They also experienced culture clash as a result of the differences between their home lives and the world of college. To diminish this disjuncture, Jalomo proposes that individuals not totally separate but instead be supported to transit between two cultures.

Levy-Warren (1988) provides additional perspectives to the concept of separation. In analyzing disruptions that people experience in separating from their cultures of origin (culture loss, culture shock), Levy-Warren indicates that the passage involves cultural dislocation and relocation, a disjunctive process that is both internal and external. The internal level involves identity formation—an individual is shedding a part of the self and assuming a new, redefined identity. The external level is the actual move from one geographical location to another and involves the loss of familiar objects and people. Cultural relocation may be highly traumatic if the move is made before the individual has established mental representations of culture. That is, individuals must be able to distinguish differences between their own world and the new world. Consequently, Rendón (1996) argues that rather than asking students to disassociate themselves from their culture, they should be assisted to make modifications in their relationships. The passage to college needs to be gradual, giving students time to slowly break away and move toward healthy individualization.

Theoretically, the concept of dual socialization seriously challenges the assumptions of separation. In addition, there are retention policy considerations. Navigating two landscapes, one of which is almost entirely different from home realities, requires both individual and institutional responsibility. To this end, the critical role of the institution cannot be overstated, yet is often diminished in retention and involvement studies. Tinto highlights the importance of the classroom as a learning community in his 1993 model. However, as noted earlier, Tinto's revised model has yet to gain widespread attention of the higher education research community. Connecting the world of the student to the world of college means that students must be able to find animate and inanimate objects in the new college culture that might evoke a sense of comfort that originates in their early cultural upbringing. That is why events and programs such as Black History Month, Women's Studies, and Cinco de Mayo celebrations are so important. Converging two worlds requires the use of cultural translators, mediators, and role models to (1) provide information and guidance that can help students decipher unfamiliar college customs and rituals, (2) mediate problems that arise from disjunctions between students' cultural traits and the prevailing campus culture, and (3) model behaviors that are amenable with the norms, values, and beliefs of the majority and minority cultures (Jalomo 1995; Rendón 1996; de Anda 1984).

The Assumption of a Dominant Culture

Tierney's (1992) critique of the Tinto model substantiates de Anda's convergence perspective. Tierney argues that Tinto did not consider an important point in Van Gennep's theory. The point was that Van Gennep uses the term *ritual* to speak of rites of passage within the same specific culture, i.e., some Indian cultures have puberty rituals designed specifically for girls and others specifically for boys. Here, the ritual is nondisruptive. However, Tinto employs the use of *ritual* in a way that "individuals from one culture, such as Apache, are to undergo a ritual in another culture, such as Anglo" (p. 609). In this case the transition constitutes a disjuncture—in effect, students from a minority culture enter a majority world that is vastly different from their sociocultural realities.

However, in his 1993 revised model Tinto argues that the majority of colleges are made up of several, if not many, communities or "subcultures." Rather than conforming to one dominant culture in order to persist, students would have to locate at least one community in which to find membership and support. Further, Tinto notes that membership does not require a full sharing of values. Instead, only some degree of consensus is necessary. Consequently, Tinto explains that the use of the term *membership* is more applicable than *integration*. Of course, safe havens and enclaves have their benefits and drawbacks. One of their key benefits is that they help students break down the institution into manageable parts. However, special communities and programs do not address the real challenge of today's institutions: the total transformation of colleges and universities from monocultural to multicultural institutions. This requires more convergence between the minority student's world and the college world. Further, Hurtado (1997) notes that research based on assimilation/acculturation views group contact as unidirectional in nature (i.e., the ethnic group changes to reflect the mainstream/dominant/white group). Hurtado argues that "this type of approach effectively blocks the possibility that cultural contact can indeed bring change in both the minority and majority groups" (p. 305). In some areas of the nation and in some colleges and universities, minorities are the majority or are rapidly on their way to acquiring majority status. While white students have normally been viewed as the dominant or majority group, future research will have to take into account how group identities and power relationships are changing and the overall impact on student persistence.

The Membership Assumption

It is also important for scholars to consider that de Anda's concept of "dual socialization"—where individuals both develop and sustain membership in new and old cultures—has been the reality of behavior for most Americans who maintain an ethnic identity while coexisting within the dominant culture. In short, many minority students are not likely to give up their affiliations and lose contact with their cultural groups in order to find membership in a new college world. Just as many Latino immigrants maintain extensive and frequent contact with Mexico (Hurtado 1997), many minority students experience multiple associations with their own cultures and their new college realities. Tierney (1992) indicates that American Indian students value group membership over the individualized process of separation. In many Latino cultures separation is often not a viable option, as family is a source of rootedness and strength. This view that both minority and majority groups coexist and actually hold similar attitudes, values, and perceptions has been obliquely (indirectly) established by Nora and Cabrera (1996). Within this context, similarities between white and nonwhite students were noted in attitudes regarding the influence of family, perceptions of discrimination on campus, and educational goals and commitments. Nora and Cabrera's (1996) research validates de Anda's (1984) notion that groups (or minorities) do not need to break all ties with past communities in order to attain membership status in a new or an alien culture, as in the case of minority students who retain their sense of identity and cultural values while integrating in a predominately majority educational environment.

Moreover, the membership option often represents a false choice given the lack of acceptance of racial/ethnic minorities in many dimensions of college life. In fact, many minorities leave college due to "cultural assaults" (Zambrana 1988) to their sense of identity and self-esteem that lead to stress and tension. Though some students may leave, others may exhibit differential patterns of behavior. Some will become subservient to the codes of others, and others may deny their cultural heritage. Still others will manage to turn a negative into a positive—developing a strong sense of ethnic consciousness, i.e., pride in their cultural heritage and awareness of racism, discrimination, sexism, and elitism prevalent in higher education systems (Zambrana 1988).

While more research is needed to substantiate the multiple varieties of external and internal group memberships and their impact on retention, research has substantiated the view that different forms of encouragement and support from family and friends from the students' past communities not only continue to influence students during college enrollment but are instrumental in affecting persistence. These associations negate discriminatory experiences, enhance the social and academic integration of students, and positively affect students' commitments to earning a college degree (Nora and Cabrera 1993, 1996; Nora et al. 1996; Nora, Kraemer, and Itzen 1997; Cabrera, Nora, and Castañeda 1993; Cabrera et al. 1992).

Theoretical Considerations Regarding Academic/Social Integration

Separation and transition are the initial processes associated with Tinto's student retention model. The next stage involves incorporation in institutional life. Tinto (1987) notes that "eventual persistence requires that individuals make the transition to college and become incorporated into the ongoing social and intellectual life of the college" (p. 126). Incorporation is analogous to integration. The term "integration can be understood to refer to the extent which the individual shares the normative attitudes and values of peers and faculty in the institution and abides by the formal and informal structural requirements for membership in that community or in the subgroups of which the individual is a part" (Pascarella and Terenzini 1991, p. 51). To learn more about how incorporation came about, Tinto turned to French sociologist Emile Durkheim (1951) and the study of suicide. Durkheim was interested in the character of the social environment, including social and intellectual characteristics, and its relationship to individual behavior, such as suicide. To draw an analogy between suicidal and dropout behavior, Tinto employed Durkheim's view of "egotistical suicide." Individuals who committed egotistical suicide were unable to become socially or intellectually integrated within communities of society. As noted earlier, interactionalist theory, when used to study minority student retention, has been called into question given that some of the theory's premises are based on an assimilation/acculturation framework.

Problems with the Use of an Acculturation/Assimilation Framework

Hurtado (1997) notes that during the 1960s an assimilation framework was the impetus of research on ethnicity, especially for Mexican Americans. Since assimilation was contingent on the minority group becoming incorporated into the life of the majority group, assimilation scales were developed to measure the quickest and most efficient ways to assimilate immigrants. In 1964 Gordon advanced the notion that individuals could be highly acculturated in one group but remain unassimilated in other dimensions of society. In short, biculturality became a viable option. But the assimilation/acculturation framework had multiple problems, which are listed below.

Focus on Academic Failure as Opposed to Success

Hurtado (1997) indicates that assimilation/acculturation research has focused on the left tail of the normal distribution curve, "that is, it has focused on cultural adaptations that are not particularly healthy, ones for which the only solutions are to assimilate to the dominant mainstream or spend a lifetime of psychological and social alienation" (p. 312). Some of the recent research (primarily within the past five to ten years) has called for a focus and examination of a variety of adaptations leading to academic success in addition to the repository of traditional research approaches examining academic failure (Hurtado and Garcia 1994).

Exclusion of Contextual and Historical Forces

Zambrana (1988) notes that during the 1960s and 1970s studies on racial/ethnic communities were in large part descriptive and ahistorical. These descriptions were in line with the cultural deficit model that emphasized the problems or "deficiencies" within these communities, for the most part pathological and disruptive. It was believed that these deficits led to a self-perpetuating cycle of poverty and deprivation. When applied to education, the cultural deficit model suggests that cultural patterns of marginalized groups are essentially inferior and predispose students within those groups to poor academic performance; de Anda (1984) notes that the discrediting of the cultural deficit model led to the ascendance of the cultural difference model that emphasized the uniqueness of each minority culture. An inherent assumption with both of these models was that upward mobility and acculturation were possible to the extent that minority groups approximated the values and norms of the dominant society. However, a model known as "internal colonialism" (Almaguer 1974; Blauner 1972) argued that cultural adaptations of ethnic/racial groups were due more to the organization of economics, labor, and power in the capitalist way the nation was structured than to differences in traits between minority and majority groups. As such, groups that had the experience of conquest were subject to race discrimination in every dimension of organized society, including education (Hurtado 1997).

In her review of cultural studies, Zambrana (1988) notes that "the most limiting aspect of the majority of studies has been their neglect of the relationship of racial/ethnic groups to the social structure" (p. 63). The lives of racial/ethnic minorities are shaped by social forces such as racism, sexism, and discrimination. Yet many researchers tend to view people of color as if they have all the options and privileges of white, middle-class Americans, when this is not often the case.

Lack of Focus on Systemic Barriers

Rather than focusing on systemic issues in the lives of oppressed people, most past researchers employing an assimilation/acculturation framework have tended to focus on perceived cultural traits or differences (i.e., poor motivation, academic deficiencies) as the source of a group's ability or inability to succeed and be upwardly mobile. This view suggests that students who possess or adopt mainstream cultural norms are capable of moving farther along the educational pipeline than those who lack these cultural traits (Nieto 1996). In opposition to this view, more recent educational research has documented that systemic barriers such as tracking, low expectations, and funding inequities, among others, play a critical role in hindering the educational achievements of ethnic/racial minorities (Oakes 1985; Brint and Karabel 1989; Nieto 1996). Nonetheless, perceptions of minority student inferiority persist to this day and have even been used as a rationale to place restrictions on college access for minorities.

Failure to Challenge Theoretical Assumptions and Paradigms

Even when minorities are studied, researchers often fail to challenge the philosophical assumptions made in traditional paradigms that are often grounded or developed from studies based on full-time, traditional-age, residential, middle-class, white, male students and/or fail to consider current research that presents a more comprehensive and contextual view of minority student lives and educational experiences. The lack of a grounded historical perspective has led to the frequent omission of minority groups, or else they are identified as a source of their group's problems (a deficit perspective). Myths and stereotypes continue to prevail for racial and ethnic groups simply because there is a void in the incorporation of roles, characteristics, and perceptions of these subgroups. Many times variables are operationally defined in the same manner for all groups involved, thus excluding any cultural or racial differences in perceptions and attitudes. Rather than conducting culturally and racially based studies that can uncover new variables and that can offer insightful and meaningful findings to transform institutional structures that preclude academic success for minority students, invisible hierarchies are left intact. In these cases, minority students are measured simply by scales that reveal their level of acculturation and integration, or lack thereof (Zambrana 1988; Hurtado 1997).

Failure to Connect Theory to Practice

In his 1993 theory review Tinto acknowledges the importance of policy-relevant research and the importance of the institution in enhancing retention. When theoretical propositions are not compared across different subgroups or when diverse and culturally driven theoretical views are not incorporated in retention studies, institutional policies and practices cannot truly detect or address differences among student groups. Theories developed without using minority student perspectives and/or without "member checks" from the field may miss important details and nuances about the connection between student cultural realities and collegiate experiences. Tierney (1992) elaborates: "The search for an understanding about why students leave college is not merely of theoretical interest; if a model may be built that explains student departure then it may be possible for colleges to retain students" (p. 604).

Conceptual Issues in Interactionalist Theory

There are at least three conceptual problems with social/academic interactionalist theory as used in Tinto's (1975, 1987, 1993) student departure model.

Individual Responsibility as Opposed to Institutional Responsibility

The first conceptual problem is overemphasis on individual responsibility for change and adaptation. In 1987 Tinto emphasized the following points:

> The problems associated with separation and transition to college are conditions that, though stressful, need not in themselves lead to departure. It is the individual's response to those conditions that finally determines staying or leaving. Though external assistance

may make a difference, it cannot do so without the individual's willingness to see the adjustments through. (p. 98)

To adapt Durkheim's work to the question of individual departure from institutions of higher education we must move to a theory of individual behavior. (p. 105)

To move to a theory of individual suicide, and therefore to a theory of individual departure, one has to take account of the personal attributes of individuals which predispose them to respond to given situations or conditions with particular forms of behavior. (p. 109)

While Tinto (1987) does indicate that "differences in institutional rates of departure may arise out of discernible differences in the structure of institutional academic and social systems" (p. 107), the overall tone of social/academic integration theory is that individuals, not the system, are responsible for departure. Elaborating on this point, Tierney (1992) argues that social integrationists tend to use anthropological terms in an individualist, rather than a collective, manner. Individuals attend college, become integrated or not, leave or stay, fail or succeed. Absent from the traditional social integrationist view are the distinctions among cultures; differences among students with regard to class, race, gender, and sexual orientation; and the role of group members and the institution in assisting students to succeed.

Nora, Kraemer, and Itzen (1997) and Nora and Cabrera (1993) argue that current quantitative models must include factors that are able to differentiate among racial and ethnic groups or must include measurement approaches (and techniques) that provide indicators of constructs that reflect racial, ethnic, and cultural differences. In a study of student persistence at an exclusively Hispanic two-year institution Nora, Kraemer, and Itzen (1997) employed a different and more culturally sensitive set of items that more closely reflected the manner in which the study's Hispanic students became integrated on their campus. In doing so, the researchers reduced misspecification in the model. The researchers elaborate: "The measures of academic integration used to form the scale not only [represented] possible academic interest and involvement with faculty and staff, but . . . also [reflected] those circumstances (both financial and academic) that [were] prevalent among [the] Hispanic group" (p. 15).

Problems Associated with the Concept of Student Involvement

While interactionalist theory is concerned with the interaction among individuals and institutions, involvement is the mechanism through which student effort is engaged in the academic and social lives of the college. Tinto explains that the 1993 model is "at its core, a model of educational communities that highlights the critical importance of student engagement or involvement in the learning communities of the college" (1993, p. 132). Consequently, it becomes important to address problematic issues related to the involvement dimension implicit in the Tinto model.

Alexander Astin's (1985) theory of student involvement is perhaps the most widely adopted college impact model of student development. According to involvement theory, "the individual plays a central role in determining the extent and nature of growth according to the quality of effort or involvement with the resources provided by the institution" (Pascarella and Terenzini 1991, p. 51). Astin's involvement theory is based on the Freudian notion of cathexis, in which individuals invest psychological energy in objects outside themselves such as friends, families, schooling, jobs, and the like. Astin (1984) defines involvement as "the amount of energy that the student devotes to the academic experience" (p. 27). Indeed, research indicates that the more time and energy students devote to learning and the more intensely they engage in their own education, the greater the achievement, satisfaction with educational experiences, and persistence in college (Pascarella and Terenzini 1991; Tinto 1987).

While both Tinto and Astin would agree that the institution plays an important role in facilitating involvement, and in fact Tinto's 1993 revised model emphasizes this point, practitioners have concentrated on the aspect of individual responsibility. The result is that practitioners have resorted to offering programs to help students get involved but have not focused on active outreach to students. Consequently, few dropout-prone students actually get involved. If practitioners accept the cultural separation assumption without understanding its inherent trauma for nontraditional students, then practitioners will tend to see involvement as a relatively easy task since they will also assume that all students, regardless of background, are ready, willing, and able to get involved.

Researchers who have studied nontraditional students (Terenzini et al. 1994; Rendón 1994; Jalomo 1995) have contributed important findings and modifications to involvement theory. While the importance of involvement cannot be negated, these researchers note that many students, especially nontraditional students, find it difficult to get involved. Important differences between traditional and nontraditional students were not explained in the original conception of student involvement theory. Traditional students often come from upper- to middle-class backgrounds, are predominantly white, and come from families in which at least one parent has attended college and the expectation of college attendance is well established. For traditional students college attendance is a normal rite of passage and a part of family tradition. Consequently, they are more likely to understand and manipulate the values, traditions, and practices of college to their academic advantage. Involvement theory does not emphasize the fact that most two- and four-year colleges are set up to facilitate involvement for traditional students.

On the other hand, nontraditional students often come from working-class backgrounds, are older, work at least part-time, and are predominantly minority and first-generation—the first in their families to attend college (Rendón 1994; Terenzini et al. 1993; Jalomo 1995). Jalomo's (1995) study of Latino first-year community college students found that involvement was difficult for students who found the transition to college troublesome or whose background characteristics did not "fit" the traditional student profile found on most college campuses today. Table 1 portrays the characteristics of students who found college involvement difficult. Moreover, Jalomo (1995) found that students required the assistance of cultural translators, mediators, and role models in order to survive or succeed in their first semester in college.

Rendón (1994) found that validation, as opposed to involvement, had transformed nontraditional students into powerful learners. While it is likely that most white and traditional students can become involved on their own in an institutional context that merely affords involvement opportunities (i.e., tutoring centers, clubs and organizations, extracurricular activities), nontraditional students expect active outreach and intervention in order to become involved. Rendón explains: "It appears that nontraditional students do not perceive involvement as *them* taking the initiative. They perceive it when someone takes an active role in assisting them" (p. 44).

Presenting a model of validation, Rendón (1994) notes that what had transformed nontraditional students into powerful learners and persisters were incidents in which some individual, either inside or outside class, had validated them. Validating agents made use of interpersonal and academic validation. Validating agents took an active interest in students. They provided encouragement for students and affirmed them as being capable of doing academic work and supported them in their academic endeavors and social adjustment. The critical role of the institution and its agents is underscored in Rendón's validation model. The role of the institution is not simply to offer involvement opportunities, but to take an active role in fostering validation. Faculty, counselors, coaches, and administrators take the initiative to reach out to students and design activities that promote active learning and interpersonal growth among students, faculty, and staff (Rendón 1994).

Table 1

Characteristics of Latino Students Who Found It Difficult to Get
Involved in Their Community College

Married students with family obligations

Single parents

Students who have been out of school for some time

Students who are the first in their families to attend college

Students who never liked high school or who were rebellious in high school

Students who have had negative experiences with former teachers or administrative staff in elementary and secondary schools

Students who were not involved in academic activities or student groups during high school

Students who did not participate in school-based social activities or student programs during high school

Students who are afraid or feel out of place in the mainstream college culture

Students who have had negative interactions with college faculty or administrative staff

Students who have a hard time adjusting to the fast pace of college

Students who take evening courses when little or no services are available

Students who lack the financial resources to take additional courses or participate in campus-based academic and social activities in college

Source: Jalomo 1995

Focus on the Negative Impact of the External Community

A third conceptual problem with interactionalist theory is that external forces and cultures are seen as distinct and having mainly a negative impact on student involvement. Tinto (1987) acknowledges that family and culture may play an important part in student decisions to depart from college. However, what Tinto (1987) stresses (and what scholars and practitioners are likely to emphasize) is that "in some situations, external social systems may work counter to the demands of institutional life. When the academic and social systems of the institution are weak, the countervailing external demands may seriously undermine the individual's ability to persist on completion" (p. 108). Even in his 1993 revised model, Tinto argues that external elements are secondary to those in college, conditioning but not determining the character of the experience on campus. Researchers have validated some of the negative effects of the external environment. For example, Terenzini et al. (1993) found that "friends who did not attend college could complicate the transition by anchoring students to old networks of friends and patterns of behavior rather than allowing them to explore and learn about their new college environment" (p. 5). Similarly, parents who feel anxious about students leaving home may function as liabilities. Nora et al. (1996) found that minority students who needed to work off-campus for financial reasons were 36 percent more likely to drop out of college than those who did not. Moreover, researchers found that female students, as opposed to male students, who were required to leave campus immediately after class to help care for family members were 83 percent more likely to withdraw.

However, not everything external is a liability. For example, Terenzini et al. (1993) found that precollege friends performed a "bridge function," providing support and encouragement. And with few exceptions, students named family members when asked "Who are the most important people in your life right now?" Jalomo (1995) found that there were more out-of-class agents helping students to make connections on campus than in-class agents. Clearly, much more research is needed to assess the positive and negative influences of the external environment and how students negotiate external influences, not only during the first year of college but throughout the student's collegiate experience.

Taking Retention Theory to a Higher Level

The conceptual issues presented in this chapter, based both on empirical evidence and conceptual critiques, substantiate that Tinto's college student retention theory needs to be taken to an even higher level of theoretical development. Tinto has done this through extensions and refinements of his theory (Braxton, Sullivan, and Johnson 1997). However, Attinasi (1989, 1994) and Tierney (1992) would likely go as far as rejecting the theory and building another that is capable of reflecting subtle processes (particularly cultural and political and emerging from qualitative analysis) involved in persistence. We believe that with all that is now known about student retention, it is quite possible that a totally new theory is needed to take Tinto's theory to a different level. Moreover, knowledge from disciplines other than education can also be used to develop new theoretical perspectives regarding student retention. For example, Hurtado (1997) has developed a "social engagement model [that] takes into account gender as well as other significant social identities like ethnicity/race, class, and sexuality to study how groups change as they come into contact with each other" (p. 299).

Employing a social psychology perspective, Hurtado (1997) advocates that understanding cultural transformations in an increasingly complex and multicultural society, as in the case when students from one group enter the sphere of social engagement of another group, requires not an assimilation/acculturation framework, but a social engagement model. Hurtado (1994) has employed a social engagement framework to study the participation of Latino parents in school. Hurtado's analysis of Latino parents' participation in school is quite similar to how one might analyze college student retention.

For example, research findings illustrate that working-class Latino students are not as likely to get involved in the academic and social domains of the college as often as whites do. Engagement is usually defined as participating in clubs and organizations, meeting with faculty in and out of class, etc. Hurtado would argue that this narrow definition of student engagement is predominately based in the dominant group's perspective and not from the Latino students' view of what is possible and desirable for them. Indeed, Rendón (1994), Jalomo (1995), and Terenzini et al. (1994) have found that involvement is not easy for nontraditional students from working-class backgrounds and that both in- and out-of-class validation were essential to their engagement and persistence. Validation is a powerful, interactive process involving a student and a validating agent. Much of the validation occurred out of class (with friends, parents, spouses, etc.), substantiating that there are other forms of engagement that can have a positive impact on persistence. These researchers employed qualitative methods that allowed students to express who and what was making a difference in their academic lives and why this was so.

If these researchers had relied only on an assimilation/acculturation framework (i.e., narrowly measuring student traits that restricted minority group involvement), then they most likely would have reached the following conclusions:

1. Latino students from working-class backgrounds are not as academically and socially integrated in college as are white students, leading to their higher dropout rate.

2. Traditional, primarily white students from upper- and middle-class backgrounds are more engaged in college than Latino students, which accounts for their higher levels of educational adjustment and attainment.

3. Consequently, we need to encourage working-class Latino students to avail themselves of services and opportunities that can increase their college retention rates. Further, because white students score the highest on scales of college involvement, they are the models all students should emulate.

An assimilation/acculturation framework would not allow Latino students to contribute their own perceptions and definitions of all that constitutes integration. Nor would their definitions influence the views of white students. We would also not be able to discuss the internal variations of each group, i.e., there are Hispanic students who exhibit very high achievement and engagement levels, and there are white students who do not. Many studies may not capture much of the variability in withdrawal decisions because of the misspecification of important constructs. Findings may turn out to be statistically significant, even though very little of the variance is explained. In these cases what may be most interesting is not what was statistically significant. Rather, the most important finding could be that there are other multiple, unaccounted factors that may be influencing retention.

Hurtado (1997) explains that a social engagement model, which has at its core a definitional approach to differences in social adaptations, would yield different results. Besides standard measures of college integration, there would be measures that allowed different groups of students to provide their own definitions of what they consider to be engagement and why. It could very well be that Latino students would report that they considered cultural activities, external relationships with family and friends, and race-based programs as essential and vital to their personal and academic development. Students could also identify the systemic barriers to integration. Similarities among the different ethnic/racial groups in terms of engagement and barriers related to involvement could also be identified. These variables could then be incorporated into quantitative models for statistical testing. Strategies for facilitating in- and out-of-class involvement for *both* minority and majority students could be generated from these findings. The key issue is that the sole use of an acculturation/assimilation framework to study retention does not go far enough.

Taking existing retention/involvement theory to a more sophisticated level will require a thorough, thoughtful, and critical analysis of all the quantitative and qualitative data that have been generated to date. Rather than operate in isolation, quantitative and qualitative researchers should be open to each other's methods, share findings, and probe further into the meaning of their results. We should also be open to theory developments in fields other than education. Multimethod approaches to the study of retention are likely to lift the current corpus of college persistence research. In short, we believe that the future of college student retention research offers exciting and viable possibilities both to uncover the dynamics involved in retention and to use data to shape practice and policy.

Conclusion

Researchers employing quantitative models based on Tinto's (1975, 1987) depiction of student persistence have conceptually advanced some of the factors and interrelationships postulated in Tinto's model (i.e., Nora and Cabrera 1993, 1996; Nora et al. 1996; Cabrera and Nora 1995; Cabrera, Nora, and Castañeda 1992, 1993). Qualitative studies also provide some support to Tinto's propositions (Terenzini et al. 1993; Jalomo 1995). But while traditional theories of student retention and involvement have been useful in providing a foundation for the study of persistence, they need to be taken further, as much more work needs to be done to uncover race, class, and gender issues (among others) that impact retention for diverse students in diverse institutions. Certainly, the theoretical issues regarding separation, transition, and incorporation presented in this chapter provide avenues for conducting future research. Yet we stress that the ideas presented here are intended to go beyond stirring intellectual discussion that will lift theory and research.

Minority students are altering the nature of higher education in many ways. Over the past twenty years we have witnessed dramatic changes in the classroom and the curriculum (with the inclusion of ethnic/ racial perspectives and the use of learning communities), in student services (with race-based programs), and in faculty and staff composition, among other areas. While we believe that theory building is important, out of scholarly discussions and research should come advances in the development and dramatic transformation of academic and student services. Assuming that good social scientists are also caring humanitarians, the goal of student retention research transcends making conceptual modifications in theoretical models. In the end, students will elect to stay or leave college not so much because of a theory, but because college and university faculty and administrators have made transformative shifts in governance, curriculum development, in- and out-of-class teaching and learning, student programming, and other institutional dimensions that affect students on a daily basis. Consequently, connecting retention research to field practitioners and policy makers in new and creative ways that involve collaborative relationships and mutual learning experiences can take student retention research to a whole new level of theoretical accuracy and applicability.

References

Allen, W. R. 1984. Race consciousness and collective commitments among black students on white campuses. *Western Journal of Black Studies* 8 (3): 156–166.

Almaguer, T. 1974. Historical notes on Chicano oppression: The dialectics of racial and class domination in North America. *Aztlán* 5 (1–2): 27–56.

Astin, A. 1984. Student involvement: A developmental theory for higher education. *Journal of College Student Personnel* 12 (July): 297–308.

Astin, A. 1985. *Achieving educational excellence: A critical assessment of priorities and practices in higher education.* San Francisco: Jossey-Bass.

Attinasi, Jr., L. 1989. Getting in: Mexican Americans' perceptions of university attendance and the implications for freshman year persistence. *Journal of Higher Education* 60 (3): 247–277.

Attinasi, Jr., L. 1994. Is going to college a rite of passage? Paper presented at the annual meeting of the American Research Association, New Orleans, La.

Belenky, M., B. Clinchy, N. Goldberger, and J. Tarule. 1986. *Women's ways of knowing.* New York: Basic Books, Inc.

Blauner, R. 1972. *Racial oppression in America.* New York: Harper & Row.

Braxton, J. M., A. V. S. Sullivan, and R. M. Johnson. 1997. Appraising Tinto's theory of college student departure. In J. C. Smart (ed.), *Higher education: A handbook of theory and research,* vol. 12, pp. 107–164. New York: Agathon Press.

Brint, S., and J. Karabel. 1989. *The directed dream: Community colleges and the promise of educational opportunity in America, 1900–1985.* New York: Oxford University Press.

Cabrera, A. F., and A. Nora. 1994. College students' perceptions of prejudice and discrimination and their feelings of alienation. *Review of Education, Pedagogy, and Cultural Studies* 16: 387–409.

Cabrera, A. F., A. Nora, and M. B. Castañeda. 1992. The role of finances in the student persistence process: A structural model. *Research in Higher Education* 33 (5): 571–594.

Cabrera, A. F., A. Nora, and M. B. Castañeda. 1993. College persistence: Structural equations modeling test of an integrated model of student retention. *Journal of Higher Education* 64 (2): 123–139.

Cabrera, A. F., M. B. Castañeda, A. Nora, and D. Hengstler. 1992. The convergent and discriminant validity between two theories of college persistence. *Journal of Higher Education* 63 (2): 143–164.

Caplan, N., and S. Nelson. 1973. The nature and consequences of psychological research on social problems. *American Psychologist* 28 (3): 199–211.

de Anda, D. 1984. Bicultural socialization: Factors affecting the minority experience. *Social Work* 29 (2): 101–107.

Durkheim, E. 1951. *Suicide: A study in sociology.* Edited by G. Simpson. Translated by J. A. Spaulding and E. Simpson. Originally published in 1897. Glencoe, Ill.: The Free Press.

Fleming, J. 1984. *Blacks in college.* San Francisco: Jossey-Bass.

Galindo, R., and K. Escamilla. 1995. A biographical perspective on Chicano educational success. *The Urban Review* 27 (1).

Gandara, P. 1993. *Choosing higher education: The educational mobility of Chicano students.* Report to the Latina/Latino Policy Research Program, California Policy Seminar. (ERIC Document Reproduction Service No. ED 374 942).

Gordon, M. M. 1964. *Assimilation in American life: The role of race, religion, and national origins.* New York: Oxford University Press.

Gurin, P., and E. Epps. 1975. *Black consciousness, identity and achievement.* New York: John Wiley & Sons.

Harvey, W. B., and L. Williams. 1989. Historically black colleges: Models for increasing minority representation. *Journal of Black Studies* 21 (3): 238.

Hurtado, A. 1997. Understanding multiple group identities: Inserting women into cultural transformations. *Journal of Social Issues* 53 (2): 299–328.

Hurtado, A., and E. Garcia. 1994. *The educational achievement of Latinos: Barriers and successes.* Santa Cruz: Regents of the University of California.

Jalomo, R. 1995. *Latino students in transition: An analysis of the first-year experience in community college.* Ph.D. diss., Arizona State University, Tempe.

Kraemer, B. A. 1997. The academic and social integration of Hispanic students into college. *Review of Higher Education* 20: 163–179.

Kuh, G., and E. Whitt. 1988. *The invisible tapestry: Culture in American colleges and universities.* ASHE-ERICD Higher Education Report.

Levy-Warren, M. H. 1988. Moving to a new culture: Cultural identity, loss, and mourning. In Bloom-Fesback & Associates (eds.), *The psychology of separation and loss.* San Francisco: Jossey-Bass.

London, H. 1978. *The culture of a community college.* New York: Praeger.

London, H. 1989. Breaking away: A study of first generation college students and their families. *American Journal of Education* 97 (February): 144–170.

Lowe, M. (1989). *Chicano students' perceptions of their community college experience with implications for persistence: A naturalistic inquiry.* Ph.D. diss., Arizona State University, Tempe.

Melchior-Walsh, S. 1994. *Sociocultural alienation: Experiences of North American Indian students in higher education.* Ph.D. diss., Arizona State University, Tempe.

Mow, S., and M. Nettles. 1990. Minority student access to, and persistence and performance in, college: A review of the trends and research literature. In J. C. Smart (ed.), *Higher education: A handbook of theory and research,* vol. 6, pp. 35–105. New York: Agathon Press.

Nettles, M., C. Gosman, A. Thoeny, and B. Dandrige. 1985. *The causes and consequences of college students' attrition rates, progression rates and grade point averages.* Nashville, Tenn.: Higher Education Commission.

Nieto, S. 1996. *Affirming diversity: The sociopolitical context of multicultural education.* 2d ed. New York: Longman.

Noel, L., R. Levitz, and D. Saluri. 1985. *Increasing student retention: Effective programs and practices for reducing the dropout rate.* San Francisco: Jossey-Bass.

Nora, A. 1987. Determinants of retention among Chicano college students: A structural model. *Research in Higher Education* 26 (1): 31–59.

Nora, A., and A. F. Cabrera. 1993. The construct validity of institutional commitment: A confirmatory factor analysis. *Research in Higher Education* 34 (2): 243–262.

Nora, A., and A. F. Cabrera. 1996. The role of perceptions of prejudice and discrimination on the adjustment of minority students to college. *Journal of Higher Education* 67 (2): 119–148.

Nora, A., and L. I. Rendón. 1988. Hispanic students in community colleges: Reconciling access with outcomes. In L. Weis (ed.), *Class, race, and gender in U.S. education,* pp. 126–143. New York: State University Press.

Nora, A., and L. I. Rendón. 1990. Determinants of predisposition to transfer among community college students: A structural model. *Research in Higher Education* 31: 235–255.

Nora, A., L. Attinasi, and A. Matonak. 1990. Testing qualitative indicators of precollege factors in Tinto's attrition model: A community college student population. *Review of Higher Education* 13 (3): 337–356.

Nora, A., B. Kraemer, and R. Itzen. 1997. Factors affecting the persistence of Hispanic college students. Paper presented at the annual meeting of the Association for the Study of Higher Education, November.

Nora, A., A. F. Cabrera, L. Hagedorn, and E. T. Pascarella. 1996. Differential impacts of academic and social experiences on college-related behavioral outcomes across different ethnic and gender groups at four-year institutions. *Research in Higher Education* 37 (4): 427–452.

Oakes, J. 1985. *Keeping track. How schools structure inequality.* New Haven, Conn.: Yale University Press.

Ogbu, J. U. 1978. *Minority education and caste: The American system in cross-cultural perspective.* New York: Academic Press.

Ogbu, J. U. 1987. Variability in minority school performance: A problem in search of an explanation. *Anthropology and Education Quarterly* 18 (4): 312–334.

Olivas, M. 1979. *The dilemma of access: Minorities in two year colleges.* Washington, D.C.: Howard University Press.

Pascarella, E. T. 1980. Student-faculty informal contact and college outcomes. *Review of Educational Research* 50: 545–595.

Pascarella, E., and P. Terenzini. 1991. *How college affects students: Findings and insights from twenty years of research.* San Francisco: Jossey-Bass.

Pavel, M. 1992. The application of Tinto's model to a Native American student population. Paper presented at the annual meeting of the Association for the Study of Higher Education in November.

Polgar, S. 1960. Biculturation of Mesquakie teenage boys. *American Anthropologist* 62: 217–235.

Rendón, L. I. 1982. *Chicano students in south Texas community colleges: A study of student- and institution-related determinants of educational outcomes.* Ph.D. diss., University of Michigan, Ann Arbor.

Rendón, L. I. 1994. Validating culturally diverse students: Toward a new model of learning and student development. *Innovative Higher Education* 19 (1): 23–32.

Rendón, L. I., and R. O. Hope. 1996. *Educating a new majority.* San Francisco: Jossey-Bass.

Rosaldo, R. 1989. *Culture and truth: The remaking of social analysis.* Boston: Beacon Press.

Terenzini, P., K. Allison, P. Gregg, R. Jalomo, S. Millar, L. I. Rendón, and L. Upcraft. 1993. *The transition to college: Easing the passage. A summary of the research findings of the Out-of-Class Experiences Program.* University Park, Pa.: National Center on Postsecondary Teaching, Learning, & Assessment.

Terenzini, P., L. I. Rendón, L. Upcraft, S. Millar, K. Allison, P. Gregg, and R. Jalomo. 1994. The transition to college: Diverse students, diverse stories. *Research in Higher Education* 35 (1): 57–73.

Thomas, G. E. 1984. *Black college students and factors influencing their major field choice.* Atlanta: Southern Education Foundation.

Tierney, W. 1992. An anthropological analysis of student participation in college. *Journal of Higher Education* 63 (6): 603–618.

Tierney, W. 1993. *Building communities of difference: Higher education in the 21st Century.* Westport, Conn.: Bergin & Garvey.

Tinto, V. 1987. *Leaving college: Rethinking the causes and cures of student departure.* Chicago: University of Chicago Press.

Tinto, V. 1993. *Leaving college: Rethinking the causes and cures of student attrition.* Chicago: University of Chicago Press.

Valadez, J. 1996. Educational access and social mobility. *Review of Higher Education* 19 (4): 391–409.

Valentine, C. A. 1971. Deficit, difference, and bicultural models of Afro-American behavior. *Harvard Educational Review* 41 (2): 137–157.

Van Gennep, A. 1960. *The rites of passage.* Translated by M. B. Vizedom and G. l. Caffee. Chicago: University of Chicago Press.

Weis, L. 1985. *Between two worlds: Black students in an urban community college.* Boston: Routledge and Kegan Paul.

Wright, B. 1988. For the children of the infidels?: American Indian education in the colonial colleges. *American Indian Culture and Research Journal* 12: 1–14.

Wycoff, S. 1996. Academic performance of Mexican-American women: Sources of support that serve as motivating variables. *Journal of Multicultural Counseling and Development* 24 (July): 146–155.

Zambrana, R. E. 1988. Toward understanding the educational trajectory and socialization of Latina women. In T. McKenna and F. I. Ortiz (eds.), *The broken web: The educational experience of Hispanic American women,* pp. 61–77. Claremont, Calif.: The Tomás Rivera Center.

Investigating the Processes of Persistence

Refining Discourse Analysis as a Tool for Generating New Departure Theory

Robert M. Johnson, Jr.

The modest successes and sharp conceptual critiques of much traditional retention research, such as that based on Tinto's model, have
sparked interest in alternative approaches. However, how one would
implement these alternative approaches is a matter of speculation and debate.
Cognitive science, however, has opened a productive pathway for framing the
processes by which both individuals and groups construct meaning in the notion of cognitive mapping. The process of cognitive mapping is cultural in
origin, involving the complex tasks of ordering one's world of meanings. The
evidence of these tasks is unfolded in narrative, metaphor, and other cultural
modes of expression and interaction. By uncovering the development of these
modes of expression and interaction faculty, staff, and administrators ought to
be better able to elicit the processes of persistence of groups at an institution.
Where Attinasi (1989, 1992) and Tierney (1992) have introduced discourse
analysis as a preferred mode of inquiry, this chapter pursues the refinement of
these formulations as a promising framework for generating a grounded theory (Glaser and Strauss 1967) of college student departure.

Every year prospective college students receive volumes of materials
from a variety of institutions, and every year college administrators fund
research and research-based interventions in order to cut down on the rate
of student departure. Yet nearly one out of every four college freshmen
leaves the institution he or she carefully chose to attend. The departure of

these students from college, in spite of their own preparation and the efforts of the institutions to retain them, constitutes a puzzle.

Because research into "the departure puzzle" to this point, it would appear, has done little to prevent or even diminish student attrition, the field needs rethinking. However, the direction in which the field should go is unclear. Two points in particular should play a role in determining how one might rethink the departure puzzle: first, the role of current theory in any reformulations; and second, the place of alternative approaches.

Regarding the first point, traditional research into student departure has been inadequate. Tinto's model (1975, 1982, 1986, 1987, 1988), which appears to have reached nearly paradigmatic status among traditional departure research, has been only modestly successful at explaining departure and granting tools for preventing it (Attinasi 1989, 1992; Braxton, Sullivan, and Johnson 1997). The model's internal consistency is particularly worrisome in cases involving diverse student populations, such as residential and commuter universities; in these cases support for the model has been weak. Similarly, the theory proves weak when tested across groups of female and male students. As Braxton, Sullivan, and Johnson (1997) conclude on the empirical support for Tinto's theory, "Although Tinto's theoretical perspective possesses logical internal consistency, it lacks, in the aggregate, empirical internal consistency . . . whether we consider multi-institutional or single institutional assessments of the thirteen primary propositions." Consequently, although traditional retention theory (Bean 1980, 1982, 1983; Weidman 1985), particularly Tinto's model, appeals to the commonsense view, it has not held up well to close scrutiny, nor has it delivered reliable empirical results.

As to the second point, the role of alternative approaches for the process of rethinking departure research is unclear. The principal problem for these alternatives has not been conceptual weakness, but rather the minimal empirical verification of the approaches. Among the critiques of Tinto's work and other traditional theories of student departure, studies by Louis Attinasi (1989, 1992, 1994) and William Tierney (1992) figure prominently. Both critics provide strong reasons for choosing alternative approaches to the traditional models, but neither fully develops an integrated model for understanding the departure puzzle (Braxton, Sullivan, and Johnson 1997).

In light of the modest successes of traditional research into student attrition and in light of the incomplete details surrounding alternative approaches, one might well wonder where to turn next to solve the departure puzzle. Should we extend or elaborate Tinto's model or another traditional model of retention? If the conceptual critics, Tierney and

Attinasi, are to be believed, then the problems in Tinto's model are beyond correction by theory extension or elaboration, and the remainder of the traditional theories are similarly flawed. As pointed out in Braxton, Sullivan, and Johnson (1997), many studies bear out various points in Tierney's and Attinasi's conceptual critiques. Should we start from the perspective of the critics, Attinasi and Tierney? They, too, have been rightly criticized for not piecing together a full plan. However, the building blocks for a new direction appear to be there; they simply need some refinement.

Three Building Blocks

Although Attinasi and Tierney do not agree on all points, they agree on three significant points for retention research. First, each claims that research on student departure or persistence should be qualitative, favoring a discourse-oriented approach. Second, they both argue that this discourse-oriented research must be culturally sensitive or culturally based, preserving the context within which decisions to depart or persist are made. Finally, Attinasi and Tierney independently base their own discourse-oriented research on the assumption that when students decide to persist or depart they do so within the context of a socially constructed reality. These three building blocks form a sufficient foundation for rethinking the departure puzzle and reinvigorating student departure research.

The first building block is that of the informal discourse-oriented approach. As opposed to the understanding of discourse as official, institutional rhetoric, discourse refers here to speech patterns, which are reflective of group norms. In this normative sense, discourse exists in speech communities, groups in which shared constructions of reality and expectations of interaction govern speech behaviors. Each person has memberships in more than one community of discourse, each with its own specific norms, and these communities constitute cultural groupings. Students, for example, negotiate in discourse their formal memberships in Greek societies, majors or academic communities, and clubs, and their informal memberships among social groupings, characterized by ethnic, geographic, or economic attributes.

Both Attinasi and Tierney underscore the importance of discourse. Each examines the speech of students who persist and depart, particularly with regard to the content of their speech. However, as we shall see, refining discourse analysis of persisting and departing students profits from going beyond content analysis.

The second building block in using discourse analysis to generate a new theory of student departure is that culture must be a central concern. Attinasi (1989) and Tierney (1992) affirm the cultural elements of Tinto's (1975) model and insist that culture play an even greater role in new theory building. Culture, they argue, forms the basis for student decision making; diminishing the role of culture in the decision to persist or depart unnecessarily strips the context from the decision. A discourse-oriented approach is therefore appropriate where the social theory must be cultural in nature, where theory must take the cultural context seriously.

Both Attinasi and Tierney develop the cultural aspects of research on departure and persistence. However, neither fully integrates a cultural perspective into the examination of discourse. Refining discourse analysis of a cultural tool depends on one's understanding of the relationship of culture to discourse, as we shall see later.

Finally, Attinasi (1989) and Tierney (1992) recognize that everyone constructs reality and makes decisions based on this construction. Individuals, however, do not construct reality individually but in groups, in social interaction. Reality is negotiated in every interaction—where "I" stand in relation to "you," what is meaningful, who "we" are, what is "young," what is "old," what is "good" or "bad." Discourse does not merely reflect group norms; it creates them (McConnell-Ginet 1989; Silberstein 1988). A discourse-oriented approach is, therefore, appropriate where taking into account the constructed nature of reality is important as reflective of group activity.

Although Attinasi and Tierney each recognize the importance of the construction of reality in student decisions to persist or depart, neither thoroughly pursues the process by which a student constructs reality through discourse. To refine the discourse-oriented approach, one must examine not only how a student's speech reflects norms and cultural values but also how it is a tool for constructing the same. Which reality is being constructed ought to bear a close relationship with the discourses and behaviors of persisting and departing.

A Discourse-Oriented Approach

Assuming the importance of the discourse-oriented approach, one might wonder what the features of discourse might be that would signal these negotiations of cultural membership and construction of reality. Discourse exists on more than one level, opening analysis to several possible angles of observation. For example, discourse exhibits content, pragmatic, and metaphorical features.

Content features are the most common in the analysis of discourse; simply put, content analysis asks, "What did the speaker talk about?" Attinasi, for example, does a fine job of separating content into themes, which illustrated for the population that he studied how each person followed a particular path for the first year of college. Perhaps more important to the study of culture, however, are the modal features of the discourse, aspects of student discourse that both Attinasi and Tierney hint at but fail to pursue in detail.

Pragmatic features are the modal and structural features of speech. Simply put, the pragmatic analysis of speech asks, "How did the speaker make the utterance?" These linguistic and sociolinguistic cues involve the sorts of details one might miss explicitly while understanding implicitly. These details include the types of verbs the speaker uses, the pronominal references the speaker makes, and the speaker's attention to politeness factors (Brown and Levinson 1987).

Types of Verbs Used

The type of verb a student uses is an important indicator for one's belief about his or her role in events. When the speaker uses action or state verbs, at which points the speaker uses active or passive verbs, and how the speaker identifies agents or agency—all communicate aspects of his or her construction of reality. For example, in answer to the interview question "How was your experience in the classroom?" a student might, among many possible responses, answer:

1. "My teacher flunked me."
2. "I flunked."

While the content of statement 1 is similar to that of statement 2, the two statements communicate a different sense of whether the student perceives himself or herself as one who only responds to things that happen or as one who makes things happen. In the types of verbs used, a student communicates a great deal about his or her perceptions of locus of control and personal efficacy. While one might argue that these beliefs are individual and personal, a person develops these beliefs in community, either experiencing the rejection of the beliefs as false or the perpetuation of them as normative for the community.

Similarly, in response to the interview request "Tell me about your schoolwork," the following two examples convey similar propositions:

1. "Everything is fine."
2. "I'm making good grades."

Statement 1 employs a state verb, which carries no aspect of agency. Statement 2, on the other hand, features an active verb, necessitating agency. While the content of the two statements in context is similar, in contrast to statement 1, the speaker identifies agency in statement 2. Agency implies responsibility, but it also implies efficacy. A student who uses active verbs, particularly in response to direct questions about his or her circumstances, is making a statement about the ability of agents to shape those circumstances. This factor is important in analyzing that student's processes in making sense of those events. The types of verbs used and when the student uses them are mildly illustrative of the student's processes of persistence. These observations are more powerful when they are matched with the pronouns a student uses.

Pronouns Used

Pronouns are important discursive indicators of the processing of experience. When a speaker uses "I," "you," "we," or "they" implies how he or she has negotiated membership, inclusion and exclusion, and entitlement. In an interview, while eliciting a narrative of a student's experiences, one might record either of the following statements:

1. "If you want financial aid, they make you fill out all these forms."
2. "I had to fill out a number of forms to get financial aid."

While the two statements communicate related propositions, the two reflect quite different understandings of the same process. To attend exclusively or even primarily to the content of a student's utterances would fail to take note of the oppositional implications of statement 1 and the personal efficacy of statement 2.

Similarly, in eliciting a narrative on social life, one might observe either of the following utterances:

1. "We think the social life here is a joke."
2. "I think the social life here is a joke."

While with respect to content each statement communicates a negative judgment of the social life on campus, statement 1 assumes a corporate opinion. In context, this use of the first-person plural pronoun might signify either an expression of affiliation or the expression of an absence of identity.

Pronouns indicate cultural understanding of social location and agency. Not only do pronouns divide and combine groups into "we" and "they," pronouns also indicate subject ("I") and object ("me"), depending upon the type of verb the speaker uses. One can determine from these types of evidence whether the speaker is one to whom things happen or one who makes things happen. Again, understandings of this sort are negotiated in groups.

Politeness Factors

When observing the conversation of students in focus groups or in naturally occurring interactions, politeness factors in speech are subtle indicators of students' understandings of their "places" in the conversation. Politeness factors are a subset of those aspects of speech that satisfy the "metagoals" of communication. These metagoals are higher order goals of interaction that govern lower order, more immediate goals. For example, a speaker's goal of defending his or her personal image in public might entail insulting one person but complimenting another. The speaker's metagoal remains constant while the strategy for meeting the goal shifts. One's metagoals influence personal style of interaction, which is a "mixture of strategies which shift in response to shifting situations" (Tannen 1982, p. 218). The most comprehensive development of the study of metagoals in communication is politeness theory.

In the study of linguistic pragmatics, *politeness* refers to those sociocultural goals that lead people to express opinions and preferences in varying forms (Tannen 1982). Penelope Brown and Stephen Levinson (1987) developed their theory of politeness to describe their observations of certain pragmatic and interactional notions of language use, and their theory has led to fruitful analyses of cultural variance in speech (Deuchar 1988). Brown and Levinson (1979) argue that speakers select discourse strategies to meet metagoals according to three variables. The first two variables concern the relationship between the speaker and the hearer: vertical social distance, or power; and horizontal social distance, or solidarity (Brown and Gilman 1989). The third variable refers to the intrinsic extremity of a face-threatening act (Brown and Levinson 1987). Speakers select various strategies, paying increasingly greater attention to politeness as vertical, horizontal, and face-threatening aspects of communication increase. For the weaker member of a conversation, or the speaker sensing the lack of solidarity more acutely, the risk of imposition or threat to face is greater and the consequent need for an indirect means of getting what one wants or needs is more acute.

Examples of attention to politeness factors based on social distance and threat to face include the use of hedges and tag questions ("like," "don't you?," "if you don't mind," "okay?"); these discursive devices function by mitigating the perceived effect of a statement, question, or demand. For example:

1. "I was, like, all embarrassed in class."
2. "I think such-and-such is a complete waste, don't you?"
3. "Would you close the door, if you don't mind?"

By eliciting or observing student conversational interactions, one can isolate those cues in speech that indicate the speakers' beliefs and decision-making patterns. Students might express beliefs and processes that they might not be able to articulate in a manner detectable from simple content analysis. Consequently, attention to politeness factors is invaluable for understanding how a student is constructing reality in community.

Discourse analytic techniques are applicable to any form of qualitative research design that involves the observation or solicitation of speech. Whether in the informal process of observing two students interacting or in the more structured context of an interview, attention to the manner in which students express themselves is crucial to determining how the students are constructing their realities. Some aspects of discourse are more relevant to certain types of interaction. For example, the types of verbs and pronouns a student uses are particularly relevant to interview designs because the student is relating a narrative. Attention to politeness factors in a student's speech, however, are far more revealing in student-to-student interaction where the students are involved in mutual negotiation of social "truths."

Each of the three categories or features of a speaker's utterances send various signals negotiating the terms of his or her membership in a discourse community—negotiating, in fact, the discourse community itself. These features communicate aspects of one's processing of experiences, and each feature can be manipulated by the speaker to participate in various communities and to participate on more than one level in those communities. These aspects of speech indicate deeper structures of discourse than content and deliver more information about the speaker's understanding of cultural belonging and decision making. However, one further, deep structure aspect of discourse is metaphor.

Metaphorical features of discourse underlie both pragmatic and content features of discourse. As opposed to the sense of the term *metaphor* as a poetic or rhetorical device, metaphor refers here to the "language of thought" (Lakoff 1987; Lakoff and Johnson 1980). As Lakoff and Johnson (1980) argue, metaphor is inescapable; reality itself is defined by metaphor, and as metaphors vary from culture to culture, so do the realities they define. The metaphors not only describe reality, they help construct and perpetuate it (McConnell-Ginet 1989; Silberstein 1988). Metaphor, therefore, structures the actions we perform; metaphor provides a vocabulary of motivation.

When we are able to elicit narratives from college students and, essentially, audit their speech for metaphor, then we begin to unlock the realities the students are constructing. We begin to place a cultural context around the decisions they make. Metaphor, therefore, is a contact point or entry point for understanding the cultural basis of a discourse community. Cognitive scientists refer to this basis as the "cognitive map" (Lakoff 1987; Lakoff and Johnson 1980).

The term *cognitive map* has referred to any number of constructs. For example, Attinasi uses the term to refer to "instructions on how to negotiate new environments" (1989, p. 272), and he claims that these maps "exhibit considerable interpersonal variation" (p. 268). Such a concept is more consistent with the psychological notions of schemata. Schemata are "knowledge structures abstracted from previously encountered stimuli that provide a goal-directed form of information processing." In short, a schema is a constantly revised set of instructions for dealing with the cognitive complexity of any real-life situation. We all use schemata in order to manage the complexity of each article we read; schemata allow us to be selectively attentive, but they are only indirectly related to the more important cultural determinants of discourse and decision making.

Cognitive maps, on the other hand, differ from schemata in that cognitive maps are long-term, rarely revised knowledge structures, whereas schemata are short-term, frequently revised knowledge structures. Cognitive maps are cultural in their origin, whereas schemata are personal and individual in origin. While investigating schemata is valuable for understanding one's sense of order, investigating cognitive mapping is more productive for examining one's sense of meaning. Cognitive maps are products of "deep structure processes," whereas schemata are products of "surface structure" processes. Schemata, therefore, are more closely connected with content analysis, and cognitive mapping is more closely aligned with discourse analysis.

Cognitive mapping, consequently, has proved to be productive in rethinking theory and theory building across many disciplines because it helps to explain the existence and formative processes of reality construction. The notion provides the theoretical framework for analyzing a reality other than one's own through the study of metaphor. The connections to the pragmatic aspects of discourse are complex; the cognitive map affects one's metagoals and perceptions of strategies, whereas schemata are likely to affect only the choice of perceived strategies.

In inferring the cognitive maps of a student, one would want to pay attention to metaphors of connection or alienation, centrality or marginality. Does the student use familial expressions in regard to faculty relationships or residence life, or does she use metaphors of chaos or simply disinterest? What connections or transitions does the speaker make between topics? Does the speaker take narrative from a subject of contest or conflict to discussions of the classroom, thus making conflict a metaphor for the classroom? By observing closely the links the speaker makes between words and topics, one can begin to map out the meaning the speaker is making of his or her experiences.

Confirming the cues of cognitive maps requires a great deal more observation than brief interviews or focus groups. Identifying the patterns of metaphor is a detailed task requiring many utterances in more than a few contexts over an extended period of time. The benefit of making the connection between cognitive maps and a student's construction of reality is that one gains greater insight into the processes of persistence at a deep structure level.

Summary

In contrast to traditional research on student departure, a discourse-oriented approach demonstrates a completely different understanding of speech norms from that which is characteristic of most traditional research on student departure. In the Tinto tradition, for example, speech or discourse is an artifact of group membership. One makes the transition into a group by learning its behaviors and norms, including speech behaviors and norms. Tinto's theory, however, does not account for the fact that the boundaries of the group are constantly being negotiated. The group's norms and behaviors are not static or codified except in formal societies. Consequently, the periphery or boundaries, the margins of the group, are always being extended, withdrawn, or redefined. A new student creates the university or the residence hall or the student body by being a part of it.

In extending Attinasi's and Tierney's approach of discourse analysis, one may focus on "deep-structure" processes; attending to pragmatic and metaphorical aspects of speech as opposed to content alone reflects a significant refinement of the method of analysis. The more thorough the understanding of the evidence, the more appropriate the response will be. Most interventions and measures, such as orientation, are oriented to the individual, psychological processes of schema production. A thorough understanding of the process of forming such cognitive structures uncovers their pertinence for understanding the depths of the cultural divide faced by some students. This understanding also demonstrates the importance of addressing these students within the terms of their cultural, cognitive maps, because faculty, staff, and administrators may hinder students' persistence through appealing to the wrong means, the wrong metaphors, and the wrong policy "levers."

In sum, through the examination of student narrative or interactive discourse regarding students' experiences, one should be able to generate a grounded theory (Glaser and Strauss 1967) that is more sensitive to cultural distinctions and acknowledges the constructed nature of reality, giving us a context for student persistence. Knowing what a student's experiences are is inadequate; one must also know what those experiences mean to the student before making a judgment on the student's decision-making processes or designing appropriate interventions for supporting that student.

Attinasi (1989, 1992) and Tierney (1992) make significant strides beyond traditional methods for generating departure theory by introducing discourse analysis as an important analytical tool. By refining the role of this tool, one can uncover students' group identities and culturally conditioned mechanisms for organizing and evaluating their experiences. One learns these things not merely from what is said but from the way it is said and which shared meanings students reference. Rather than focusing on the attributes of persisting or departing students, one can rethink the departure puzzle dramatically by attending to the processes of persistence, focusing on culture, cognition, and the structure of meaning through discourse analysis.

References

Attinasi, L. C., Jr. 1989. Getting in: Mexican Americans' perceptions of university attendance and the implications for freshman year persistence. *Journal of Higher Education* 60: 247–277.

Attinasi, L. C., Jr. 1992. Rethinking the study of the outcomes of college attendance. *Journal of College Student Development* 33: 61–70.

Attinasi, L. C., Jr. 1994. Is going to college a rite of passage? Paper presented at the annual meeting of the American Educational Research Association, New Orleans, La.

Bean, J. P. 1980. Dropouts and turnover: The synthesis and test of a causal model of student attrition. *Research in Higher Education* 12: 155–187.

Bean, J. P. 1982. Conceptual models of student attrition: How theory can help the institutional researcher. In E. T. Pascarella (ed.), *Studying student attrition*, pp.17–33. San Francisco: Jossey-Bass.

Bean, J. P. 1983. The application of a model of turnover in work organizations to the student attrition process. *Review of Higher Education* 6: 129–148.

Braxton, J. M., A. V. S. Sullivan, and R. M. Johnson. 1997. Appraising Tinto's theory of college student departure. In J. C. Smart (ed.), *Higher education: A handbook of theory and research*, vol. 12, pp. 107–164. New York: Agathon Press.

Brown, P., and S. Levinson. 1987. *Politeness: Some universals in language use*. Cambridge: Cambridge University Press.

Brown, R., and A. Gilman. 1960. The pronouns of power and solidarity. In T. A. Sebeok (ed.), *Style in language*, pp. 253–276. Cambridge, Mass.: MIT Press.

Brown, R., and A. Gilman. 1989. Politeness theory and Shakespeare's four major tragedies. *Language and Society* 18: 159–212.

Deuchar, M. 1988. A pragmatic account of women's use of standard speech. In Coates and Cameron (eds.), *Women in their speech communities: New perspectives on language and sex*, pp. 27–32. New York: Longman.

Glaser, B. G., and A. L. Strauss. 1967. *The discovery of grounded theory: Strategies for qualitative research*. New York: Aldine.

Lakoff, G. 1987. *Women, fire, and dangerous things: What categories reveal about the mind*. Chicago: University of Chicago Press.

Lakoff, G., and M. Johnson. 1980. *Metaphors we live by*. Chicago: University of Chicago Press.

McConnell-Ginet, S. 1989. The sexual (re)production of meaning: A discourse-based theory. In F. Frank and P. Treichler (eds.), *Language, gender, and professional writing: Theoretical approaches and guidelines*, pp. 35–50. New York: Modern Language Association.

Silberstein, S. 1988. Ideology as process: Gender ideology in courtship narratives." In A. Todd and S. Fisher (eds.), *Gender and discourse: The power of talk*, pp.125–149. Norwood, N.J.: Ablex.

Tannen, D. 1982. Ethnic style in male-female conversation. In J. J. Gumperz (ed.), *Language and social identity*, pp. 217–231. Cambridge, U.K.: Cambridge University Press.

Tierney, W. G. 1992. An anthropological analysis of student participation in college. *Journal of Higher Education* 63: 603–618.

Tinto, V. 1975. Dropout from higher education: A theoretical synthesis of recent research. *Review of Educational Research* 45: 89–125.

Tinto, V. 1982. Limits of theory and practice in student attrition. *Journal of Higher Education* 53: 687–700.

Tinto, V. 1986. Theories of student departure revisited. In J. C. Smart (ed.), *Higher education: A handbook of theory and research,* vol. 2, pp. 359–384. New York: Agathon Press.

Tinto, V. 1987. *Student leaving: Rethinking the causes and cures of student attrition.* Chicago: University of Chicago Press.

Tinto, V. 1988. Stages of student departure: Reflections on the longitudinal character of student leaving. *Journal of Higher Education* 59: 438–455.

Weick, K. E. 1979. The social psychology of organizing. 2d ed. Reading, Mass.: Addison-Wesley.

Weidman, J. 1985. Retention of non-traditional students in postsecondary education. Paper presented at the annual meeting of the American Educational Research Association, Chicago.

Where Is the Student?

Linking Student Behaviors, College Choice, and College Persistence

Frances K. Stage and Don Hossler

R esearch conducted in the past twenty years has examined student persistence in college extensively (Attinasi 1989; Cabrera, Stampen, and Hansen 1990; De Los Santos, Montemayor, and Solis 1980; Bean and Metzner 1985; Nora 1987; Olivas 1986; Pascarella and Terenzini 1977, 1991; Stage 1989; Terenzini and Pascarella 1980; Tinto 1975, 1987, 1988; Tracey and Sedlacek 1987). Throughout the 1980s and 1990s increasingly sophisticated statistical techniques and ethnographic approaches have been more widely used (Pascarella and Terenzini 1983, 1991). Out of that period of study grew assuredness regarding factors that were key in the persistence of many college students, such as relationships with faculty and positive academic and social experiences on campus (Terenzini et al. 1995; Tinto 1987).

Additionally, during roughly the same time period but in a separate line of inquiry, researchers turned increasingly sophisticated analytic skills toward explanation of students' decisions to attend and choice of colleges (Carpenter and Fleishman 1987; Chapman 1981; Ekstrom 1985; Hossler, Braxton, and Coopersmith 1989; Litten 1982; McDonough 1997; Ortiz 1986; Paulsen 1990; Solomon and Taubman 1973; Trent and Medsker 1967). In the past decade researchers developed models to explain those decision processes. Some of those models demonstrated overlap with the sociologically based status attainment models (Chapman 1981; Hossler and Gallagher 1987). Studies of college choice employed a number of theoretical approaches to develop models and to conduct research. For example, Jackson's (1982) model of college choice and Hossler and Gallagher's (1987) model draw heavily on status attainment research. Hearn's (1984) work on college choice also relies upon variables and constructs derived from the status attainment tradition. However, studies of college choice have also been conducted using economic theory (Manski and Wise 1983), Bourdieu and Passeron's (1977) concept of cultural capital (McDonough 1997), and consumer behavior (Young and Reyes 1987).

In his study of the college entrance and subsequent persistence of Mexican American college students, Attinasi (1989) provides a link between research on student college choice and the study of persistence. He also provides theoretical leads for connecting these two lines of research when he describes students going through "getting ready" behaviors and, later, "getting in" behaviors. His student respondents ascribed their eventual success in college to these earlier behaviors. In addition, Braxton, Vesper, and Hossler (1995) found that when the expectations formed by prospective students prior to matriculation were met, they were more likely to be committed to graduating from the college in which they had enrolled. The authors posit that the expectations students form of the collegiate experience (which are in part shaped by the admissions and recruitment process that is part of the college choice process) in turn influence their subsequent assessments of whether or not the campus academic and social communities fulfill their expectations. These assessments in turn influence plans to persist. Hamrick and Hossler (1996) learned that high school students who had greater access to information about colleges later reported greater satisfaction with the colleges in which they had enrolled. Also, Williams (1996) found a positive relationship between lack of information prior to enrollment in college and subsequent disillusionment with college choice.

Other researchers have called for an examination of college choice and college persistence as one process. Stage and Rushin (1993) presented and tested a combined model based on a model of college choice and college persistence using the High School and Beyond data set. Parental encouragement to attend college while a senior in high school was a significant predictor of graduation from college within six years of high school graduation. More recently St. John, Paulsen, and Starkey (1996) observed that variables and constructs derived from status attainment theory are used to frame both persistence and college choice research. In addition, St. John and Hossler (1998) have conceptualized the process of student college choice and student persistence decisions as a sequence of student choices. They posit a sequence of student choices including formation of postsecondary aspirations, the opportunity to attend (access), choice of college, choice of major, persistence, and graduate education as a sequence of interrelated student choice options that are influenced by many of the same variables. Paulsen and St. John (forthcoming) have further explored the connections among these student choices. But to date no one has presented a comprehensive model that links the processes of student college choice and college persistence.

We view the similarities across both processes as important rather than incidental. We further propose that college preparation and college choice, to the degree that the student actively engages in them, provide an important actual and conceptual basis for later college success. This chapter reviews higher education literature focusing on student college choice and college student experiences leading to persistence. Common constructs from these areas of research are used to link the concepts into one causal process. But we wish to focus beyond the educational experiences of students, which are commonly emphasized in many retention studies. Therefore, we draw on Bandura's (1997) construct of self-efficacy to discuss the ways students develop their sense of being college students and on Fishbein and Ajzen's (1975) Behavioral Model of Intention to describe the development of educational intentions and attendant behaviors of students. Using both theories we focus on students as active agents as opposed to passive recipients of experiences. We suggest the use of measures of activities and behaviors engaged in by students themselves as they make their way through the educational process. Our model, based on student behaviors, focuses on traditional-age high school and college students. Clearly the decisions involved in college choice and college departure processes differ for nontraditional students (Bean and Metzner 1985; Valadez 1996). The theory presented in this chapter traces the educational process from predisposition to college attendance through college, and to college persistence or dropout. Finally, we make suggestions for refinement, measurement, and testing of the model.

Context

Background for this model combines over two decades of research on both status attainment and college student persistence and over one decade of research on college choice. The model is also informed by conceptual work by

Braxton, Sullivan, and Johnson (1997), Tierney's (1992) criticism of college student persistence research, and Tinto's (1987) reflections on his initial model. DiMaggio's (1982) work on cultural capital informs conceptualizations regarding family background of students. Key to our model is the description of students' behaviors in the educational process; students are viewed as active rather than passive participants.

Conceptualizations that focus on precollege students' activities such as "getting ready" (Attinasi 1989; Hossler and Maple 1993) and those that focus on college students rather than institutions as actors (Pace 1979, 1997) inform the process aspects of the model. We incorporate literature that relates student academic behaviors to success in college, referring in particular to Fishbein and Ajzen's (1975) model that relates behaviors to intentions and to Bandura's (1986, 1997) model of self-efficacy as a regulator of motivation.

Behaviors and Self-efficacy

Key to our model is the psychological concept of human agency—persons, in this case students, exercising control over what they do. "Based on their understanding of what is within the power of humans to do and based on their own capabilities, people try to generate courses of action to suit given purposes" (Bandura 1997, p. 3). The key feature of personal agency in this case is the power within the student to generate actions that will result in his or her success. Often that power is called motivation. We acknowledge that students are not the sole controllers of their behavior; they must interact with individuals, groups, and institutions. Fishbein and Ajzen's (1975) discussion of the role of social pressures in influencing motivation enriched the combined model we advance in this chapter.

Fishbein and Ajzen (1975) developed a basic behavioral intention model to demonstrate that behaviors of individuals are preceded by intentions to perform those behaviors. Behavioral intentions are influenced by attitudes toward those behaviors and by subjective norms concerning the behaviors. The attitude component is comprised of the beliefs of respondents about performing the acts and is a function of the acts' perceived consequences. Fishbein and Ajzen, however, do not assert that behavioral intentions alone account for the actions of individuals. They note that the behaviors are influenced by norms present in the social environment. The normative component deals with the influence of the social environment on behavior. For example, in their study of college choice in Australia,

Carpenter and Fleishman (1987) also drew upon Fishbein and Ajzen's work. The empirical model they tested included students' perceptions of community social norms toward college attendance as one of the predictor variables.

In over two decades of research Bandura (1986, 1994, 1997) refined the relationship of beliefs about self to motivation. He described self-efficacy as individuals' "beliefs about their capabilities to produce designated levels of performance that exercise influence over events that affect their lives" (Bandura 1994, p. 71). Self-efficacy is related to motivation in that if an individual believes he or she has the capability to perform a task and that performance will then lead to a positive result, the individual will be motivated to perform (Bandura 1977). Presumably what Fishbein and Ajzen describe as intention is based on the self-efficacy of the individual in question; absent a belief in ability, no intention would be formulated and no action taken. Beliefs about one's capabilities influence motivation through attributions, expectancy-values, and goals. Self-efficacy influences academic achievement through several mechanisms; it affects an individual's thoughts about, emotional approach to, selection of, and persistence at a task (see Bandura 1998).

Self-efficacy to achieve in college can be positively influenced through activities that provide opportunities for students to (1) experience mastery, (2) watch others like themselves succeed and thus experience success vicariously, (3) be persuaded by others to engage in challenging activities, and (4) develop positive emotional reactions to college situations and expectations (Stage et al. 1998). College search and preparatory behaviors described by Attinasi (1989) and by Hamrick and Hossler (1996), as well as successful academic and personal investment of time and energy once a student arrives at college, lead to an increasing belief in self-efficacy. Accordingly, a student's expectations are enhanced, intentions are developed, goals are established, and the student's motivation increases.

For successful movement into college and persistence through college, student intentions and behaviors influence and are influenced by the behavioral norms in the collegiate environment, which in turn lead to increasingly positive, or negative, expectations, goals, and beliefs about college and the ability to be successful in college. Student behaviors that provide positive academic and social results lead to increasingly positive expectations, goals, and beliefs about college and the ability to perform. We posit that the development of positive motivations (or intentions) and goals leads to educational activities and achievements (behaviors) that begin early in the educational process to persistence through or dropout from college. Key constructs of the model span a time period long before college entry. Language and the limitations of the two-dimensional presentation format require us to present our model in a manner that appears more discrete than we believe it to be. The processes and related intentions and behaviors we describe are not isolated, disjoint steps. Rather, they are cyclical and are more like a spiral than a linear progression (see figure 1).

Figure 1. Key Elements of a Student-Centered Model

The elements and processes presented in figure 1 play an important role in our behavioral model and are described briefly below.

1. Background consists of family experience including cultural and economic capital factors, student ability, and parental encouragement. These shape student beliefs and aspirations (or intentions) as well as subsequent behaviors.

2. School experiences from both middle and high school; encouragement or lack thereof from teachers, peers, and counselors; parental support; and interactions with family background create the beginnings of predisposition or intentions for postsecondary education and influence student behavior.

3. Intentions lead to a range of behaviors, seeking advice, enrolling in college preparatory classes, engaging in volunteer service, exploring career options, and college searching. Successful participation in these activities exerts a strong influence upon post–high school goals such as entering the military, work, or college matriculation. Preparation follows from the influence of family resources, student experiences, and intentions. As students prepare to select

colleges, they increasingly engage in getting-ready behaviors such as visiting college campuses and talking to peers about specific colleges. They attempt to envision new lives in new environments.

4. College entry initiates student behaviors that will determine success or dropout. Students enroll in appropriate-level courses, engage in intellectual and social activities, and establish study patterns as active or passive students. Influenced by family and school background and capitalizing on prior "getting-ready" behaviors, students enter college with motivations and goals, engage in new behaviors, engage with faculty and with their course work, and engage in the social fabric of campus.

5. Students ultimately persist or depart.

As the student moves through the educational process, he or she is at first more of a passive recipient of parental and school effects and experiences. If the previous experiences in the process were positive and developmental, the student will have strong beliefs in his or her future efficacy as a college student. Accordingly the student will formulate goals and intentions and engage in behaviors that will result in a greater likelihood of persisting. According to the model, in late grade school and early college the student assumes a more active role, and those actions and behaviors ultimately lead to success and persistence or dropout.

A Student-Centered Theory of College Completion

To move beyond current research and writing on college predisposition and college persistence as two discrete processes, we capitalize on overlapping influences to create a conceptual link. Figure 2 presents a proposed behavioral theory combining elements of college predisposition models (Hossler, Braxton, and Coopersmith 1989; McDonough 1997; Paulsen 1990) as well as college persistence models (Pascarella and Terenzini 1983; Bean 1980; Tinto 1987). Within this model, as within most college predisposition and persistence models, background characteristics of students are viewed as external. In other words, they are viewed as factors whose cause is unexplained within the model but that continue to influence later elements of the model. In this initial theoretical presentation we discuss only direct effects in a linear fashion but recognize that indirect effects as well as other direct effects such as from Background to Persistence/Dropout would be important elements of an empirical model.

Figure 2
A Student-Centered Theory of Persistence

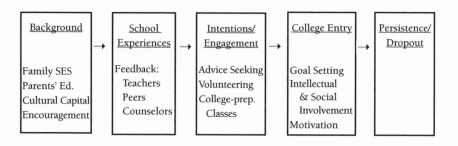

The difference between this persistence theory and others is that the combination of background characteristics includes parental encouragement, student involvement in high school, and modeling or getting-ready behaviors, which are common to some college-choice studies but not typical to persistence studies. The remaining parts of the theory resemble mainstream college student persistence research, but here we emphasize the role of the individual's psychological characteristics and include the importance of the roles of intention, expectation, goal setting, and behaviors in the college student experience. The level of commitment to goals leads (as within most college student persistence models) to a certain level of academic and social involvement in the campus environment. Unique to our description of the process is the way that we envision the measurement of the variables. In all cases we focus on activities undertaken by students to accomplish specific tasks related to the concepts at hand. Thus, we purposely use the word *involvement* rather than *integration* to emphasize the importance of personal agency on the part of students. Student-initiated activities contrast with active efforts of institutions to "integrate" students and are the results of students' beliefs about their potential success in college and their intentions to succeed. These active experiences might include study behaviors, attendance at cultural activities and academic lectures, and engagement in intellectual discussions with other students. These active measures contrast with those that characterize many studies of college student persistence (students' estimated intellectual gains or students' estimated academic growth). Results of these actions can lead to changes in self-beliefs about ability (Bandura 1997) and intentions and behaviors (Fishbein and Ajzen 1975) that ultimately lead to persistence or attrition. Finally, the theory allows for the inclusion of the influence of outside demands on commitments, activities, and persistence, similar to other persistence studies.

Below we discuss the relationships among these constructs and suggest examples of the many research questions that might be used to further develop the theory. Each question should be examined separately by racial-ethnic groups, by gender, and for socioeconomic strata to identify important differences.

Family Background and Cultural and Economic Capital Factors

In both literatures—college predisposition and college student persistence—sociodemographic variables play an important role. Few major theoretical models ignore the probable influences of factors such as family education, status, income, and student ability. These factors continue to be reliable indicators of status attainment, educational intentions, and success in college even when later experiences and behaviors are taken into account.

In general, status attainment models focus on relationships among parental education and income, family structure, and ultimate status as an adult mediated by educational achievements. Downey (1992) and Downey and Powell (1993) reported that levels of social and economic capital provided within families of eighth graders were positively related to grades and predisposition to college. Several studies found that parental education and encouragement to attend colleges and universities were strongly associated with students' intentions to attend such institutions (Carpenter and Fleishman 1987; Gaier and Watts 1969; Hossler and Stage 1992; Sewell and Shah 1978; Stage and Hossler 1989). In a nine-year longitudinal study Hossler, Schmit, and Vesper (1998) found that students who consistently reported plans to attend colleges and universities between ninth and twelfth grade were more likely to actualize their intentions and enroll. McDonough (1997) conducted case studies of women high school seniors and described cultural capital in terms of social norms within high schools and their influence on channeling lower SES students away from college or toward colleges of low prestige.

Similarly, within the college student persistence literature, parents' higher educational levels and incomes are strongly related to successful involvement in college and, indirectly, to persistence (Astin 1975; Anderson 1987; Braxton, Sullivan, and Johnson 1997; Chapman and Pascarella 1983; McDonough 1997; Pascarella, Smart, and Ethington 1986; Pavel 1991; Stage 1989; Tinto 1987; Williamson and Creamer 1988).

However, few persistence studies have examined encouragement factors in relation to persistence. An exception is Attinasi's (1989) ethnographic study of Chicana and Chicano students. A factor termed "getting ready" as well as a second factor, "familial" modeling, were described as important influences on students' success. In a quantitative test of the factors within a model of student persistence, parental encouragement was positively related to initial commitment to college and getting-ready behaviors were significantly and positively related to academic involvement and initial commitment (Nora, Attinasi, and Matonak 1990). However, getting-ready behaviors were negatively related to persistence. In general, ethnic minority students were less likely to choose to attend college (Freeman 1997; Hossler and Stage 1992; Ortiz 1986). And while typically there is not a difference across gender, black women are far more likely to attend than black men (Washington and Newman 1991). However, women in general receive less family support for their college-going plans (Stage and Hossler 1989), although they have higher aspirations than men (Hossler and Stage 1992).

In studies of persistence, minority students, particularly at predominantly white institutions, are less likely to succeed (Chacon, Cohen, and Strover 1986; Kobrak 1992; Robinson 1990) and demonstrate differing experiences and behaviors leading to persistence than their white peers (Chacon, Cohen, and Strover 1986; Hood 1992; Nora 1987; Nora and Cabrera 1996). Finally, recent work suggests that measures of academic and social integration constructs typically employed within persistence studies need to be reconceptualized for minority college students (Hurtado and Carter 1997; Kraemer 1997).

Most college persistence models emphasize college experiences, but parents' financial contributions and educational measures maintain strong influence despite the immediacy of the college experience (Stage 1989). In addition Bean and Vesper (1992) found that parental support and encouragement was the strongest predictor of persistence at a small liberal arts college that enrolled high numbers of first-generation college students. Often these factors, along with student ability, significantly influence college experiences and successes, thus indirectly influencing college persistence as well. Frequently such factors have significant direct influences on persistence.

Sample research questions from this part of the theory include:

> Do cultural capital variables influence later constructs in the theory (school experiences, intentions and engagement, college entry, and persistence)?

> To what extent are measures of cultural capital significantly related to later constructs in the theory (school experiences, intentions and engagement, college entry, and persistence)?

> To what extent do parental encouragement and economic status influence school experiences, intention, and engagement as a college student, and persistence?

> To what extent do parental and student factors interact to influence later constraints in this model?

> Do cultural capital experiences initiated by students have a greater positive effect than those initiated by parents for students?

Student Ability

Measured abilities and high school experience factors are nearly as popular as socioeconomic status in attempts to explain students' predisposition to and persistence in college. For the purposes of our behavioral model, student ability effects are complex. Student ability influences both motivation and intention of students and is also a product of behavior. Grade point average, for example, is the product not only of innate ability but also of student effort. As their grade point averages rise, students receive more parental and teacher encouragement to continue to perform well in school and to consider continuing their formal education after high school. Additionally, they receive reinforcement for their beliefs that they might be successful in college and, corresponding with Bandura (1997) and with Fishbein and Ajzen (1975), accordingly plan and undertake paths that will result in college matriculation. Researchers have also found that students of high ability are more likely to apply for admission to colleges (Carpenter and Fleishman 1987; Hause 1969; Sewell and Hauser 1975; Hossler and Stage 1992; Manski and Wise 1983). Carpenter and Fleishman (1987) found that high school grades and test scores influenced students' self-assessments of their ability to "get in" to colleges and universities. Thus grades and test scores influence students' intentions and their sense of self-efficacy.

In the college student persistence literature the role of student ability is complex. Student ability has been measured variously as high school grade point average (GPA), high school rank, and SAT scores (Chapman and Pascarella 1983; Pascarella and Terenzini 1983; Terenzini et al. 1985). Most campus-based studies show that college grade point average has a direct effect upon student persistence but that high school grades and other measures of ability are not good predictors of persistence (Nora and Cabrera 1996; Okun, Benin, and Brandt-Williams 1996; Stage 1989). However, national studies that are not limited to single institutional studies usually show that high school grades are predictors of persistence (Astin 1975; Williams 1996; Williamson and Creamer 1988).

Sample research questions from this part of the theory include:

What are the relationships among student grades, test scores, and rank and intentions toward postsecondary education?

What are the relationships among student grades, test scores, rank, students' beliefs about ability, and college search behaviors?

What are the relationships among student grades, test scores, and rank; students' beliefs about ability; subsequent engagement in college search behaviors; and persistence in college?

School Behaviors and Experiences

The second part of the theory focuses on school behavioral measures as well as education-related experiences of students. Research on this area is somewhat limited in the college-choice literature. Some research uncovered a relationship between high school "ability tracks" in which students are enrolled and their educational aspirations (Alexander and Eckland 1977; Falsey and Heyns 1984; McDonough 1997). School tracks are not solely a function of student ability because both the extent of tracking and the impact of school guidance counselors influence the course-taking patterns and aspirations of students within high schools. McDonough's (1997) recent ethnographic work on the college decision-making process indicates that the high school context, images of "acceptable" colleges within various high schools, and the interactions among students, teachers, and counselors can have a powerful impact on which colleges students consider attending.

In addition, the activities that students are involved in can have an impact on the college plans of students. Hearn (1984) and Hossler and Stage (1992) report that the degree of involvement in high school activities was related to intentions to attend college. Additionally, Marsh (1992), Camp (1990), and Spady (1971) found, in general, positive relationships between several measures of activity participation and achievement and college aspirations. However, Lisella and Serwatka (1996) found a negative relationship between high school activity participation and achievement levels for minority men but not for women. Additionally, Hamrick and Stage (1998) analyzed a model of predisposition to college and found that for minority students in poor schools, high school activities were not good predictors of predisposition. We draw special attention to the effects of student involvement on college choice decisions and later college student involvement and persistence. In our review of student persistence research many of the measures of academic and social integration are behavioral measures that also assess levels of student involvement. However, persistence studies have not included measures of students' high school involvement as predictor variables.

Sample research questions from this part of the theory include:

How do teacher (counselor) attitudes and feedback (unrelated to student ability) influence students' college search behaviors?

What kinds of school activities and experiences are associated with students' intentions to attend college, college search behaviors, and subsequent experience in college?

Student Information-Gathering Activities/Search for College

In addition to student and family factors and secondary-school experiences, research suggests that the extent to which students actively engage in searching for colleges and gather information about educational options influences their choice of colleges, subsequent satisfaction, and possibly ultimate persistence. Although the link to student retention may not immediately be apparent, student information gathering and searching for important college characteristics are consistent with Tinto's early theory of student departure (1975) and later emphases on student involvement (Astin 1985; Kuh et al.

1991; Pace 1990; Pascarella and Terenzini 1991). Tinto (1975) notes that a theoretical model of persistence must take into consideration the "expectational and motivational attributes of students" (p. 93). The degree to which students engage in these activities can be viewed as an indicator of intent. In addition, the extent of students' involvement in their education has consistently been validated as a primary determinant of educational outcomes (Astin 1985; Pace 1990; Pascarella and Terenzini 1991). Information gathering and search activities are early manifestations of students' motivation and their involvement in their education.

Schmit (1991) identifies a number of important factors associated with student information-gathering activities. Hamrick and Hossler (1996) and Williams (1996) report that students who engaged in more information-gathering activities about college and who reported knowing more about postsecondary educational institutions were more likely to report being enrolled in their first-choice institutions and to be satisfied with those institutions. As of yet, however, no empirical tests between information gathering and persistence have been found.

Sample research questions from this part of the theory include:

To what extent do students' beliefs about their likely success as college students influence involvement in information gathering and active searching for college?

Are students who have spoken to family members and older friends about college more likely to engage in their own independent college search activities?

Are students who engage in their own independent college search activities more likely to envision themselves in the role of college students?

To what extent are students who engage in their own independent college search activities more likely to engage in college experiences and to persist in college?

College Behaviors and Experiences

As students move through late high school and into college, ideally we would see a shift from dependence to independence in initiation of behaviors. Student intentions and some behaviors form the foundation of most campus-based research on student persistence. In examining constructs of Tinto's theory of student departure, behavioral measures of academic and social integration provide a robust anchor for the model. In a recent modification of that model Tinto (1997) adds greater emphasis to student-initiated efforts. The degree of interaction with faculty, peers, and other socializing agents of universities is frequently the best predictor of student persistence (Braxton, Sullivan, and Johnson 1997; Hurtado and Carter 1997; Pascarella and Terenzini 1977). We assert that student-initiated interactions are even more predictive than those in which the student engages more passively. Tinto's theory also posits that goal commitment and institutional commitment as well as attitudinal intention are important constructs to understanding student departure. In 1980 Bean incorporated Fishbein and Ajzen's (1975) construct of intention and demonstrated that by late spring semester, intent to reenroll the following semester was a robust predictor of fall reenrollment. Tinto incorporated this concept of intention into a revised theory of student departure in 1987. Here we use Fishbein and Ajzen's construct to focus on student intent and then behavior as played out in students' everyday lives. Choices students make on a daily basis and then the ways they follow through on those choices with actions that lead to success are predictors of overall success.

Additionally, students' views of self play a role in their degree of active, self-initiated participation in their education. Various measures of self-efficacy have consistently demonstrated to have positive relationships to student behaviors and to global measures of academic success (Forsyth and McMillan 1991; Hackett et al. 1992; Lucas 1990; Sexton and Tuckman 1991; Zimmerman and Bandura 1994). Simmons (1996) examined the effects of low-achieving college students' beliefs and attitudes on their approaches to learning and their use of study and learning strategies. Students with a strong sense of academic self-efficacy were more likely to pursue learning goals that emphasized subject mastery and to use learning strategies to effectively manage their learning. Students who were more confident of their academic competence were also more certain of their academic majors than were those with lower levels of self-efficacy. Finally, in an ethnographic study of college students with learning disabilities, Stage and Milne (1996) found that students' beliefs about their abilities to succeed were important to them in explaining their study behaviors and their success at the college level.

Sample research questions from this part of the theory include:

What is the relationship between intention or commitment to various goals (earning a good grade in a class, getting to know an interesting professor, socializing with fellow students) and engaging in activities that promote those goals?

Can an institution have an influence on student intention, thereby promoting positive behaviors on the part of students?

Do students who have strong beliefs about their abilities as college students also have strong intentions and therefore engage in behaviors that will likely lead to college success?

Academic Involvement

The term *involvement* emphasizes the importance of behavior rather than perception and of student-initiated rather than institution- or class-initiated activity. Past examination of students' academic success incorporated not only grades but a host of other variables as well (Astin 1975; Ballesteros 1986; Pascarella and Terenzini 1983). Although many of the measures of the academic experience of college students are behavioral, they are rarely measured this way in college student persistence research. These behavioral measures include the utilization of academic support facilities (Churchill and Iwai 1981; Leon 1975), contacts with faculty members (Feldman and Newcomb 1969; Pascarella 1978; Pascarella and Terenzini 1983; Stage 1989; Terenzini and Pascarella 1980), participation in academic activities (Pascarella and Terenzini 1983; Stage 1989), effort put forth both inside and outside the classroom (Sailes 1990; Simmons 1996; Stahl and Pavel 1992), and other academic realms (Pace 1984; Tinto 1997). Often these factors have proven significantly influential singly as well as in combination with other measures in models of persistence behavior.

In the college persistence literature student behaviors, especially those related closely to academic interests of students, are strong predictors of academic success and retention (Camp 1990; Lisella and Serwatka 1996; Marsh 1992; Terenzini et al. 1995; Tinto 1997). However, much of this research employs more passive measures of academic integration such as students' perceptions of academic development or the degree to which they believe they are achieving academic goals. These more abstract measures could account for the relative weakness of academic integration in many college student persistence models (Braxton, Sullivan, and Johnson 1997).

Sample research questions from this part of the theory include:

Do student-initiated academic activities (getting to know faculty members, attending lectures or concerts, visiting art museums) relate positively to persistence?

Are student study behaviors positively related to persistence?

Are students who have stronger beliefs about themselves as college students more likely to engage in self-initiated academic activities and study behaviors?

Are student-initiated activities better predictors of persistence than student perceptions of academic growth and intellectual development?

Social Involvement

Again, our use of the term *involvement* emphasizes the importance of behavior rather than perception and of student-initiated rather than institution- or class-initiated activity. Recent longitudinal studies of college student persistence included social integration as an important factor in influencing students' satisfaction with institutions as well as persistence. In general, students who felt they were socially well integrated persisted (Pascarella 1978; Pascarella and Terenzini 1983). In contrast with academic integration measures many measures of social integration are behavioral, and that behavioral emphasis may be the reason social integration has proven to be a strong element of persistence studies (Braxton, Sullivan, and Johnson 1997). For example, living on campus, most often a student choice, was positively correlated with persistence (Astin 1975; Stage 1989). Additionally, development of informal relationships with faculty, often student initiated (Pascarella 1978; Pascarella and Terenzini 1977), and participation in social activities are frequently found to be positively related to persistence (Rendón 1994; Tinto 1997).

Sample research questions from this part of the theory include:

Do student-initiated social activities (informal contact with faculty members, joining clubs, going on weekend field trips) relate positively to persistence?

Are students' socializing behaviors positively related to persistence?

Are students who have stronger beliefs about themselves as college students more likely to engage in self-initiated social activities and behaviors?

Are student-initiated activities better predictors of persistence than student perceptions of friendship development and integration?

Discussion

In an examination of initial differences among students by major field groups, Feldman and Weiler (1976) spoke of the "accentuation effect" of college. They found that initial differences by major across student groups were accentuated across the four college years. Similarly, in an analysis of College Student Experiences Questionnaire (CSEQ) data from two hundred institutions, Pace (1997) found that measures of academic and intellectual growth and satisfaction with college were more strongly related to type of major than to college type. Referring to Holland personality type, Pace suggests that students bring important differences with them to college and that those differences influence students' college experiences and should not be ignored. Essentially, modeling college persistence from earliest influences—family factors and intentions to attend college through graduation—focuses on a similar, though more general, effect. Do students whose backgrounds, attitudes, and behaviors suggest an early predisposition to college attendance also have a greater probability of graduating? In other words, do the differences in background and experiences that exert influence on the college enrollment decisions of students also affect the college experience? Do they have an accentuation effect on the probability of persistence of college students?

Much of the work here is based on Bandura's (1994, 1997) work on individuals' beliefs in their own efficacy in certain life roles. We suggest that students' experiences in high school in preparation for college can help them with their efficacy (1) by creating successes in collegelike courses; (2)

by allowing them to view siblings and friends like themselves who have succeeded in college; (3) through persuasion of counselors, teachers, friends, and family that they will be successful in college; and (4) by developing positive rather than fearful feelings about the college experience (Stage et al. 1998). Through these positive experiences and activities students gain confidence, set higher goals, and work to achieve those goals. Of course, negative experiences in any of these realms will have the opposite effect.

In this review we focused on (1) precollege characteristics, attitudes, experiences, and behaviors; (2) college experiences and behaviors; and (3) their interactions that result in college success. Characteristics that were already in place, such as family status, money, and ancestral postsecondary experience, continue to influence students throughout college. Linking these two lines of inquiry has the potential for helping scholars focus more productively on the unfolding of the status attainment process. Although many studies have used status attainment models to study educational aspirations, few studies have systematically examined the variables and experiences associated with enacting the educational plans of students. To test this behavioral model, longitudinal data sets that permit the linking of college choice processes with student persistence and that measure students' activities in college at the level sought here are needed.

The evidence presented here suggests that, rather than being the great equalizer, in many instances the entire process of developing college aspirations, getting ready to go to college, and the college experience accentuates differences among students. Based on the theory offered in this chapter, students of lower socioeconomic status, those whose parents have not attended college, and those who are minority are not likely to consider college as an option early in their educational process and are also less likely to persist if they enroll. While these statements might seem obvious, they require empirical testing. We suggest the need for a fundamental change in the way many researchers construct their studies. A sample for a college student persistence analysis that includes *all* students electing to go a given college would only reinforce the existing research already described here. In addition, research questions should focus on specific populations of interest. To answer the question "What leads to college graduation for first-generation college attenders?" one must select only first-generation attenders for study. To identify factors that help more minorities be successful in college, we would select minority students and ask, "What helps this particular type of student to attend *and* succeed in college?" Fortunately, large longitudinal databases now give us that luxury. Such analysis would allow us to base our interventions and programs on knowledge gained from the experiences of the students whom we seek to aid in their educational attainment.

Answers to these questions might provide suggestions to administrators who hope to attract and educate traditionally disenfranchised students. Research that treats the decision to go to college and the decision to persist as a continuous process may lead to precollege interventions beyond academic preparation that may enhance student-institution fit and student persistence. In this chapter we focus on the individual experiences of students, specifically related to their own activities both before and during college. We hope that as we learn more about students' individual experiences and activities, we can move from broad prescriptive notions of what it means to be a successful college student and learn more about the college student of today. By changing perspectives and focusing on behavioral measures that are more directly observable, perhaps we can provide answers for some of the critical issues of access and achievement that we currently face on college campuses.

References

Alexander, K. L., and B. K. Eckland. 1977. High school context and college selectivity: Institutional constraints in educational stratification. *Social Forces* 56 (1): 166–188.

Anderson, K. L. 1987. Persistence, student background, and integration/commitment: Variation by definition of persistence and institutional type. Paper presented at the annual meeting of the Association for the Study of Higher Education, Baltimore, November.

Astin, A. 1975. *Preventing students from dropping out*. San Francisco: Jossey-Bass.

Astin, A. W. 1985. *Achieving educational excellence*. San Francisco: Jossey-Bass.

Attinasi, L., Jr. 1989. Getting in: Mexican Americans' perceptions of university attendance and the implications for freshman year persistence. *Journal of Higher Education* 60 (May/June): 247–277.

Ballesteros, E. 1986. Do Hispanics receive an equal educational opportunity? The relationship of school outcomes, family background, and high school curriculum. In M. Olivas (ed.), *Latino college students*, pp. 296–324. New York: Teachers College Press.

Bandura, A. 1978. Self-efficacy: Toward a unifying theory of behavior change. *Psychological Review* 84: 191–215.

Bandura, A. 1986. *Social foundations of thought and action: A social cognitive theory*. Englewood Cliffs, N.J.: Prentice-Hall.

Bandura, A. 1994. Self-efficacy. In V. S. Ramachaudran (ed.), *Encyclopedia of human behavior*, vol. 4, pp. 71–81. New York: Academic Press.

Bandura, A. 1997. *Self-efficacy: The exercise of control.* New York: Freeman & Co.

Bean, J. 1980. Dropouts and turnover: The synthesis of a causal model of student attrition. *Research in Higher Education* 12: 155–187.

Bean, J., and B. Metzner. 1985. A conceptual model of nontraditional undergraduate student attrition. *Review of Educational Research* 55: 485–539.

Bean, J. P., and N. Vespe. 1992. Student dependency theory: An explanation of
student retention in college. Paper presented at the annual meeting of the Association for the Study of Higher Education, Minneapolis, October.

Bourdieu, P., and J. Passeron. 1977. *Reproduction in education, society, and culture.* Beverly Hills, Calif.: Sage.

Braxton, J., N. Vesper, and D. Hossler. 1995. Expectations for college and student persistence. *Research in Higher Education* 13: 595–612.

Braxton, J. M., A. V. S. Sullivan, and R. M. Johnson. 1997. Appraising Tinto's theory of college student departure. In J. C. Smart (ed.), *Higher education: A handbook of theory and research,* vol. 12, pp. 107–164. New York: Agathon Press.

Cabrera, A. F., J. O. Stampen, and W. L. Hansen. 1990. Exploring the effects of ability to pay on persistence in college. *Review of Higher Education* 13 (3): 303–336.

Camp, W. G. 1990. Participation in student activities and achievement: A covariance structural analysis. *Journal of Educational Research* 83 (5): 272–278.

Carpenter, P., and J. Fleishman. 1987. Linking intentions and behavior: Australian students' college plans and college attendance. *American Educational Research Journal* 24 (spring): 79– 105.

Chacon, M. A., E. G. Cohen, and S. Strover. 1986. Chicanas and Chicanos: Barriers to progress in higher education. In M. Olivas (ed.), *Latino college students,* pp. 296–324. New York: Teachers College Press.

Chapman, D. 1981. A model of student college choice. *Journal of Higher Education* 52: 490–505.

Chapman, D. W., and E. Pascarella. 1983. Predictors of academic and social integration of college students. *Research in Higher Education* 19 (3): 295–322.

Churchill, W., and S. Iwai. 1981. College attrition, student use of campus facilities, and a consideration of self-reported personal problems. *Research in Higher Education* 14: 353–365.

De Los Santos, A., Jr., J. Montemayor, and E. Solis. 1980. *Chicano students in institutions of higher education: Access, attrition, and achievement.* Research Report Series, vol. 1, no. 1. ERIC 205–360. Austin: Office for Advanced Research in Hispanic Education, College of Education, University of Texas.

DiMaggio, P. 1982. Cultural capital and school success: The impact of status culture participation on the grades of U.S. high school students. *American Sociological Review* 47: 189–210.

Downey, D. B. 1992. Family structure, the transfer of parental resources, and educational performance. Ph.D. diss.

Downey, D. B., and B. Powell 1993. Do children in single-parent households fare better living with same-sex parents? *Journal of Marriage and the Family* 55: 55–71.

Ekstrom, R. 1985. *A descriptive study of public high school guidance report to the commissions for the study of precollegiate guidance and counseling.* Princeton, N.J.: Educational Testing Service.

Falsey, B., and B. Heyns. 1984. The college channel: Private and public schools reconsidered. *Sociology of Education* 57: 111–122.

Feldman, K., and T. Newcomb. 1969. *The impact of college on students.* San Francisco: Jossey-Bass.

Feldman K., and J. Weiler. 1976. Changes in initial differences among major-field groups: An exploration of the accentuation effect. In W. Sewall, R. Hauser, and D. Featherman (eds.), *Schooling and achievement in American society,* pp. 373–407. New York: Academic Press, Inc.

Fishbein, M., and I. Ajzen. 1975. *Belief, attitude, intention, and behavior: An introduction to theory and research.* Reading, Mass.: Addison-Wesley.

Forsyth, D., and J. McMillan. 1991. Practical proposals for motivating students. In R. Menges and M. Svinicki (eds.), *College teaching: From theory to practice.* New Directions for Teaching and Learning, no. 45. San Francisco: Jossey-Bass.

Freeman, K. 1997. Increasing African Americans' participation in higher education: African American high-school students' perspectives. *Journal of Higher Education* 68 (September/October): 523–550.

Gaier, E. L., and W. A. Watts. 1969. Current attitudes and socialization patterns of white and Negro students entering college. *Journal of Negro Education* 38 (4): 342–350.

Hackett, G., N. Betz, Casas, and Rocha-Singh. 1992. Gender, ethnicity, and social cognitive factors predicting the academic achievement of students in engineering. *Journal of Counseling Psychology* 39 (4): 527–538.

Hamrick, F., and D. Hossler. 1996. Active and passive searching in postsecondary educational decision making. *Review of Higher Education* 19 (2): 179–198.

Hamrick, F., and F. K. Stage. 1998. Student predisposition to college in high minority, high free lunch participation schools. *Review of Higher Education* 21 (4): 342–357.

Hause, J. 1969. Ability and schooling as determinants of lifetime earnings; or if you're so rich why aren't you smart? *American Economic Review* 23: 289–298.

Hearn, J. 1984. The relative roles of academic ascribed and socioeconomic characteristics in college destinations. *Sociology of Education* 57: 22–30.

Hood, D. W. 1992. Academic and noncognitive factors affecting the retention of black men at a predominantly white university. *Journal of Negro Education* 61 (1): 12–23.

Hossler, D. 1984. *Enrollment management: An integrated approach.* New York: College Board.

Hossler, D., and K. Gallagher. 1987. Studying student college choice: A three-phase model and the implications for policy makers. *College and University* 62 (3): 207–221.

Hossler, D., and S. Maple. 1993. An investigation of the factors which differentiate among high school students' plans to attend a postsecondary educational institution and those who are undecided. *Review of Higher Education* 16 (3): 285–307.

Hossler, D., and F. Stage. 1992. Family and high school experience factors' influences on the postsecondary plans of ninth grade students: A causal model of predisposition to college. *American Educational Research Journal* 29.

Hossler, D., J. Braxton, and G. Coopersmith. 1989. Understanding student college choice. In J. C. Smart (ed.), *Higher education: A handbook of theory and research,* vol. 5. New York: Agathon Press.

Hossler, D., J. Schmit, and N. Vesper. 1998. *Going to college: How social, economic, and educational factors influence the decisions students make.* Baltimore, Md.: Johns Hopkins University Press.

Hurtado, S., and D. F. Carter. 1997. Effects of college transition and perceptions of campus racial climate on Latino college students' sense of belonging. *Sociology of Education* 70: 324–345.

Jackson, G. A. 1982. Public Efficiency and Private Choice in Higher Education. *Educational Evaluation and Policy Analysis.* 4: 237–247.

Iwai, S., and W. Churchill. 1982. College attrition and the financial support systems of students. *Research in Higher Education* 17: 105–113.

Kobrak, P. 1992. Black student retention in predominantly white regional universities: The politics of faculty involvement. *Journal of Negro Education* 61: 509–530.

Kraemer, B. A. 1997. The academic and social integration of Hispanic students into college. *Review of Higher Education* 20 (2): 163–179.

Kuh, G. K., J. S. Schuh, E. J. Whitt, R. E. Andreas, J. W. Lyons, C. C. Strange, L. E. Krehbiel, and K. A. Mackay. 1991. *Involving colleges: Successful approaches to fostering student learning and personal development outside the classroom.* San Francisco: Jossey-Bass.

Leon, D. 1975. Chicano college dropouts and the educational opportunity program. *High School Behavioral Science* 3: 6–11.

Lisella, L. C., and T. S. Serwatka. 1996. Extracurricular participation and academic achievement in minority students in urban schools. *Urban Review* 28 (1): 63–80.

Litten, L. 1982. Different strokes in the applicant pool: Some refinements in a model of student choice. *Journal of Higher Education* 53: 383–402.

Lucas, A. F. 1990. Using psychological models to understand student motivation. In M. Svinicki (ed.), *New directions for teaching and learning,* no. 42. San Francisco: Jossey-Bass.

Manski, C., and D. Wise. 1983. *College choice in America.* Cambridge, Mass.: Howard University Press.

Marsh, H. W. 1992. Extracurricular activities: Beneficial extension of the traditional curriculum or subversion of academic goals? *Journal of Educational Psychology* 84 (4): 553–562.

McDonough, P. M. 1997. *Choosing colleges: How social class and schools structure opportunity.* Albany: State University of New York Press.

McNeal, R. B., Jr. 1995. Extracurricular activities and high school dropouts. *Sociology of Education* 68: 62–81.

Nora, A. 1987. Determinants of retention among Chicano college students: A structural model. *Research in Higher Education* 26 (1): 31–59.

Nora, A., and A. Cabrera. 1996. The role of perceptions of prejudice and discrimination on the adjustment of minority students to college. *Journal of Higher Education* 67 (March/April): 119–148.

Nora, A., L. Attinasi, and A. Matonak. 1990. Quantification and testing of qualitative measures of precollege factors in Tinto's model of student attrition among a community college student population. *Review of Higher Education* 13 (3): 337–355.

Okun, M. A., M. Benin, and A. Brandt-Williams. 1996. Staying in college: Moderators of the relation between intention and institutional departure. *Journal of Higher Education* 67 (September/October): 577–596.

Olivas, M. A. 1986. Introduction—A theoretical framework and inquiry. In M. Olivas (ed.), *Latino college students.* New York: Teachers College Press.

Ortiz, V. 1986. Generational status, family background, and educational attainment among Hispanic youth and non-Hispanic white youth. In M. Olivas (ed.), *Latino college students,* pp. 29–46. New York: Teachers College Press.

Pace, C. R. 1979. *Measuring outcomes of college: Fifty years of findings and recommendations for the future.* San Francisco: Jossey-Bass.

Pace, C. R. 1990. *The undergraduates: A report of their activities and progress in college in the 1980s.* Los Angeles: University of California, Center for the Study of Higher Education.

Pace, C. R. 1997. Connecting institutional types to student outcomes. Paper presented at the annual meeting of the Association for the Study of Higher Education, Albuquerque, November.

Pascarella, E. 1978. Student-faculty informal contact and college outcomes. *Review of Educational Research* 48: 49–101.

Pascarella, E., and P. Terenzini. 1977. Patterns of student-faculty informal interaction beyond the classroom and voluntary freshman attrition. *Journal of Higher Education* 48: 540–552.

Pascarella, E., and P. Terenzini. 1983. Predicting voluntary freshman year persistence/withdrawal behavior in a residential university: A path analytic validation of Tinto's model. *Journal of Educational Psychology* 75 (April): 215–226.

Pascarella, E., and P. Terenzini. 1991. *How college affects students: Findings and insights from twenty years of research.* San Francisco: Jossey-Bass.

Pascarella, E., J. Smart, and C. Ethington. 1986. Long term persistence of two-year college students. *Research in Higher Education* 24: 47–71.

Paulsen, M. B. 1990. *College choice: Understanding student enrollment behavior.* ASHE-ERIC Monograph Series, no. 6. Washington, D.C.: George Washington University.

Pavel, M. 1991. Assessing Tinto's model of institutional departure using American Indian and Alaskan Native longitudinal data. Paper presented at the annual meeting of the Association for the Study of Higher Education, Boston, October.

Rendón, L. 1994. Validating culturally diverse students: Toward a new model of learning and student development. *Innovative Higher Education* 19 (1): 33–51.

Robinson, T. 1990. Understanding the gap between entry and exit: A cohort analysis of African American students' persistence. *Journal of Negro Education* 59: 207–218.

Sailes, G. 1990. An investigation of black student attrition at Indiana University. ERIC Document ED338747.

St. John, E. P., and D. Hossler. 1998. Higher education desegregation in the post-*Fordice* legal environment: A critical-empirical perspective. In R. Fossey (ed.), *Race, the courts, and equal education: The limits of the law.* Readings on Equal Education, vol. 15, pp. 101–122. New York: AMS Press.

St. John, E. P., M. B. Paulsen, and J. B. Starkey. 1996. The nexus between college choice and persistence. *Research in Higher Education* 37 (2): 175–220.

Sewell, W., and R. Hauser. 1975. *Education, occupation and earnings: Achievement in early career.* New York: Academic Press.

Sewell, W. H., and V. P. Shah. 1978. Social class, parental encouragement, and educational aspirations. *American Journal of Sociology* 3: 559–572.

Sexton, T. L., and B. W. Tuckman. 1991. Self-beliefs and behavior: The role of self-efficacy and outcome expectation over time. *Personality and Individual Difference* 12 (7): 725–736.

Simmons, A. B. 1996. Beliefs and academic performance of low-achieving college students. Ph.D. diss., Indiana University, Bloomington.

Smart, J. C. 1986. College effects on occupational status attainment. *Research in Higher Education* 24 (1): 73–95.

Smart, J. C., and E. T. Pascarella. 1986. Socioeconomic achievements of former college students. *Journal of Higher Education* 57 (5): 527–549.

Solomon, L.C., and P. J. Taubman. 1973. *Does college matter?* New York: Academic Press.

Spady, W. G. 1971. Dropouts from higher education: Toward an empirical model. *Interchange* 2: 38–62.

Stage, F. K. 1989. Motivation, academic and social integration, and the early dropout. *American Educational Research Journal* 26 (fall): 385–402.

Stage, F. K., and D. Hossler. 1989. Differences in family influences on college attendance plans for male and female ninth graders. *Research in Higher Education* 30 (3): 301–315.

Stage, F. K., and N. Milne. 1996. The experience of college students with learning disabilities. *Journal of Higher Education* 67 (4): 426–445.

Stage, F. K., and P. W. Rushin. 1993. A combined model of student predisposition to college and persistence in college. *Journal of College Student Development* 34: 276–281.

Stage, F., P. Muller, J. Kinzie, and A. Simmons. 1998. *Creating a learning centered classroom: What does learning theory have to say?* Washington, D.C.: ASHE/ERIC.

Stahl, V. V., and M. D. Pavel. 1992. *Assessing the Bean and Metzner model with community college student data.* ERIC Document ED344639.

Teachman, J. D. 1987. Family background, educational resources, and educational attainment. *American Sociological Review* 52: 548–577.

Terenzini, P., and E. Pascarella. 1980. Toward the validation of Tinto's model of college student attrition: A review of recent studies. *Research in Higher Education* 12: 271–282.

Terenzini, P., E. Pascarella, C. Theophilides, and W. Lorang. 1985. A replication of a path analytic validation of Tinto's theory of college student attrition. *Review of Higher Education* 8 (summer): 319–340.

Terenzini, P. T., L. Springer, E. T. Pascarella, and A. Nora. 1995. Academic and out-of-class influences on students' intellectual orientations. *Review of Higher Education* 19 (1): 23–44.

Tierney, W. G. 1992. An anthropological analysis of student participation in college. *Journal of Higher Education* 63 (6): 603–618.

Tinto, V. 1975. Dropout from higher education: A theoretical synthesis of recent research. *Review of Educational Research* 45: 89–125.

Tinto, V. 1987. *Leaving college: Rethinking the causes and cures of student attrition.* Chicago: University of Chicago Press.

Tinto, V. 1988. Stages of student departure: Reflections on the longitudinal character of student leaving. *Journal of Higher Education* 59 (July/August): 438–455.

Tinto, V. 1997.Classrooms as communities: Exploring the educational character of student persistence. *Journal of Higher Education* 68 (6): 599–623.

Trent, J., and L. Medsker. 1967. *Beyond high school: A psychological study of 10,000 high school graduates.* San Francisco: Jossey-Bass.

Valadez, J. R. 1996. Educational access and social mobility in a rural community college. *Review of Higher Education* 19 (4): 391–409.

Washington, V., and J. Newman. 1991. Setting our own agenda: Exploring the meaning of gender disparities among blacks in higher education. *Journal of Negro Education* 60: 19–35.

Williams, J. 1996. Project C.A.R.E.: A university commitment to African-American student retention. *College Student Journal* 13 (1): 44–57.

Williamson, D. R., and D. G. Creamer. 1988. Student attrition in 2- and 4-year colleges: Application of a theoretical model. *Journal of College Student Development* 29 (3): 210–217.

Young, M. E., and P. Reyes. 1987. Conceptualizing enrollment behavior. *Journal of Student Financial Aid* 17 (3): 41–49.

Zimmerman, B. J., and A. Bandura. 1994. Impact of self-regulatory influences on writing course attainment. *American Educational Research Journal* 31 (4): 845–862.

A Cultural Perspective on Student Departure

George D. Kuh and Patrick G. Love

V incent Tinto's (1993) theory is the paradigm of choice when examining student departure. Yet empirical support for the theory is relatively soft (Braxton, Sullivan, and Johnson 1997). This suggests that alternative approaches to looking at student departure are warranted, especially as this topic continues to be a high priority for institutions and policy makers. In this chapter we examine student departure using a cultural lens. First, we review the limitations of the popular approaches to understanding student departure and argue for using culture as an analytical framework. We then set forth propositions based on cultural constructs and processes that yield insights into the transactions between students and their institutions related to persistence and student departure. Special attention is given students from historically underrepresented groups and others who are among those at greatest risk of premature departure. We conclude with recommendations for researchers, institutional leaders, and policy makers for using a cultural lens when examining student departure phenomena.

The Warrant for Additional Perspectives on Student Departure

Going to college typically requires negotiating unfamiliar environments and becoming acquainted with strangers. The extent to which students do this well and adapt to institutions' academic and social demands is thought to be related to satisfaction, achievement, and educational attainment (Pascarella and Terenzini 1991). In Tinto's (1993) theory of student departure two constructs, academic and social integration, represent the process of student acclimation to institutions. Academic integration represents the extent to which students are doing reasonably well in their classes (academic achievement), perceive their classes to be relevant and have practical value (e.g., prepare them for jobs), and are satisfied with their majors. Social integration refers to students' levels of social and psychological comfort with their colleges' milieus, association with or acceptance by affinity groups, and sense of belonging that provides the security needed to join with others in common causes, whether intellectual or social. These two clusters of behaviors influence students' overall performances and affective responses to the college experience.

Thus it was surprising that Braxton, Sullivan, and Johnson (1997) did not find much empirical support for the theoretical propositions related to academic and social integration. In fact, in reviewing single-institution studies, they found support for only one of the six propositions involving either academic or social integration: social integration was positively related to a student's subsequent commitment to graduating from the institution. They did not find support for any of the six propositions in multiple institutional studies. In part, the lack of empirical support for the Tinto model may be a function of the manner in which researchers have operationalized academic and social integration (Hurtado and Carter 1997). Perhaps survey items developed to measure these constructs do not capture the complexities and subtleties of the interactions between students and institutions that affect persistence.

Tierney (1992) points to other shortcomings of the Tinto theory, observing that it inappropriately adapted anthropological constructs. For Tinto, integration into the dominant institutional culture was an a priori assumption of success. That is, in order to survive or persist to graduation newcomers must successfully negotiate certain "rites of passage" to become full members of institutions and learn how to behave consistent with the institutions' established ways of doing things. The operating assumption is that students would and should adapt to their institutions' dominant systems of values and mores. Tierney argues that this interpretation is inconsistent with the anthropological notion that rites of passage are experiences specific to social groups that mark the end of one stage and the beginning of another. These experiences are exclusively intracultural transitions, not cross-cultural transitions as Tinto's theory suggests. The Tinto expectation of integration is particularly problematic when trying to understand and explain the experiences of students from historically underrepresented groups. Moreover, Tierney concludes that this interpretation and the

assumption on which it is based have had the unintended negative consequence of placing a disproportionate amount of responsibility on students
to adapt, attributing little or no responsibility to the institutions to modify
their policies and practices to respond to the changing needs and characteristics of students.

In sum, the leading model of student departure lacks robust empirical
support, may be inadequately operationalized (i.e., academic and social integration), and is based on assumptions that understate institutional responsibility for creating hospitable learning conditions. Alternative approaches to
studying student departure may help to move beyond the status quo.

A Cultural Perspective

Over time all groups and organizations, including colleges and universities,
develop cultures, more or less coherent, widely accepted ways of doing
things which shape how people think and behave. In higher education culture can be thought of as "the collective, mutually shaping patterns of
norms, values, practices, beliefs, and assumptions that guide the behavior
of individuals and groups . . . and provide a frame of reference within which
to interpret the meaning of events and actions on and off campus" (Kuh and
Whitt 1988, pp. 12–13). An institution's culture represents both product
and process. That is, it is manifested in accumulated understandings acquired and expressed through daily interactions and routines, common
symbols, and special ceremonies and traditions. At the same time, culture is
constantly evolving, albeit imperceptibly, shaped by interactions between
old and new members and contact with other people from other organizations and cultures. Thus, from a cultural perspective when an individual
joins a group, interactions between people influence the larger institutional
environment and its subenvironments. In other words, interactions between people influence and subsequently change both the students and the
larger institutional environments and subenvironments. This position is
consistent with the campus ecology view (Banning 1980), which views the
student experience as a series of transactions between people and their environments, broadly defined to include all forms of physical, biological, and
human exchanges between and among students, faculty, staff, and so on.

One of culture's most important functions is to insure a group's survival
and to protect its relative position with other groups and the larger culture
in which it is ensconced (Bourdieu and Passeron 1977). Culture can also be
thought of as a form of social control in that it induces "a state of conscious

and permanent awareness of expectations and social repercussions" (Rhoads 1994, p. 28) of doing and talking about matters in accepted ways. As a result, an institution of higher education, or a subgroup within the institution, that possesses a strong, dominant culture exerts a conforming press on its members to adopt the group's norms and attitudes. Thus, cultural influences are rooted in acquired frames of reference, normative behaviors, and values.

One advantage of using a cultural perspective to examine student departure is that it accounts for student behavior resulting from the interactions of cultural properties, specifically the effects of these interactions on process variables—involvement, effort, and perceived belonging (Attinasi 1989; Hurtado and Carter 1997). Moreover, using a cultural lens means defining the issue of student departure primarily as a sociocultural phenomenon, rather than an individual, psychological experience (Tierney 1992). That is, while decisions to voluntarily leave institutions are made by individuals, such decisions are also shaped by cultural forces. Some of these forces are inextricably linked to previous experiences with families, neighborhoods, ethnic and racial groups, social classes, churches, and schools and in anticipation of groups and organizations that individuals hope to join, such as institutions, major fields, social clubs or organizations, and social-oriented affinity groups. For this reason the concept of a single dominant institutional culture that defines "the standards of judgment for all members of the institution" (Tinto 1993, p. 60) has only limited utility because it cannot account for the experiences of members of different groups, especially those that may interact frequently with multiple subcultures. Martin (1992) provides three perspectives that can be used to discover and better understand the complexities of the multiple influences of culture: integration, differentiation, and fragmentation.

The integration perspective emphasizes consensus, that is, those activities and interpretations about which almost everyone agrees or sees the same way. Ambiguous and conflicting aspects of group life are usually overlooked, inadvertently overstating the degree to which values and interpretations are shared. The differentiation perspective shows that within any group of adequate size and with some history, subgroups develop with values, attitudes, and norms that differ to varying degrees from those of the larger dominant group and other subgroups. The group's particular combination of values, interests, and activities sets them apart from other groups, as illustrated by athletes and fraternities on many campuses. However, to identify these subgroups, investigators must look for them (i.e., adopt a differentiation perspective). The fragmentation perspective is sensitive to pockets of dissensus that often characterize aspects of group existence, even within affinity groups. That is, affinity groups or subcultures comprised of peers (e.g., fraternities) can be marked by relatively "strong" conforming cultures but have some members whose views and interpretations of group life differ from those of other members in terms of their meaning and significance. In other words, even within "islands of clarity" (i.e., members of peer groups who see things pretty much the same way) (Martin 1992) people differ from one another in the ways in which they interpret aspects of group life.

Tinto's theory tacitly endorses an integration view of culture in that students are expected to adapt to the institution's dominant cultural code or norms in order to succeed, be satisfied, and persist. In Tinto's (1993) words, "the closer one is to the mainstream of the academic and social life of the college, the more likely is one to perceive oneself as being congruent with the institution generally. . . . Conversely . . . the more marginal one's group is to the life of the college, the more likely is one to perceive oneself as being separate from the institution" (p. 60). Tierney's (1992) argument is consistent with Martin's differentiation perspective—that is, although institutions may have what appears to be a dominant culture, emphasizing the need to adapt and adopt the dominant culture's values does little to prompt administrators and faculty to change institutional policies and practices in order to help newcomers succeed, especially members of marginalized groups such as racial and ethnic minorities, many of whom bring a different culture to the institution. Braxton, Sullivan, and Johnson (1997) point out that while Tierney's critique of Tinto's model from a cultural perspective had merit, he failed to move beyond critique and provide information on what a cultural-based view of the student departure process would look like. In the next section we present a set of cultural propositions about student departure consistent with Martin's differentiation perspective.

Cultural Propositions Related to Premature Student Departure

The eight propositions that follow are consistent with the research on college student persistence as interpreted through a cultural lens. The propositions (table 1) do not constitute a theory nor are they the products of an exhaustive, comprehensive account of all cultural influences on persistence. Rather, their purpose is heuristic. Proposition 1 emphasizes the role of the individual in understanding and engaging with an institution's culture. That is, while culture is a product of a group's or organization's history and daily life, individuals carry and interpret culture. Propositions 2 and 3 acknowledge that students have different cultural backgrounds (cultures of origin) and that colleges and universities are made up of multiple, overlapping cultures. Propositions 4, 5, and 6 articulate the concept of cultural distance, which accounts for many of the challenges students face when they go to college. Finally, propositions 7 and 8 address the process of cultural connections that are necessary to succeed in college.

Table 1
Cultural Propositions about Premature Student Departure

1. The college experience, including a decision to leave college, is mediated through a student's cultural meaning-making system.

2. One's cultures of origin mediate the importance attached to attending college and earning a college degree.

3. Knowledge of a student's cultures of origin and the cultures of immersion is needed to understand a student's ability to successfully negotiate the institution's cultural milieu.

4. The probability of persistence is inversely related to the cultural distance between a student's culture(s) of origin and the cultures of immersion.

5. Students who traverse a long cultural distance must become acclimated to dominant cultures of immersion or join one or more enclaves.

6. The amount of time a student spends in one's cultures of origin after matriculating is positively related to cultural stress and reduces the chances they will persist.

7. The likelihood a student will persist is related to the extensity and intensity of one's sociocultural connections to the academic program and to affinity groups.

8. Students who belong to one or more enclaves in the cultures of immersion are more likely to persist, especially if group members value achievement and persistence.

Proposition 1. The college experience, including a decision to leave college, is mediated through a student's cultural meaning-making system.

An institution's structural or organizational properties per se do not induce premature student departure. Rather, it is what students make of them that determines their affective and behavioral responses. The meaning-making system is informed by one's cultures of origin—family (immediate and ancestral), school, community, and so forth. The meaning-making system is comprised of values, assumptions, and beliefs about what to expect from college, the role of being a college student, and the value of a college degree.

Students with ill-defined meaning-making systems about college and college-going will likely have vague or inaccurate notions of college and what will occur. Such students may appear to be committed to the institution, but this "commitment" is based on inaccurate information, which may account for the lack of an empirical relationship between initial institutional commitment on the part of low-income, African American (Donovan 1984), and Native American/Alaskan Native students (Pavel 1991).

Proposition 2. One's cultures of origin mediate the importance attached to attending college and earning a college degree.

As with new employees (Van Maanen 1984), new students try to understand their new environments using an interpretive scheme or sense-making system developed through experiences in their cultures of origin. For example, do the families and/or others in the cultures of origin (school-teachers, relatives, neighbors) value attending and graduating from college? Is college supported, or congruent with, the families' values and aspirations? Is college important primarily to get good jobs? Or does it hold some other meaning, such as cultivating aesthetic sensibilities or developing new worldviews? Is college appropriate for both men and women? What are the students' pictures of the institutions? Answers to these questions reveal cultural forces that can affect students' aspirations, motivation, and willingness to persevere in the face of obstacles.

When the values of one's cultures of origin support the goals of college education, they encourage persistence (Bean and Vesper 1992; Roth 1985). Students may come from cultures whose values and behavioral expectations are counter to those perceived as dominant in the culture of American higher education and yet those students persist at higher than expected rates. This may be due, in part, to the strong value held for pursuing higher education in the cultures of origin and may account for the relatively higher rates of persistence among recent Asian immigrants. In cases where students' parents did not go to college (a negative predictor of success in college), parents and other family members may enthusiastically encourage college attendance, which is a source of motivation to graduate. Supportive families have been found to be better predictors of African American students' educational aspirations than parental education or occupation (Clark 1983; Ginsburg and Hanson 1986; Martin 1986). Maintaining family relationships and support was vital to the successful transition and adjustment to college of academically talented Latino students (Hurtado, Carter, and Spuler 1996). Nora, Castañeda, and

Cabrera (1992) found that family support increased the chances that students would engage socially and academically with faculty and peers.

Proposition 3. Knowledge of a student's cultures of origin and the cultures of immersion is needed to understand a student's ability to successfully negotiate the institution's cultural milieu.

Prior experiences play a major defining role in determining whether and where a student goes to college and whether he/she will persist to graduation. Cultures of origin are primary sources of cultural capital (Bourdieu and Passeron 1977) related to higher education—intellectual resources (values, assumptions, and expectations), interpersonal resources (e.g., access to valued individuals who espouse the importance of higher education, use of language, styles of interaction), and physical resources (e.g., libraries, books, educational opportunities). Higher levels of cultural capital are favorable to the development of accurate meaning-making systems related to college and college-going and explain in part why socioeconomic background and first-generation status have different effects on persistence. That is, students from lower SES backgrounds have less knowledge about what to expect, how things are done at college, and so forth. On the other hand, individuals with considerable tacit knowledge about the college experience often learn what college will be like from their parents, siblings, family friends, and peers (Persell, Catsambis, and Cookson 1992).

What type of college should one attend? How does one prepare for college? How does one survive and thrive? Where can one get help with financial problems? How does one manage interpersonal conflicts with roommates or others, especially if these people are different from oneself? These are "getting-ready" competencies, behaviors that engender a college-going frame of mind, model college-going behavior, or simulate the experience of going to college (Attinasi 1989). For some students, college attendance and graduation may be only moderately important, yet their cultures of origin have developed relatively accurate meaning-making systems about college and college-going. From parents, siblings, and neighbors who attended college, by attending high school programs about college, and by absorbing information from their teachers and guidance counselors, they know what it takes to negotiate the culture space of college and what it takes to succeed. Whether or not institutional commitment is an accurate predictor of persistence depends on the amount of students' tacit knowledge about the college experience.

Proposition 4. The probability of persistence is inversely related to the cultural distance between a student's culture(s) of origin and the cultures of immersion.

Most students attend college within two hundred miles of where they went to high school or their families live. But geographical distance is not the same as cultural distance. For some students the cultural distance is negligible because college-going was stitched into the fabric of their cultures of origin. That is, their cultures of origin effectively prepared them to expect and deal with the institutions' values, attitudes, beliefs, assumptions, and expectations. Other students must travel a great distance, an experience that can be arduous, threatening, and intimidating. This is more likely for students who perceive that elements of the cultures of immersion (the institutions and their subcultures) conflict with aspects of their cultures of origin in the context of their meaning-making systems. For many Native American students, the values of traditional American higher education (e.g., individualism, competition, autonomy, challenging authority) are counter to the values of their tribes' cultures (Tierney 1992). By speaking out in class and working independently to attain high grades, students must do things that prior to this point in their lives they learned were wrong. Students from other group-oriented cultures such as Asian and Hispanic/Latino may also find these expectations alien to their cultures of origin. Tinto (1993) addresses this issue with the example of a white child of a college-educated family who looks forward to and is rewarded for making the transition to college whereas a Native American child from a poor family senses that she is rebelling against the wishes of her family and local community by going to college.

Proposition 5. Students who traverse a long cultural distance must become acclimated to dominant cultures of immersion or join one or more enclaves.

Through a process of socialization newcomers come to adopt values, attitudes, beliefs, and assumptions of the groups or institutions they are joining. This view is consistent with the traditional notion of social and academic integration in that students are expected to move toward the cultures of the institutions in order to succeed and survive. In cases where the dominant cultures of origin are distinct or countercultural to the institution's dominant cultures or academic and social mainstream (Tinto 1993), becoming socialized may require denying or renouncing some aspect of the cultures of origin. For example, London (1989) found that first-generation students needed to break away from certain family and neighborhood norms to make the transition to college.

A person's willingness and ability to leave one cultural setting may be necessary conditions for subsequent persistence in another cultural setting.

Another way to negotiate cultural distance is to join a group or subculture that has values, attitudes, beliefs, and assumptions that are congenial with one's culture(s) of origin. This can effectively reduce the cultural distance a student must travel and make navigating the institutional culture on a daily basis less intimidating. We call these groups cultural enclaves.

Thus, premature departure of some students can be explained as the result of students' inability to manage the distance between their cultures of origin and the institutions' dominant cultures. Students either reject the institutions' attempts to socialize them or they have not found cultural enclaves from which they can draw support and guidance as they try to negotiate "alien" cultures. Some students who leave institutions of higher education, especially during or at the end of the first year, never really "arrived" in the first place. They did not complete the journey across the cultural distance from the cultures of origin to those of the institutions.

Proposition 6. The amount of time a student spends in one's cultures of origin after matriculating is positively related to cultural stress and reduces the chances they will persist.

Many students who live at home or nearby while attending college do not travel the cultural distance between their cultures of origin and institutional cultures of immersion. Rather, many simply add an additional sphere to their existing cultural universe, which may require renegotiating competing values, expectations, and assumptions as well as juggling competing roles and time demands (Anderson 1981). For students from cultures with values and mores that are distinct from, or counter to, the dominant cultures of the institutions, the need to shift between distinct cultural meaning-making systems (i.e., the ones that they are socialized to at the institutions and the ones in which they interact outside the institutions) adds to their stress and contributes to decisions to depart. For older students, the cultural distance may be defined by distance of relevance of study to their lives outside the classroom. That is, the more relevant one's studies are to a job or other life circumstances (family, community involvements), the easier it is to manage the divide between cultures of origin and immersion.

Proposition 7. The likelihood a student will persist is related to the extensity and intensity of one's sociocultural connections to the academic program and to affinity groups.

Consistent with Tinto's view, students navigate cultural distance by connecting to an institution's culture in some fashion. However, connecting to the institution differs to an important degree from being integrated into the institution's culture, which is more akin to what Hurtado and Carter (1997) call a "sense of belonging." Although integration means combining parts into a whole, in both Tinto's theory and the American sociopolitical realm (Williams 1988) the word has come to mean one part being absorbed into the whole—that is, students are integrated into institutions or "minorities" are integrated into schools. From a cultural perspective, this is akin to being socialized to the institutions. As indicated above, this meaning and the use of the word *integration* imply little or no responsibility on the part of the institutions or their stakeholders to accommodate and adapt policies and practices to respond to newcomers.

In the latest iteration of Tinto's theory, the definition of integration is positively correlated with institutional membership. Cultural connection focuses on a subjective sense of membership or affiliation with others in the institution. There is a sense of belonging to one or multiple groups in that there are shared values, assumptions, perspectives, beliefs, and meaning-making systems related to negotiating the cultural spheres of the institution and its components. Cultural connection may translate to a sense of belonging to the institution as a whole but ultimately is mediated through students' interpersonal interactions with faculty, peers, and others.

All colleges and universities have complex social and academic systems. The social system is a pattern of interpersonal interactions and relationships among organizational members and the subgroups and organizations that define a college or university as an organizational entity and meet the membership needs of organizational participants (Tinto 1993). From a cultural perspective the academic system is best understood as a subset of the social system. That is, students connect with their academic programs through processes similar to those through which they connect with peers and the social life of the institution. Perhaps the lack of empirical support for Tinto's propositions related to academic integration is due to interpreting certain behaviors to be exclusive to social integration (e.g., interacting with peers in class and study groups, with faculty in and out of class, with academic advisers, with academic-related discussions with peers). Nora (1993) took a different approach by assigning student interactions with faculty and academic staff and participation in academic organizations to social integration. A similar interpretation was advanced by Hurtado and Carter (1997), who discovered that higher grade performance by Latino students did not enhance their sense of belonging.

Proposition 8. Students who belong to one or more enclaves in the cultures of immersion are more likely to persist, especially if group members value achievement and persistence.

As Tinto (1993) suggests, one way students manage cultural distance is to join enclaves or affinity groups that have values, attitudes, beliefs, and assumptions similar to those of the students' cultures of origin, or those the students find appealing. Enclave membership is critical for fitting in, for developing a sense of belonging to one or multiple groups and perceiving that there are people there with similar values, assumptions, perspectives, beliefs, and meaning-making systems. Students with close friends who are doing well academically and like college life are more likely to persist. This positive pull toward persistence is even greater when the group has formal status, such as a departmental club, or if the group has official responsibility for institution functioning, such as resident assistants or student government officers. Some groups such as fraternities and athletic teams are orthogonal or countercultural (Kuh and Whitt 1988) in that their values and activities do not complement the institution's espoused values and academic missions (Kuh and Arnold 1993). Nonetheless, the network of social relations these groups form among their members supports persistence. That is, these students would rather be in college than doing anything else at this point in their lives largely because of the friendships they enjoy.

In their study of Latino students, Hurtado and Carter (1997) discovered that high degrees of membership or sense of belonging in particular groups (i.e., religious organizations and Greek organizations) appeared to involve higher levels of individual commitment. This could also be evidence of membership in particular groups involving varying degrees of cultural connection. Kraemer (1997) discovered that issues of importance to the persistence of adult Hispanic students at a two-year institution were the presence of Hispanic faculty and staff, access to other Hispanic students, and the availability of Hispanic cultural activities. Attinasi (1989) found that Mexican American students became connected to their institution because they formed collective affiliations with students similar to themselves, which helped them to "scale down" the institution and to acquire the skills necessary to negotiate the social, physical, and cognitive landscape of the campus.

Hurtado and Carter (1997) found that activities typically associated with persistence for white students were not related to the perceived sense of belonging of Latino students. They discovered that those Latino students who reported working on an independent research project, working with a faculty member on a research project, or being a guest in a professor's home did *not* report a greater sense of belonging to the college. Perhaps Latino students experienced or viewed these activities as conflicting with their cultures of origin and exacerbated the fragmented nature of their experience, making it more difficult to negotiate the new cultures of immersion.

Implications of Adopting a Cultural Perspective

Cultural forces influence individual students and their affinity groups or cultural enclaves in myriad and sometimes conflicting ways. Thus, using a cultural perspective on persistence invariably introduces more complexity and ambiguity into attempts to understand the process and modify institutional policies and practices to enhance persistence rates. Further complicating matters is that it is impossible to draw distinct boundaries around cultural forces. Moreover, students (as well as faculty and administrators) belong to multiple cultural groups, multiple layers of culture exist, and the strength of these cultural groups and layers varies. With this complexity in mind, in this section we consider some implications of the cultural approach for institutional policy and practice and for research into student departure.

Policy and Practice

A few decades ago there was a tacit agreement that colleges and universities were repositories of knowledge, dispensers of certificates of vocational training (if not the skills themselves), and engines of social democracy, institutions where the people from lower socioeconomic backgrounds could mingle with others more advantaged and learn how to navigate "the system" so that they could improve their social and economic positions. However, the proportions of people who seek higher education have burgeoned without a guaranteed immediate return on investment (e.g., good jobs). Add the changing characteristics of undergraduates—increasing numbers of people from underrepresented racial and ethnic groups, more students oriented primarily to practical job skills than intellectual pursuits as compared with their predecessors (or so faculty believe), more students with learning styles different than the majority of the faculty (Schroeder 1993)—and the prospects are good for divergent meaning-making systems and multiple, divergent subcultures.

The undergraduate experience has traditionally been thought of as a developmentally powerful period of change and transformation. However, the question arises as to how much we should expect students to change their values, attitudes, perspectives, and beliefs. Some students need to make only relatively minor adjustments in order to fit into most institutions. For other students the magnitude of the adjustment is substantial and threatens to cut them off from their cultures of origin. These issues of cultural diversification and student change present a dilemma: to what degree can or should a college remake or diversify its culture without jeopardizing its core organizing premises and values; maintain a steady, clear focus on what is to be learned; maintain a curriculum with integrity; and encourage student development and personal transformation? Can institutions intentionally change the very aspects of their organizational lives that essentially define them and enable them to be successful in the first place? Therefore, the first implication for policy makers and institutional leaders is that these important policy questions need to be examined.

Virtually all colleges and universities espouse a commitment to diversifying their student bodies, faculty, and curricula. Yet an underlying assumption persists that those from cultural backgrounds different from that of the institution's dominant culture need to adapt to the institution. To enhance the quality of the undergraduate experience and increase persistence rates, most institutions must challenge this assumption and the institutional policies and practices that flow from it. This means that not all students should or will adapt to an institution's preferred way of conducting business.

An initial institutional challenge is to make the strange seem familiar as soon as possible through the initial exposure and cultural learning that come through contacts with admissions, orientation, registration, and initial advising procedures, as well as through the subsequent immersion that occurs through classes, faculty contact, peer groups, and residence halls. A student's first weeks on campus are key. Institutions can reduce the cultural distance for students by cultivating "communities of difference" (Tierney 1993), embracing the multiple cultures that already exist and encouraging the development of others. This means that institutions must become multicultural organizations. Such a view makes traditional definitions of community almost irrelevant, especially the romanticized notion that all members of a college should see things the same way and have the same values.

Institutions can assist students in crossing long cultural distances through the process of enclave extension. Using this process an institution, as represented by a cultural enclave, intentionally reaches across cultural distance to assist students in bridging that distance. An example is Kent State University's Kupita/Transiciones program, which is grounded in Hispanic culture and is designed to help Hispanic matriculants bridge the cultural distance between their cultures of origin and the predominantly white host institution.

Research

Given the conditional nature of the propositions offered in this chapter, their validity and utility for guiding policy and practice must be determined. Much of this work will necessarily be qualitative (Attinasi 1992) in order to discover the relevant factors associated with college attendance and persistence (e.g., individual meaning-making systems, the impact of various cultures of origin, gauging cultural distance, describing the process of cultural connection). One student may be involved in a whole series of activities yet not be connected to peers or faculty. Another student may be strongly connected to a single subculture and have a strong sense of belonging to the larger institution. The various propositions can generate focused research questions.

Action research on student departure grounded in a cultural perspective would also be welcome. Institutional members can conduct cultural audits (Kuh, Schuh, Whitt, and Associates 1991; Whitt 1993) to discover what elements of the cultures of immersion are encouraging students to persist, what elements are having a negative influence, the characteristics of enhancing enclaves and affinity groups, which groups alienate certain students from the institution's academic or social system, whether the cultures of some academic departments make it difficult for certain groups of students to persist, and whether some faculty behaviors alienate certain groups of students.

Conclusion

A cultural perspective extends and is in many ways consistent with Tinto's view of student departure. Its promise lies in the fact that it reconceptualizes the process from a predominantly individualistic process to a more group-oriented process. Examining student departure from a cultural perspective will give researchers, policy makers, and institutional leaders a better understanding of the complex phenomena that influence the decision process and reveal aspects of institutional functioning that can be changed to promote higher rates of student persistence and educational attainment.

References

Anderson, K. L. 1981. Post–high school experiences and college attrition. *Sociology of Education* 54: 1–15.

Attinasi, L. C., Jr. 1989. Getting in: Mexican Americans' perceptions of university attendance and implications for freshman year persistence. *Journal of Higher Education* 60: 247–277.

Attinasi, L. C., Jr. 1992. Rethinking the study of the outcomes of college attendance. *Journal of College Student Development* 33: 61–70.

Banning, J. H. 1980. The campus ecology manager role. In U. Delworth and G. R. Hanson (eds.), *Student services: A handbook for the profession*, pp. 209–227. San Francisco: Jossey-Bass.

Bean, J. P., and N. Vesper. 1992. Student dependency theory: An explanation of student retention in college. Paper presented at the annual meeting of the Association for the Study of Higher Education, Minneapolis, October.

Bourdieu, P., and J. Passeron. 1977. *Reproduction in education, society, and culture*. Newbury Park, Calif.: Sage.

Braxton, J. M., A. V. Sullivan, and R. M. Johnson, Jr. 1997. Appraising Tinto's theory of college student departure. In J. C. Smart (ed.), Higher education: A handbook of theory and research, vol. 12, 107–164. New York: Agathon Press.

Clark, R. M. 1983. *Family life and school achievement: Why poor black children succeed or fail*. Chicago: University of Chicago Press.

Donovan, R. 1984. Path analysis of a theoretical model of persistence in higher education among low-income black youth. *Research in Higher Education* 21 (3): 243–259.

Ginsburg, A. L., and S. L. Hanson. 1986. *Values and educational success among disadvantaged students*. Contract No. 300–83–0211. Washington, D.C.: U.S. Department of Education.

Hurtado, S., and D. F. Carter. 1997. College transition, campus racial climate perceptions, and sense of belonging among Latino college students. Unpublished manuscript.

Hurtado, S., D. F. Carter, and A. J. Spuler. 1996. Latino student transition to college: Assessing difficulties and factors in successful adjustment. *Research in Higher Education* 37: 135–157.

Kraemer, B. A. 1997. The academic and social integration of Hispanic students into college. *Review of Higher Education* 20: 163–179.

Kuh, G. D., and J. A. Arnold. 1993. Liquid bonding: A cultural analysis of the role of alcohol in fraternity pledgeship. *Journal of College Student Development* 34: 327–334.

Kuh, G. D., J. H. Schuh, E. J. Whitt, and associates. 1991. *Involving colleges*. San Francisco: Jossey Bass.

Kuh, G. D., and E. J. Whitt. 1988. *The invisible tapestry: Culture in American colleges and universities*. ASHE-ERIC Higher Education Report, no. 1. Washington, D.C.: Association for the Study of Higher Education.

London, H. 1989. Breaking away: A study of first-generation college students and their families. *American Journal of Education* 97: 144–170.

Martin, J. 1992. *Cultures in organizations: Three perspectives.* New York: Oxford University Press.

Martin, O. L. 1986. An analysis of black high school students' postsecondary plans: Educational excellence or economic survival? Paper presented at the annual conference of the American Educational Research Association, San Francisco, April.

Nora, A. 1993. Two year colleges and minority students' educational aspirations: Help or hindrance? In J. C. Smart (ed.), *Higher education: A handbook of theory and research,* vol. 9, pp. 212–247. New York: Agathon Press.

Nora, A., M. Castañeda, and A. Cabrera. 1992. *Student persistence: The testing of a comprehensive structural model of retention.* Paper presented at the annual meeting of the Association for the Study of Higher Education, Minneapolis, November.

Pascarella, E. T., and P. T. Terenzini. 1991. *How college affects students.* San Francisco: Jossey Bass.

Pavel, M. 1991. Assessing Tinto's model of institutional departure using American Indian and Alaskan Native longitudinal data. Paper presented at the annual meeting of the Association for the Study of Higher Education, Boston, November.

Persell, C. H., S. Catsambis, and P. W. Cookson, Jr. 1992. Differential asset conversion: Class and gendered pathways to selective colleges. *Sociology of Education* 65: 208–225.

Rhoads, R. A. 1994. *Coming out in college: The struggle for a queer identity.* Westport, Conn.: Bergin & Garvey.

Roth, M. 1985. Immigrant students in an urban commuter college: Persisters and dropouts. Ph.D. diss., Adelphi University, Garden City, N.Y.

Schroeder, C. C. 1993. New students—new learning styles. *Change* 25 (4): 21–26.

Tierney, W. G. 1992. An anthropological analysis of student participation in college. *Journal of Higher Education* 64: 604–618.

Tierney, W. G. 1993. *Building communities of difference: Higher education in the twenty-first century.* Westport, Conn.: Bergin & Garvey.

Tinto, V. 1993. *Leaving college: Rethinking the causes and cures of student attrition.* 2d ed. Chicago: University of Chicago Press.

Van Maanen, J. 1984. Doing old things in new ways: The chains of socialization. In J. Bess (ed.), *College and university organization: Insights from the behavioral sciences,* pp. 211–247. New York: New York University Press.

Whitt, E. J. 1993. "Making the familiar strange": Discovering culture. In G. D. Kuh (ed.), *Cultural perspectives in student affairs work,* pp. 81–94. Lanham, Md.: American College Personnel Association.

Williams, J. B., III. 1988. *Desegregating America's colleges and universities.* New York: Teachers College Press.

Power, Identity, and the Dilemma of College Student Departure

William G. Tierney

College student departure is one of the most studied areas in the higher education literature.* Our practical concern is generally to maintain a constant flow of students into the "pipeline," on the one hand, and to stem the premature tide of students out of academe, on the other. Our theoretical concern is often based on trying to understand the functions of various phenomena and their relationships to college leave-taking. What has come to be known as "Tinto's model" (Tinto 1975, 1993; Braxton, Sullivan, and Johnson 1997) has had the most pervasive influence on our thinking about why students leave and what institutions might do to ensure that they stay. The crux of the model hinges on ideas related to rituals of academic and social assimilation into the mainstream of college life.

I have critiqued Tinto's model from a cultural perspective that is informed by critical theory (Tierney 1992a, 1992b). My purpose here is neither to rehash concerns raised in previous work nor to offer yet another exegesis on the lessons of critical theory and postmodernism (Tierney 1993; Tierney and Rhoads 1993). Rather, I have three objectives. I first will consider the idea of culture and how it influences our conceptions of student departure. I then will posit a model based on critical notions of power and community. I conclude by examining how such a model might be employed as an intervention for those students who are most at risk of departing from college—low-income, urban, black, and Hispanic youth.

*The author would like to thank James Antony, John Braxton, Vincent Garcia, Alexander Jun, Dean McGovern, and Greg Tanaka for comments on an earlier draft of this chapter.

My goal is straightforward. The model offered in this chapter stands in contrast to some of the basic tenets of a functional model of dropouts. Yet certain characteristics of the model interact with or extend what the functionalists appear to suggest. The model also demonstrates what a cultural view involves in the "real world"; rightfully so, one of the major criticisms of critical theory is that individuals cannot often envision what abstract ideas look like when they are employed.

The scaffolding for the model derives from a college preparation program I have studied for the last year that is located in south central Los Angeles—the Neighborhood Academic Initiative (NAI). As will be elaborated in the final section, NAI accurately reflects a commitment to cultural integrity and educational reform in a manner distinctly different from traditional mainstream efforts at helping urban youth get into and graduate from college. My assumption is that if we can understand the basic tenets of what works for college preparation programs for low-income minority youth, we will be able to use such a model for those same individuals once they set foot on college campuses.

The Cultural Construction of Dropouts

We often forget that however "real" classrooms, schools, and universities may be, at their base we build them through cultural constructions of what we mean by words such as *classroom, school,* and *university.* The words we use to infuse such entities with meaning vary by time, circumstance, and context. A simplistic way to make sense of such a comment is to create a taxonomy about the different meanings people have of similar words. From this perspective, a classroom in Guatemala is organized differently from a classroom in south central Los Angeles. How teachers organize students and how they conduct their classes in an upper-class high school in Beverly Hills are certainly different from the high school classrooms I observed in a poor neighborhood in south central Los Angeles. The educational expectations, including degree attainment, that an upper-class family has for a son or daughter differ greatly from those of parents in rural Guatemala or inner-city Los Angeles who may never have graduated from high school, much less college.

Words and ideas mean something different as well. There is a saying in the Koran: "The teacher is like the prophet and you must respect him." Surely the authority of a teacher in an Islamic country is greater than that of a teacher in the United States where television shows frequently ridicule or make fun of the teaching profession. In some cultures the idea of "dropout" does not exist, whereas in the educational system in the United States it is a filter that sorts and separates individuals according to certain loaded variables that have consequences.

And yet by referring to the "cultural construction" of dropouts I mean something more than merely that different people do things differently. The culture in which we live, work, and learn is not inherited out of whole cloth and unchangeable. In large part we are involved in the creation of meaning throughout our lives, and the interpretations we bring to different organizations offer our own unique insights about events, people, and actions. "All Guatemalans" do not see the world in a particular manner any more than "the upper class" or "believers of Islam" act in one, lockstep manner. McDermott and Varenne (1995) are helpful here: "The coherence of any culture is not given by members being the same, nor by members knowing the same things. Instead, the coherence of a culture is crafted from the partial and mutually dependent knowledge of each person caught in the process and depends, in the long run, on the work they do together. Life in culture, Bakhtin reminds us, is polyphonous and multi vocalic; it is made of the voices of many, each one brought to life and made significant by others" (p. 326).

Culture is the difficult negotiation between understanding the implicit interpretations that have been built over time and our reconstruction of such meanings. On the one hand, if we believe that culture is fixed and determined and that all people act in one fashion, then we do injustice to the rich fabric of individuals and groups that exists in any one culture at a given time. Human agency is denied, and individual action accounts for little more than appearing as if we are all bit players in an absurdist drama. On the other hand, to ignore the very real cultures that we step into and out of in our daily lives and in our organizations suggests that individuals are free to make of life whatever they want regardless of history, culture, or social context.

Those who adhere to a structural view of the world subscribe to the former notion, and most important for the purpose of this text, those who call upon Tinto's model utilize the latter. As noted previously (Tierney 1992a), Tinto's model calls upon individualistic theoretical notions such as the idea of suicide proposed by Durkheim (1951). The focus of attention is the individual who commits suicide (or drops out) and not the culture that makes such acts possible or interprets them in a particular manner. One interprets the universe and then changes it according to desires and goals.

However much we might like to feel that we can change the world, my concern is that without struggling to understand how that world has been constructed we are doing little more than reinscribing notions of power and privilege for those who have had an active hand in determining those very relations of power. The assumption is that individual struggle is certainly essential in order for one to succeed; yet we cannot overlook the fact that individual actions exist within sociohistorical cultural constraints that have denied opportunity to some and afforded others great benefits. Issues of racism and sexism, among others, have been embedded in the way American education has been structured throughout our history. However much we struggle to change our present contexts we must also acknowledge that current actions are framed in light of historical and cultural parameters.

Such a concern is particularly germane to discussions about education in general and dropouts in particular. The framework for what we desire of education and what we mean by *drop out* has been developed by way of our culture. There is no scientific law, for example, that asserts that when a group of individuals composes a cultural category called "students" and they participate in another cultural term labeled "school" some of those "students" will "drop out." Surely we could have developed a system in which everyone stayed to completion. Or we could have developed a system from which everyone drops out; we might have created a system in which individuals come and go into educational settings throughout their lives and the length of period for which an individual stays at any one time is irrelevant. Instead, we have created a system in which there are winners and losers—some students stay; others drop out.

Increasingly, the consequences of dropping out are quite severe. As manufacturing jobs move to the third world, workers in the United States need to rely on advanced skills often learned in postsecondary education. In 1979, for example, a male college graduate earned 49 percent more than a male with only a high school degree, and today that gap has grown to over 83 percent (Tierney 1998). Although I am not suggesting that everyone must have a four-year degree, I am highlighting that the consequences are more severe today than ever before for those who drop out. Such a realization provokes at least three commentaries. The structuralist often has the fewest responses; if the system is predetermined, then there is little we can do short of revolution to change systemic shortcomings to stem the flow of dropouts. My concern with this position is that it denies human agency and suggests that whatever actions we take are fruitless. As I will suggest, there are programs that have made differences in overcoming historical in-equities; to do nothing verges on nihilism.

The functionalist devises ways to mend the perceived problem. It is from this perspective that we act on models such as Tinto's and try to put to-gether ways to enable more individuals to stay first in high school and then in college. My concern is that we inadequately address the structures and meanings of the world. In effect, the system is hemorrhaging, and rather than treat the problem we try to slow the bleeding. The metaphor is pur-poseful. I certainly appreciate campus-based programs that try to stop indi-viduals from dropping out of college, but those of us involved in campus remediation efforts need to act less like emergency-room medics and more like preventive physicians. We need to redesign a system whose effect is that it casts individuals aside if they do not meet predetermined criteria. In a culture we all have a hand in creating, our challenge is to ensure that everyone has a fruitful role in society that enables voice and empowerment.

The third response, and the one I elaborate on here, is acceptance of the consequences of dropping out while at the same time striving to alleviate painful consequences for individuals involved in the system. Nevertheless we accept that terms such as *drop out* are neither neutral nor scientific. The import of a cultural view of terms such as *drop out* is twofold. First, we move from an individualistic analysis to one that also incorporates under-standing of groups, power, and oppression. Surely previous research on tracking (Oakes 1985; Oakes, Gamoran, and Page 1992; Fine 1991) under-scores how students are sorted and filtered not so much according to their abilities, but in a binary fashion because of who they are, be they girls, eth-nic minorities, poor, or their counterparts—boys, Anglos, the upper class. When we define some individuals as "disabled" either implicitly or explic-itly we also have defined others as "abled."

A cultural view of schooling seeks to expose and understand what terms such as *dropout* mean beyond surface interpretations. In this light, *dropout* means something more than merely that a student is no longer in school. We learn, for example, that the supposedly neutral term *dropout* is identified with those who are most often powerless and disabled by the cul-ture in which they live and participate.

Once we learn that culture exists through powerful definitions that enable some and disable others, we are then able to investigate issues such as the hidden curriculum, the social organization of classrooms, and in-herent pedagogical practices that occur every day. From such studies we learn how power operates through culture's webs. We find, for example, that "low ability groups are taught less frequently and are subjected to more control by the teacher. Students in low-ability reading groups spend more reading time on decoding activities, whereas students in high-ability groups spend more time on text comprehension and deriving the meaning of stories" (Mehan et al. 1996, p. 6). Our understanding of what works and how we are to help people learn takes on a new approach. "Culture is not a property of individuals-as-conditioned" (McDermott and Varenne 1995, p. 344). Instead, we investigate the properties and interpretations of the culture in order to come to terms with how some are silenced and others privileged.

Of consequence, a cultural response to stem the tide of dropouts takes on a different framework. We surely seek to enable students to come to grips with the multiple phenomena that hold them back. In effect, we aim to equip students with the necessary cultural capital to succeed within the system that exists, but in doing so we seek to disrupt the process. Rather than have students reproduce the social order of the classroom that divides some as haves and others as have-nots, the struggle becomes to obviate a culture that organizes individuals in such a way. In what follows I suggest a framework that incorporates a cultural view of the world whereby students hold on to and affirm their own embedded identities while they function and succeed within the received culture of multiple kinds of educational institutions at the turn of the century.

Culture Framed

The framework developed here follows from the assumption that power's grasp has a direct relationship with the achievement that minority students face in educational settings in general and postsecondary institutions in particular. That is, power relations already existent in the larger society frequently get transformed in educational organizations as failures for those who are on the margins. The model proposed stands in contrast and yet ultimately complements what has been previously delineated with regard to college student leave-taking. In the past researchers have suggested that students need to be integrated into the fabric of the institution, that both academic and social integration needs to take place, and that we ought to view college as a ritualistic transition point from one stage to another. In large part the onus in such a model is on the individual. The individual integrates; the individual undergoes the ritual; the individual finds ways to fit into the academic and social milieu of the institution.

What I am suggesting is that we turn the model on its head—that we develop a framework which has the negotiation of identity in academe as central to educational success. The interactions that students, teachers, parents, and families have and how we approach the definitions of these interactions are key to students' success, failure, leave-taking, or completion. Rather than a model that assumes that students must fit into what is often an alien culture and that they leave their own cultures, I argue the opposite. The challenge is to develop ways in which an individual's identity is affirmed, honored, and incorporated into the organization's culture. Of necessity, we must seek ways not only to aid the individual in succeeding, but also in developing ways for the organization's culture to adapt to new individuals and groups. The model rests on five key points: (1) collaborative relations of power; (2) connections across home, community, and schooling; (3) local definitions of identity; (4) challenge over remediation; and (5) academic support.

Collaborative Relations of Power

Power has too often been viewed as a fixed quantity that operates within a zero-sum logic. The problem with the idea of fixed relations of power is that some groups and their practices end up as deviant and subordinate while others are mainstream and superior. The only possibility for those without power is to become more like those in power or to express resistance by way of leave-taking or behavior that is likely to be deemed "antisocial." Simply stated, either someone adapts and assimilates or he remains aloof and is maladapted.

I am suggesting that we consider an alternative logic. Under this approach power is neither fixed nor predetermined. This approach acknowledges that people generate power by way of the cultures in which they operate. Consider again the comment above by McDermott and Varenne (1995) that "culture is not property of individuals-as-conditioned." Culture is polyphonous; what culture becomes is determined by the multiple individual and group relations in which people function and develop meaning. As Cummins (1997) notes, "participants in the relationship are empowered through their collaboration such that each is more affirmed in his or her identity and has a greater sense of efficacy to create change in his or her life or social situation" (p. 424). The elaboration of one's identity, rather than ignoring such issues or trying to incorporate identity work into unquestioned organizational norms, becomes central. The challenge in programs that seek to prevent dropouts is not to develop ways for people to integrate into the system, but instead to change that system by way of programs, activities, events, and curricula that affirm and honor individual identities. As I will discuss, the definitions that educators develop when working from a collaborative perspective are dramatically different from a framework that seeks to assimilate individuals into a static social context in which power goes unquestioned and identity is assumed.

Connections across Home, Community, and Schooling

One viewpoint works from the assumption that where an individual comes from is relatively unimportant, perhaps even harmful. From this perspective, a school or university has arbitrary rules, standards, procedures, and definitions of excellence. What one merits in this organization depends entirely upon an individual's efforts. Accordingly, if we want students to succeed we emphasize skills. Since there are limited resources, time, and programs, the challenge is to ensure academic success.

Tinto's model highlights that social integration is also critical, but the limitation in this approach is that such integration begins from the institutional perspective rather than from the vantage point of the individual. Thus, social integration works from the idea that the kinds of social activities and the forms of these events are relatively unimportant; what matters is that students become integrated. As with Durkheim's (1951) work on anomie, the overriding factor in success (or prevention of suicide) is incorporation into a larger social order. But overlooking Durkheim's analysis, the functionalist model of drop-out prevention assumes that the background of an individual is relatively unimportant as long as he or she can identify with social activities in the college or university.

The approach suggested here, however, begins by pointing out the critical importance of affirming student identity. Successful programs cannot be developed unless we acknowledge the particular backgrounds of those whom we seek to educate. To decontextualize the activities developed for learning from students' lives is to assume that identity is similar and static—or should be—and that if those who participate cannot fit in then they have failed. An alternative framework is to develop programs that are palpably local in definition. We begin by working from where students are. The assumption that a ritual of transition is necessary for students to succeed is rejected in favor of activities that affirm the identities, homes, and communities in which individuals live and grow.

Local Definitions of Identity

I cannot emphasize enough the importance of beginning where students are—intellectually, socially, emotionally—rather than working toward academic abstractions. Low-income minority youth, be they Native American students from an Indian reservation, inner-city black adolescents who grow up in a housing project, Mexican immigrants who live in a barrio, or any number of other individuals who see themselves as part of a group that considers postsecondary campuses as alien territory, need to have teachers, tasks, and pedagogies that affirm who they are. In a text about successful community-based organizations McLaughlin (1993) notes that "localness assumes strong ties to the community so that programs can shape and be shaped by their context" (p. 58). Although the settings may differ somewhat for different colleges and universities, the emphasis needs to be the same. Teachers, curricula, and organizational frameworks incorporate the identities of students into their frameworks.

What might such a comment imply? I have previously pointed out how teachers of Native American students may be well versed in their particular subject areas—for instance, geology, calculus, European history—but they frequently have no understanding of the students whom they teach (Tierney 1992c). If one wants to be not merely a purveyor of information and subject matter but also a transformative intellectual who seeks to challenge and engage students to perform to the best of their ability, then of consequence one must come to terms with the backgrounds and forces that have shaped those individuals who sit in classes. Department chairs, deans, and hiring committees will take into account how teachers view students and how the organization teaches new instructors about the backgrounds of their students. Compare such an idea to what actually happens: all but a handful of institutions have neither discussions nor programs that orient faculty to how to improve learning based on student identity. Social integration of this sort may well not reside in programs where race is "whited out" but instead work to enhance multicultural programming and understanding for all students (Cummins 1986).

The framework assumes that "students from dominated societal groups are empowered or disabled as a direct result of their interactions with educators" (Cummins 1986, p. 21). The manner in which we empower students is based on a cultural understanding of their local contexts and how such understandings might be incorporated into the basic fabric of the institution. Obviously, I am not suggesting that educators mindlessly

include all aspects of someone's local context into educational programming and curricula. Dysfunctional families, neighborhoods, and communities reside with all groups, regardless of race, income, or locale. Abusive
relationships are certainly not to be celebrated. Indeed, one function of
progressive programming is to enable students to feel safe enough to discuss the problems they face and help them filter out destructive aspects of
their locales such as drugs and crime and still affirm their core identities.
When black students equate being black with crime and drug use, we work
from a deficit model that assumes a particular group is subordinate; in
order for them to succeed they must "act white." Steele (1997) has pointed
out how such stereotypes shape intellectual identity and performance and
has coined the phrase "stereotype threat" (p. 614) to highlight the detri-
mental consequences to those who are stereotypes—be they women in
math and science classes or minority youth in college. The approach called
for here breaks the equation of race and deviant behavior and actively
works to form an inclusive identity.

Challenge over Remediation

One additional factor with which educators must contend with students labeled "at-risk" or who are in danger of dropping out is the lowering of expectations so that one's aspirations are leveled rather than raised. Steele
(1997) notes, "Giving challenging work to students conveys respect for
their potential and thus shows that they are not regarded through the lens
of an ability-demeaning stereotype" (p. 625). With such an approach teachers, programs, and institutions convey high expectations to students and
create a climate within the classroom and on campus that gives the message
that everyone can learn and will succeed. In inner-city schools we often find
the opposite messages being transmitted to students. Discussions about college are infrequent, and when they occur they often revolve around attendance at a community college rather than four-year institutions. To be sure,
community colleges have a valid and important role to play in the panoply
of postsecondary education; but students should be encouraged to consider
all types of institutions, not merely those that are considered the least academically challenging. College preparation classes are frequently nonexistent. When students arrive at an institution they find themselves labeled in
one way or another that inevitably lowers their own and their teachers' expectations. Faculty spend less time demanding excellence from their students and coaching individuals about how to improve their study skills.

Over the last generation we have heard frequent attacks on equity-based policies such as affirmative action or "remedial" education on college campuses. One of the main critiques is that such policies and their recipients lower standards and dilute excellence. I suggest that no one is well served if beneficiaries of affirmative action or other policies aimed at increasing minority representation in academe do not set high, measurable standards. The problems do not reside with programs such as affirmative action, but with those who interpret them as anything less than methods to achieve high performance (Tierney 1997). Program effectiveness means nothing if in stemming the tide of dropouts from college or increasing college-going for different groups the students have not been placed in programs that enable them to flourish to their highest potential.

Academic Support

The model I am trying to develop works from the idea that those individuals who have been labeled "at-risk" or are likely to drop out have much greater potential than previous frameworks suggest. Programs that see individuals as broken and in need of repair are less likely to create the conditions for success than those programs that assume students are valuable resources to themselves and their families, communities, and society. Negative discussions about someone's shortcomings or their inability to perform are eschewed in favor of dialogues of respect that affirm the potential of the individual. The key word here is *respect*. However different in age, learning, or educational degree, those programs that honor a student's position are more likely to help the student succeed than programs that concentrate solely on erasing perceived and/or real academic shortcomings.

Respect acknowledges that even though students may have families without college degrees or formal educational backgrounds, they have knowledge and strengths in ways the teachers do not. Alliances with parents and families are essential in this model; consider how dramatically different such an approach is from one that may implicitly reject the role of families in college education or, more likely, ignore the students' families with the false assumption that because they have not been to college they cannot play a useful role in getting their child into college.

Cummins (1986) writes that a collaborative, supportive environment explicitly "encourages minority parents to participate in promoting their children's academic progress" (p. 27). Academic support becomes active, explicit. Although there are certainly egregious examples of teachers or programs that seem to set out to negate the self-worth of an individual, the larger problem that I am concerned with pertains to the more mundane aspects of educational life. We may not negate a student's background or family, but we all too often ignore or overlook it, which in a way also negates identity. This model suggests the opposite. If we are to improve academic performance, we should concentrate on the individual's identity and background.

Implementing the Model and Implications for College Retention

What are the practical consequences for the kind of model suggested in this chapter? How might such a model differ from other programs? The Neighborhood Academic Initiative (NAI), located in south central Los Angeles, has worked over the last eight years to implement the framework developed above. I have offered elsewhere a case study of the project to demonstrate how the staff works with low-income minority youth and the specific successes they have had over a longitudinal time horizon. (Tierney and Jun, in preparation). In what follows I draw on the attributes of NAI to show how one might develop a culturally responsive program. My singular caution is that I am not suggesting that one formulaic response meets the needs of all program types and students. As others have noted (Dryfoos 1990; McLaughlin 1993), the key ideas in the development of such projects are flexibility and responsiveness. Students arrive at educational settings with a multitude of issues and concerns that need to be addressed. If we are to follow the basic tenets outlined above, we need to be responsive to the learner, which in turn necessitates programmatic and personal flexibility.

The Neighborhood Academic Initiative is a college preparation program aimed at educating junior high and high school students so that they are able to enter college. Each year NAI accepts roughly thirty-five students into the program. Students are drawn from two schools in a low-income neighborhood, and they are purposefully not the honors students. All a student needs to have is a C average, the desire to enter the program, and the support of one adult guardian. Participation in the program is in addition to attendance at the "scholar's" regular school. All students take classes for two hours prior to the start of the regular school day; classes begin at 7:00 A.M. Students also have after-school activities, week-end classes, and a summer intensive program, and their parents or guardians also must attend periodic weekend workshops.

Activities range from English and math classes to individual and group counseling about personal problems and what one must do to gain entrance to college. A great deal of effort and time are spent discussing the discipline that a "scholar" needs to succeed and how everyone must help one another follow the rules of the program. Virtually every activity I have personally observed has included discussion of values clarification that affirms the importance of the youth's background and also discussion of negative behaviors (e.g., drug use, cheating). The model works from five departure points that parallel the assumptions noted above. The following discussion returns to the points listed above and offers insight into how abstract ideas such as "local definitions of identity" get enacted at NAI.

Collaborative Relations of Power: Positive Self-definitions

Teachers, counselors, and the program director constantly reiterate the strengths of the children involved in the program. All students are called "scholars" to emphasize their academic potential. Inside and outside of the classrooms teachers are valued resources who are on the students' side and will create safe spaces where learning will occur. Although the teachers and counselors remind students of the responsibility they have to succeed, students are also involved in a setting that assumes success.

Throughout the program's activities the orientation is that the youths have personal tasks that must be attended to in order to ensure that they meet their goals; nevertheless, no one exists in a climate of "sink or swim." Instead, adults guide the adolescents and constantly reaffirm the basic tenets of the program that exist in a contract each person signs (appendix 1). Parenthetically, the vast majority of students are either African American or Hispanic; the contract is written in English and Spanish. Those who direct the program have developed a rigorous structure that demands that students rise to the set standards. The program also recognizes the often difficult challenges low-income adolescents face en route to adulthood. A multitude of perplexing questions face these students—for example, How would you respond if your brother tried to get you to join a gang? or What should you do if your best friend gets pregnant? The program's thrust is twofold. The adults who run the program are models of trust and respect whom students turn to for guidance and support. The program is also a safe space that enables the students to stay focused on learning and gaining an education.

Figure 1

A Culturally Responsive Model for Educational Success

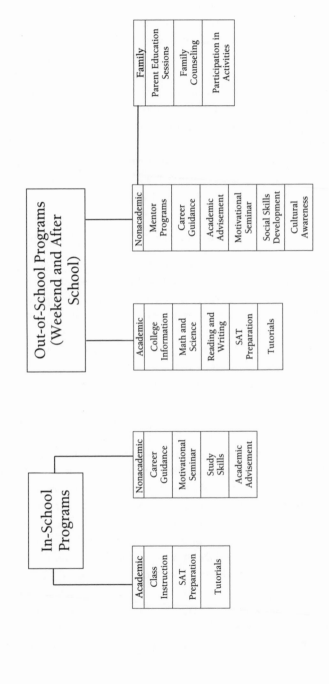

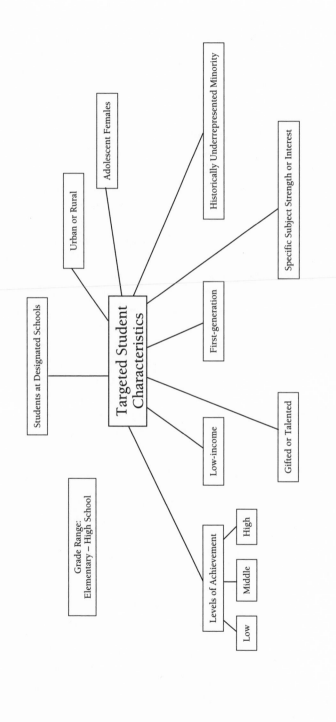

Connections: Family Involvement.

As noted, one way to work with children from low-income neighborhoods is to assume that families should be kept away or ignored. Families in which rampant drug use exists, for example, might be assumed to be unable to help young people with college work. NAI works from the opposite perspective. One component of the program is that a family member or guardian must sign on o be involved in the activities of the project. Family involvement has a double role. The directors believe that when NAI educates a student they must involve those other primary-care individuals in an educational experience as well. Oftentimes that will mean that Saturday seminars deal with topics such as how a parent might help a child by encouraging him or her to study, how to talk about sex, or how to interact with teachers in a positive and supportive way. Schools are frequently seen by families as alien institutions that do not seek the best interests of individual children. NAI works to demonstrate to families and the community how they can best get involved and support teachers and counselors, which in turn helps the children. In effect, NAI has taken the notion of cultural capital beyond merely the individual and extended it to the scholars' primary relationships. For students to be able to enter and graduate from college, it is necessary to enable multiple individuals to become involved in efforts aimed at helping the children. Another role of family involvement, in addition to educating families about their responsibilities, is conveying to students/scholars that they do not need to drop their personal identities in order to be successful. Family involvement affirms, rather than rejects or ignores, the import of identity.

Local Definitions of Identity: Dealing with Racism

NAI begins from a framework that assumes that racism exists and that low-income black and Hispanic youth in particular have a significant challenge to face if they are to succeed. At the same time, no one in the program allows students to blame racism for bad test scores or for their own particular mistakes or foibles. Indeed, one often hears comments that acknowledge the existence of discrimination while simultaneously also pointing out that the task of the NAI scholar is to figure out ways to overcome discrimination.

Matute-Bianchi (1986) has pointed out that "to participate in class discussions, to carry books from class to class, to ask the teacher for help in front of others, to expend effort to do well in school—are too often efforts that are viewed derisively, condescendingly, and mockingly" by other minority students (p. 255). Her point is that local identities reject schooling when education is seen as antithetical to one's background. NAI works assiduously to combat such stereotypes from two perspectives.

First, teachers and administrators are often African American or Hispanic. Ladson-Billings (1994) has made a similar point in her work on successful teachers of African American children. The point surely is not that white people cannot teach students in NAI, since the program has many successful white teachers; however, the program also has role models who students recognize as coming from similar backgrounds. Further, positive role models from a university or the community speak to the students stressing the importance of college education.

Second, because racism is perpetuated not only by Anglos but across all groups, one emphasis of the program is to eradicate racist tendencies with all students. Derisive language, stereotyping, and ethnic grouping of black students versus Hispanic students are vigorously rejected in favor of an approach that accentuates pride in one's heritage and respect for others.

Challenge over Remediation: Standards

NAI has been likened to a loving boot camp. Classes start on time, and a tardy student is expected to apologize to the other scholars for retarding the progress of learning. Teachers point out mistakes to students and constantly ask what students will do to overcome errors. Silence in class, adherence to rules about attendance, and a host of other policies set a tone that highlights the focus of the program: education. Noguera (1996) has spoken about a similar kind of schooling by summarizing that students noted "that the teachers they admired most were academically demanding ones who worked hard to make their classes interesting" (p. 232). Similarly, although each NAI scholar occasionally was criticized, the adolescents reiterated that the discipline and climate of the classrooms enabled them to focus on their studies and not become distracted.

In part, this focus on excellence succeeds because the students also acknowledge that everyone cares about them. The teachers, administrators, counselors, and director were portrayed by the students as understanding of the kinds of challenges the students faced and did not put them down. The safety of the learning environment was constantly reiterated as enabling students to accept their tasks and actually begin to think about going to college. One final point pertains to definitions of excellence. In some schools with a similar population, graduation from high school alone might be considered an achievement; in other schools similar students are tracked to the community college. In NAI, however, the entire emphasis is constantly on getting students into institutions that will enable them to achieve to their highest potential. Again, the point is not to put down those students who would have better educational experiences at community colleges; rather, NAI tries to help students sort out what they want to do and struggles to ensure that in a student's decision making all options exist, rather than merely ones that are environmentally circumscribed.

Academic Support: Collecting Data

Obviously, from the sketches provided, this program begins from very different premises of students than most traditional programs use. True, grade point averages and test scores play a role in student selection. How students do on quizzes and exams in their classes is also of paramount importance. The attainment of the honor roll or graduating with honors is precisely the kind of accomplishment that NAI tries to teach family members to cherish and honor.

Nevertheless, students are never reduced to numbers or simple descriptions. The scholars are looked on as unique, talented individuals who have a wealth of potential that can be tapped and utilized for personal good as well as the good of the entire community. The analysis of student progress is an intensive and multifaceted examination of the struggles each student faces, how he or she adapts to those struggles, and what the program might do to increase student productivity. Consider the focus of such a program when compared to the traditional model that assumes students need to fit in and adapt to what already exists.

On the one hand, there is a delicate balance that exists in NAI between the constant emphasis on student achievement and the rejection of excuses or laziness on a scholar's part. And yet, on the other hand, the instructors and the overall program accept the responsibility for designing success. They acknowledge that they cannot make students do their homework, listen in class, or learn to do well on examinations. The teachers and counselors also recognize that without an explicitly structured academic environment aimed at success and excellence, the chances are slim that these adolescents will be successful.

Conclusion

The demise of affirmative action programs and the fiscal cutbacks in public higher education are cause for grave concern for those of us who maintain a desire to ensure equal access and participation to postsecondary education. In this chapter a model is described that employs a cultural framework for analyzing student participation. The model has been used successfully by individuals involved in a college preparation program for low-income urban minority youth (for specific outcomes see Tierney and Jun, in preparation). My assumption is that the basic tenets of the framework apply throughout the educational life span and not only for adolescents in high school. To be sure, different groups necessitate different strategies. For an adult student, familial involvement may not require a parent's participation but rather the participation of a spouse, life partner, or supervisor at work. For a college student, a professor may play a different classroom role from that of a high school teacher. In effect, those involved with low-income minority students at a college or university need to reorient how they think about and work with such students. The tasks point to a fundamental reorientation of the culture of the organization.

A cultural model affords a theoretical and policy-oriented lens to study college student departure in a dramatically different way from the traditionalists' framework. At a time when access to public higher education is under fire, we must develop and enhance the way we see the world so that we might change that world. This chapter argues that we need a more robust discussion of what we mean by college student departure so that we might inform our actions on campuses to ensure greater equity and excellence.

References

Braxton, J. W., A. V. Sullivan, and R. M. Johnson. 1997. Appraising Tinto's theory of college student departure. In J. C. Smart (ed.), *Higher education: A handbook of theory and research,* vol. 12, pp. 107–164. New York: Agathon Press.

Cummins, J. 1986. Empowering minority students: A framework for intervention. *Harvard Educational Review* 56 (1): 18–36.

Cummins, J. 1997. Minority status and schooling in Canada. *Anthropology & Education Review Quarterly* 28 (3): 411–430.

Dryfoos, J. G. 1990. *Adolescents at risk.* New York: Oxford University Press.

Fine, M. 1991. *Framing dropouts: Notes on the politics of an urban public high school.* Albany: State University of New York Press.

Durkheim, E. (J. A. Spaulding and G. Simpson, trans.). 1951. *Suicide.* Glencoe: Free Press.

Ladson-Billings, G. 1994. *The dreamkeepers: Successful teachers of African American children.* San Francisco: Jossey-Bass.

Matute-Bianchi, M. E. 1986. Ethnic identities and patterns of school success and failure among Mexican-descent and Japanese-American students in a California high school: An ethnographic analysis. *American Journal of Education* 95 (3): 233–255.

McDermott, R., and H. Varenne. 1995. Culture as disability. *Anthropology & Education Quarterly* 26 (3): 324–348.

McLaughlin, M. W. 1993. Embedded identities: Enabling balance in urban contexts. In S. Heath and M. McLaughlin (eds.), *Identity & inner-city youth*, pp. 36–68. New York: Teachers College Press.

Mehan, H., L. Hubbard, I. Villanueva, and A. Lintz. 1996. *Constructing school success*. New York: Cambridge University Press.

Noguera, P. A. 1996. Responding to the crisis confronting California's black male youth: Providing support without furthering marginalization. *Journal of Negro Education* 65 (2): 219–236.

Oakes, J. 1985. *Keeping track: How schools structure inequality*. New Haven, Conn.: Yale University Press.

Oakes, J., A. Gamoran, and R. N. Page. 1992. Curriculum differentiation: Opportunities, outcomes, and meanings. In P. Jackson (ed.), *Handbook of research on curriculum*, pp. 570–608. New York: Macmillan Press.

Steele, C. 1997. A threat in the air: How stereotypes shape intellectual identity and performance. *American Psychologist* 52 (6): 613–629.

Tierney, W. G. 1992a. An anthropological analysis of student participation in college. *Journal of Higher Education* 63 (6): 603–618.

Tierney, W. G. 1992b. The college experience of Native Americans: A critical analysis. In L. Weis and M. Fine (eds.), *Beyond silenced voices: Class, voice, and gender in United States schools*, pp. 309–323. Ithaca: State University of New York Press.

Tierney, W. G. 1992c. *Official encouragement, institutional discouragement: Minorities in academe—the Native American experience*. Norwood, N.J.: Ablex.

Tierney, W. G. 1993. *Building communities of difference: Higher education in the twenty-first century*. Westport, Conn.: Bergin & Garvey.

Tierney, W. G. 1997. The parameters of affirmative action: Equity and excellence in the academy. *Review of Educational Research* 67 (2): 165–196.

Tierney, W. G. (ed.). 1998. *The responsive university: Restructuring for high performance*. Baltimore: Johns Hopkins University Press.

Tierney, W. G., and A. Jun. In preparation. A case study of a culturally responsive college preparation program.

Tierney, W. G., and R. A. Rhoads. 1993. Postmodern and critical theory in higher education: Implications for research and practice. In J. C. Smart (ed.), *Higher education: A handbook of theory and research*, pp. 308–343. New York: Agathon Press.

Tinto, V. 1975. Dropout from higher education: A theoretical synthesis of recent research. *Review of Educational Research* 45: 89–125.

Tinto, V. 1993. *Leaving college: Rethinking the causes and cures of student attrition*. 2d ed. Chicago: University of Chicago Press.

Appendix 1

Neighborhood Academic Initiative Pre-college Enrichment Academy Scholar's Code of Ethics

Since I am no better than any other human being, I will treat everyone, regardless of age, race, or gender, with dignity and respect.

Since I need love, kindness, consideration, and encouragement, I will strive to be loving in my relations with my fellow scholars; to be kind and considerate when they do not perform or behave in ways I expect; to offer encouragement when things go badly for them.

Since I am not perfect, I will forgive my peers and others when they behave imperfectly.

Since I am dedicated to being the most productive scholar I can be, I will conduct all of my affairs—those at the USC Pre-College Enrichment Academy, at my home school, at home, and in my community—with honesty, maturity, sincerity, and dignity.

Since I am a scholar who has a great opportunity to better my life through the acquisition of knowledge and because I am intelligent and motivated, I will succeed in all my academic and social endeavors.

As a scholar, I will not in any form or situation cheat, lie, or steal.

As a scholar, I will always be there for my peers, helping them understand the processes, procedures, and rules required to complete homework assignments, projects, and activities, but never give them the answers or conclusions until after the assignments have been turned in and graded or when the teacher gives me permission to do so.

As a scholar, I will strive tenaciously to master the skill of discerning right from wrong, actively suppressing all impulses from myself and coercion from others to behave in ways that are counterproductive; in conflict with the Scholar's Code of Ethics; and a detriment to my growth and development as an effectual, ethical, trustworthy, and moral human being.

As a scholar, I will treat every teacher, teacher assistant, counselor, and administrator with reverence and respect, arriving to class on time and adhering to their advice to work to attain the highest possible standards of excellence in and out of class.

As a scholar, I will carry myself as a person of pride and honor, never taking the easy way, the expedient way, but accepting the responsibility of always taking the right way, regardless of its academic/emotional difficulty, unpopularity with my peers, or necessity to change my overall pattern of behavior.

New Institutional Theory and Student Departure

Berta Vigil Laden, Jeffrey F. Milem, and Robert L. Crowson

T here is increasing public (and professorial) attention to college and university rankings, productivity indexes, and best-buy characteristics. Thus, it is understandable that steady and rather immutable rates of student departure would be not only a puzzle but of serious administrative and public-relations concern to persons in the field of higher education. Particularly as the field becomes increasingly diverse and struggles to integrate that diversity more deeply into organizational cultures, to speak of student departure is increasingly to speak potentially of a performance problem.

Indeed, the persistent and seemingly intractable problem of student departure in higher education might well be considered an indicator of what Meyer and Zucker (1989) label "permanently failing organizations." Permanently failing organizations are those "whose performance, by any standard," falls short of expectations—yet the organization and its accompanying problems go on and on indefinitely (p. 19). Such organizations can go on indefinitely at least in part because the various "interests that surround them become more concerned with maintaining the existing organizations than with maximizing their performance" (p. 23).

Of course, one might ask, as part of an understanding of the puzzle, whether nonretention should be at all considered an indicator of failure or of nonmaximized performance. Perhaps departure is a historically valid vestige of the culling-out function captured in infamous freshman orientation messages of: "Look to your left, look to your right; one of you will not be here next term." On the other hand, culling out is not a feature today's higher education wishes to highlight, and, if not real failure, the departure rate is now a sufficiently sensitive statistic (when turned on its head toward retention) to warrant organizational worry, college-to-college comparisons, and "we-retain-better" promotionalism. Higher education organizations (with diversity goals much in mind) do not at all wish to give the public and prospective students an impression that they may fail to retain effectively. Indeed, it is increasingly an agreed-upon performance measure. The very legitimacy and hence survival of the organization seems to ask that it seek to curb student departure.

It is just this combination of forces (an intractable problem, an organizational characteristic that is simultaneously a failure and a selling point, and a genuinely "puzzled" organization) that attracts the attention of persons interested in a rapidly developing body of organizational theory labeled "the new institutionalism." New institutional theorizing revels in the study of that which persists organizationally despite efforts toward change and that which seems to be "deeply" embedded in organizational structures and procedures (Powell and DiMaggio 1991a). Yet to be applied to the departure puzzle, new institutional theorizing may possibly offer some heretofore inadequately considered insights into this most enduring and mysterious of college and university characteristics.

The New Institutionalism

It is important to note at the outset that there are many variations of institutional theory (Scott 1987). New theorizing about institutions is now found in diverse forms that grow quite separately from the languages and traditions of sociology, economics, political science, organizational theory, and history. The approaches of these disciplines are far from compatible, and there is not even a firm agreement on just what is or is not an "institution" (Scott 1987; Zucker 1987).

There is general agreement that institutions are not the same as organizations. In the main, new institutional theorists do not tend to think in organization-specific terms. The greater concern is with categories of organizations (e.g., health care, higher education, public utilities). Similarly, the concern is more with environmental fields of forces (impacting upon organizations of common purpose) than with organization-at-a-time analyses. Nevertheless, much of the literature does address the value of new institutional theorizing in organizational inquiry, and organization-at-a-time studies have indeed been vital to the development of institutional theory (DiMaggio and Powell 1991a).

Scott (1987) identifies four different conceptualizations of the term *institution;* but a cleaner and hopefully clearer delineation, for the purposes of this chapter, is drawn from Zucker (1987) with two key distinctions. One delineation regards the larger environment of a field of organizations as its institution. The environment creates a collective normative order to which organizations conform—complete with flows of societal resources, legal and regulatory demands, legitimating expectations, and an array of rationalized myths and rituals (Meyer and Rowan 1977). Over time, in what DiMaggio and Powell (1991b, p. 64) refer to as "an inexorable push toward homogenization," individual organizations are pressured by their institutional environments to become increasingly similar (or isomorphic). By this definition all hospitals, law firms, elementary/secondary schools, and higher-education organizations will share many more within-group than between-group characteristics—inhabiting a common field.

A second delineation looks inside individual organizations toward those common structures, processes, and behaviors that tend to be highly formalized, are shared across organizations, and have continuity over time—and are thereby considered to be "institutionalized" (Zucker 1987). That which instills value (e.g., history), a shared social reality, typifications and classifications (e.g., of a clientele), things taken for granted, routines, and cultural elements (e.g., symbols, cognitive systems)—indeed, whatever assists generally in the stability and persistence of organizations over time—could well be part of its institutionalization (Scott 1987; DiMaggio and Powell 1991a).

W. Richard Scott (1987) has warned that (as an emerging body of work) there are "many faces" of institutional theory and "little agreement on specifics" (p. 493). One of the many faces has been heavily influenced by Philip Selznick (1957), who saw institutionalization as an adaptive process of "instilling value" within an organization (Scott 1987, p. 494). What might begin as an activity with merely technical or instrumental utility (e.g., a freshman orientation session, a parents' weekend, a promotion and tenure review) can become imbued over time with a sense of intrinsic worth far beyond the task or action itself. "By instilling value," summarizes Scott (1987, p. 494), "institutionalization promotes stability: persistence of the structure over time."

A second, but related face sees institutionalization as a shared definition of social reality within an organization. It is a reality, notes Scott (1987), "whose validity is seen as independent of the actor's own views or actions but is taken for granted as defining the 'way things are' and/or the 'way things are to be done'" (p. 496). An accumulation of credit hours toward graduation; a schedule of class meetings, locations, and instructors; the rhythm of registration, payment, beginning, add/drop, and ending in an academic year; a ceremonial conferring of diplomas—these are actions and categories of behavior that typify a higher-education organization. People tend to respond to these elements of social reality in similar fashion, whatever the college or university.

However, a third important face of institutional theory breaks a bit from the hint of cultural determinism suggested in notions of environments that instill value or organizational realities that become taken for granted (Scott 1987). On the one hand, it is possible to see institutionalization as a rather passive process whereby societal expectations exist and individual organizations conform to them, with behaviors that take on a "rule-like status" internally (Covaleski and Dirsmith 1988). On the other hand, organizations have and act upon powers of their own and their own special self-interests. Scott (1987) writes: "Organizations do not necessarily conform to a set of institutionalized beliefs because they 'constitute reality' or are taken for granted, but often because they are rewarded for doing so through increased legitimacy, resources, and survival capabilities" (p. 498).

Finally, a fourth face connects institutions to that which encourages the persistence and stability of societal systems (e.g., religion, work, the family, public entertainment). Much of this encouragement can be symbolic and/or ceremonial in form, and much may be closely built into the behavioral logics or repertoires of those who inhabit organizations. From the perspective of this face, everything from the credentialing function to "big-time" athletics could merit examination as elements in the maintenance of "enduring systems of social beliefs and socially organized practices" (Scott 1987, p. 499). Even the international reputation of higher education as a source of radicalism, inventiveness, and cultural change (in many of its national contexts) provides that which can serve social continuity.

In brief summary, institutionalized organizations tend to inhabit common organizational fields and tend (isomorphically) to grow increasingly similar over time, with shared cultural elements. Furthermore, four of its key faces suggest that institutionalization is (1) an adaptive process of instilling value in an organization, (2) an enculturating matter of sharing organizational definitions of social reality, (3) a political process of both conforming to and self-interestedly using organizational environments, and (4) a highly normative and symbolic endeavor to protect societal persistence and stability.

Institutionalism and Departure

"College founding in the nineteenth century," wrote historian Frederick Rudolph (1962, p. 48), "was undertaken in the same spirit as canal-building, cotton-ginning, farming, and gold-mining." Much touched by America's "faith in tomorrow" (p. 48), by religious/denominational energies, by "provincial loyalties and rivalries" (p. 51), and by increasing "requirements of middle-class life" in America (p. 57), a nineteenth-century college movement helped greatly to define the social fabric of our nation.

The growth in opportunities for attending a college or university in America has continued unabated. There were 977 institutions of higher learning in the United States at the beginning of this century that enrolled close to 240,000 students (Snyder 1993). By 1994–1995 there were 3,688 two- and four-year colleges and universities in the United States with a combined enrollment of more than 14 million persons (Hunter 1997). In 1900 about 2.3 percent of the "college-age" population (aged eighteen to twenty-four years) was actively attending school; that figure climbed to an amazing 63.7 percent by 1994 (*Statistical Abstracts of the United States* 1996). Community colleges alone represent one-third of all higher-education institutions and constitute nearly 40 percent of the total enrollment (Cohen and Brawer 1996).

It can be argued that colleges and universities as organizations and what is labeled going-to-college behavior have become thoroughly institutionalized features of our American culture (TInto 1993). Indeed, no other nation sends as large a percentage of its population on to higher learning, and the social acceptability of being a college graduate in America stands tall.

All the more intriguing, therefore, are the observations that many of those persons who enter two-year and four-year collegiate organizations depart without finishing their courses of study, indeed often leaving within the first year of study (Braxton, Sullivan, and Johnson 1997). It is surprising that, despite the social desirability of attaining a degree, many of those who leave appear to depart the college and university scene completely. Tinto (1993) writes: "Of the nearly 2.4 million students who in 1993 entered higher education for the first time, over 1.5 million will leave their first institutions without ever completing a degree. Of those, approximately 1.1 million will leave higher education altogether, without ever completing either a two- or four-year degree program" (p. 1).

Since going to college is a well institutionalized feature of our society, it is hard to understand why the second step of staying in school (and "holding" students in school) does not seem to be burdened with an equally firm set of normative, economic, and psychological imperatives. The departure puzzle, in short, is a fascinating and mysterious puzzle in institutional theorizing. How can our understandings of the new institutionalism possibly explain such two opposing sides of college attendance—going to and departure from an institution? In examining these two sides of college attendance from the perspective of new institutional theorizing, we ask two central questions and offer some recommendations for future research around a third.

1. Is retention in school an inadequately institutionalized feature of higher education?

Much of the inquiry to date into college student departure (heavily based upon Tinto's theoretical work) would suggest that (unlike going to college) the act of persisting in college may not yet have been adequately institutionalized. Tinto's (1993) adaptive (or "interactionalist") model asks students to make a "transition to college" and "an adjustment to the new world of the college." Although students enter colleges with their own attributes, observes Tinto, it is "what goes on after entry [that] matters more," for the "interactional attributes" (the academic and social communities) of the colleges "have much to do with the eventual leaving of many of their students" (Tinto 1993, p. 136).

It stands to reason, then, that some "principles" of effective student retention would seek to assure students of organizational concerns for their welfare, for the fulfillment of their personal goals, and for their integration "into the mainstream of the social and intellectual life of the institution" (Tinto 1993, p. 147). Indeed, many of the specific mechanisms for student retention (around such principles) have now (isomorphically) become rather common elements in higher education's organizational landscape—including improved preentry information systems, orientation programs, social/academic support programs, early-warning systems, and concerted efforts toward creating a sense of community on college campuses.

From the interactionalist perspective that underlies the Tinto model, a persistence of student departure (despite administrative efforts to blend individual and college attributes) may reflect an adaptive effort that has yet failed to jell. Principles of retention have been recognized and activities/programs established; however, the match of societal expectations and organizational conformity that would place staying in college on a par with going to college has failed to achieve an equally institutionalized sense of value.

It is interesting that much the same point has been made by one of the sharpest critics of Tinto's model, William Tierney (1992a). Tierney argues that the language of interaction and integration is a language of conformity to a dominant or mainstream organizational culture, generally giving little attention to group differences. Indeed, the focus of Tinto's (1993) model upon the assimilation of individuals into college cultures tends to downplay the differing experiences of cultural groups—perhaps, as Braxton, Sullivan, and Johnson (1997) put it, thereby underestimating "the cultural cost of integration to marginalized students" (p. 153).

In short, a failure to retain could very well represent an inadequate institutionalization in higher education of societal diversity, multiculturalism, and emerging divisions of power (Tierney 1992a) in ways that would be consistent with a more varied set of environmental expectations and values than are currently recognized. Hauptman and Smith (1994, p. 90) have reported, for example, that with socioeconomic background and college "preparedness" held constant, some 55.8 percent of whites in the graduating high school class of 1980 had persisted in school toward bachelor's degree completion by 1986. Comparable degree completion rates for African Americans and Hispanics by 1986 were, respectively, 30.3 percent and 32.3 percent.

A similar but even more cynical conclusion, around retention as an inadequately institutionalized feature of higher education, would ask whether many of the trappings of college and university efforts to retard departure tend to be just that—i.e., symbolic efforts to publicly legitimize through a demonstration of political correctness, with little that extends deeply into the structures and lifeways of the organization. Much of the student welcoming, support, and intervention structure of the typical university tends to be rather marginalized, inhabited by staff who must engage in ongoing battles to integrate more effectively their units and services into the core culture.

To be sure, on the individual organizational level there is much variation and choice, as will be discussed later in this chapter. An institutionalized feature, even under isomorphic pressures, does not mean absolute sameness. Colleges and universities do differ in their departure rates, and colleges do differ in their capacities and in their collective will to maneuver successfully toward enhanced retention, within the larger institutional environment. In some organizations the trappings of departure restraint may have left their symbolic and marginalized conditions, with influence upon the departure problem. Nevertheless, a second piece of the puzzle, below, would suggest that individual organizational deviation has not yet altered a long, historical feature of the problem.

2. Is student departure an institutionalized feature of higher education?

Vincent Tinto (1982) has presented some remarkable evidence indicating that the rates of student attrition from higher education in the United States have "remained strikingly constant over the past 100 years." Rates of dropout, he noted, "have remained at about 45 percent," and dropout "has remained stable despite the marked growth and alteration in the character of the higher educational system" (p. 694). He concluded: "As a national phenomenon, attrition has been a surprisingly stable feature of the higher educational enterprise. It is unlikely to be significantly altered without some massive changes in both the structure and functioning of higher education in the United States" (p. 693).

It would be difficult to find more intriguing evidence than this of the possibility that student departure from higher education, in its constancy, is itself institutionalized. Tinto (1982, p. 693) warns that "massive changes in . . . structure and functioning" may be necessary if the dropout rate is to be altered; and he suggests conservativeness in our predictions of significant change—indications again of a sense that the departure puzzle may be sufficiently enduring to warrant identification as one of the most deeply structured of characteristics in American schooling.

The central difficulty, however, in considering departure as an institutionalized characteristic is that student departure is an outcome. But an outcome of what? What are some of the core attributes of college and university organizations, and of their social environments, that (in their own institutionalization) link well with departure? Put another way, while recent theorizing stresses the stability of institutional components, and a homogeneity of organizations around such components (see Kraatz and Zajac 1996), are there some long-term and possibly persistent structures in higher education that may tend to communicate a departure thrust?

With a few notable exceptions (particularly Burton R. Clark's *The Open Door College* [1960b]), this is not a question that has received much scholarly attention. Indeed, as the Braxton, Sullivan, and Johnson (1997) review of the departure literature indicates, and with decidedly mixed results from the empirical work thus far, there is a need for much more research into linkages between organizational characteristics and student persistence. With further research called for, we can at best interpret and speculate about a possible institutionalization of departure from pieces here and there in the extant literature.

We suggest below two potential core attributes of higher education organizations that may assist in structuring an institutionalized departure-thrust into higher education. These are both gleaned from David Kamens's (1977) discussion of the role of "legitimating myths" in a structuring of higher education. Kamens's article was a first effort to bring some earlier, "classical" work in higher education (e.g., Newcombe 1943; Jencks and Riesman 1969; Bowles 1972; Blau 1973) to bear on "the social meaning attributed to university attendance for understanding organizational structure and development" (Kamens 1977, p. 217). The term "myth" is used by Kamens to denote some basic elements in the organizational belief system that helped to legitimize higher education as a system and are now structural properties of the field. We will drop the rather confusing term, however, and discuss two of Kamens's categories as structural properties at the organizational level.

A Legitimating Property: Selectivity

Astin argues that excellence in American higher education has been traditionally equated with either the academic reputation of an institution or the resources it accumulates. These resources are measured by money, faculty, research productivity, or higher-ability students. Astin argues that this traditional view of excellence results from the hierarchical nature of the higher-education system. While the American higher-education system is large, diverse, complex, and decentralized, it is remarkably homogeneous (Astin 1985). This homogeneity can be seen in similar approaches to undergraduate curricula, remarkable similarity in the training and preparation of faculty, and similar administrative structures.

These forces have led to the development of a highly refined status hierarchy in higher education comprised of a few well-known institutions at the top, a bigger group of institutions with more modest reputations in the middle, and the largest group of institutions at the bottom of the hierarchy that remain virtually unknown outside of their geographic regions (Astin 1985). Research indicates that the single best predictor of an institution's place in the hierarchy of institutions is its selectivity (or average score of the entering freshman class on the SAT) (Astin and Henson 1977). Hence, we see why students come to be viewed as a resource that will enhance an institution's reputation.

Kamens (1977) pulled all of this downward deeply into the core of what higher education organizations are "all about." It was Kamens's argument that a number of organizational structures are vital to "legitimating the idea" that students have been changed by their school experiences "independent of any actual changes" (p. 209). Among the major legitimating strategies, he argued, is the idea of selectivity—buttressed historically by "internal selection processes" that establish collegiate reputations "as highly competitive, meritocratic institutions" (p. 212). He observed:

"Flunking out large numbers of students and creating the myth of the freshman year are examples of the devices used to establish this idea among clients" (p. 212).

Although there are increased efforts today to mute the rigor and terrors of the freshman year, Tinto (1993) notes that "the largest proportion of institutional leaving" continues to occur "in that year and prior to the beginning of the second year" (p. 14). To be sure, the leaving rates vary by race, class, gender, and ethnicity (Astin 1982, 1986; Baker and Velez 1996; National Center for Education Statistics (NCES) 1997) as well as by type of institution (Allen, Epps, and Haniff 1991). However, this diversity is wrapped heavily in questions and concerns about a continuing "internal selection process" in higher education that reflects a strong historical bias toward meritocratic values (Astin 1982). "The most 'dropout-prone' freshmen," observes Astin (1986), "are those with poor academic records in high school, low aspirations, poor study habits, relatively uneducated parents, and small town backgrounds" (p. 45). The fact that student departure rates fall as admissions selectivity increases (Tinto 1993) reinforces the power of selectivity as a key value (in organizational legitimation)—above the value of student retention.

Jencks and Riesman (1968) observed three decades ago that "one of the central functions of higher education—along with providing jobs for scholars—is to control access to the upper-middle social strata." They argued further that "since demand for upper-middle class jobs and living standards far exceeds the supply, colleges must (in Erving Goffman's terminology) cool out large numbers of youngsters whose ambitions exceed their ability" (p. 99). Indeed, despite a decided lowering of job-entry expectations for college graduates, the issue of selectivity/meritocracy still appears to be well institutionalized in U.S. education—sufficiently so for Clark (1960a) to have noted a special societal function of cooling-out, as a specific role for the community college. The same issue prompted Brint and Karabel (1989) to write much later of continuing goal-definition struggles within the community college sector between training students for a selective transition into further higher education versus direct training for non-college-graduate employment.

In short, the evidence is that selectivity serves the goal of retention. Selectivity is also a property at the heart of organizational reputation and hence legitimation (Astin and Henson 1977). It is even deeply enough embedded in larger structures of social mobility, within our nation, to warrant the development of some organizations that traditionally have opened access opportunities broadly to the college-interested but have also simultaneously "cooled" many of them out. Turned on its head, then, selectivity as an institutionalized property of organizational legitimation around retention also tends to serve as a property of organizational legitimation around departure.

A Legitimating Property: Residentiality

A second, key idea identified by Kamens (1977) comes with a catch-all label, "residentiality." To be sure, not all of higher education includes the act of actually living in college residence units. Indeed there are many commuter colleges and universities with few opportunities to actually be in-residence institutions. Commuter schools tend to have rather high departure rates, but actual residence in the student-housing sense is not the narrow focus here.

There is a deeper symbolic value to the phenomenon of residency that cuts thoroughly into the history of higher education. On the one hand, notes Thelin (1982, p. 29), it has to do with a staking out of a "distinctive corporate identity" and an "institutionalization of scholarship" during the Middle Ages (complete with special privileges, a charter, licenses, seals, colors, etc.). On the other hand, it establishes symbolically a transfer of socialization authority (over students) to the school and "establishes the credibility of the claim that intense socialization is actually occurring and is under the control of the school" (Kamens 1977, p. 213).

The construct of residentiality, argues Kamens (1977), identifies the symbolic role of the college in "*removing* students physically and socially from membership and participation" in an earlier "everyday life," affirming in its place an "identity-conferring ability of the college" (p. 213). Tinto's (1993) model discusses much the same phenomenon as a "rite of passage" in higher education—with stages of separation from past associations, of transition into new memberships, and of full incorporation or integration into a culture of new association(s). "Having moved away from the norms and behavioral patterns of past associations," observes Tinto (1993), a person "now faces the problem of finding and adopting new ones appropriate to the college setting" (p. 98). Persistence is not assured; "not all new students come to be incorporated into the life of the institution" (Tinto 1993, p. 99).

Tierney (1992a) and Attinasi (1994) have expressed their difficulty with the one-best-culture assumptions accompanying the rite-of-passage construct. Indeed, Attinasi (1994) suggests that the college participation process is better described as a "territorial passage," a trip across "both physical and cultural boundaries, enter[ing] institutions of higher education as strangers" (p. 7).

It is interesting that the notions of territory, boundary, and "stranger" seem quite consistent with Kamens's (1977) earlier notion of residentiality—with its own language of removal, intensity, a socialization of "recruits," and identity-conferring structures. The negotiation of residence as a stranger in totally new territory is a theme that emerges fairly often in the extant literature. Again, actual residence in the strict sense is not the feature here—although, to be sure, residential colleges and universities do tend to fare better in retention. The feature here is the larger sense of learning the ropes of residentiality, which leaves much room for departure—for learning the ropes of residentiality is not always easily achieved. Along these lines, Tinto (1993) observes: "Though some institutions have established freshmen-year programs, it is still the case that most new students are left to make their own way through the maze of institutional life. They, like the many generations of students before them, have to learn the ropes of college life largely on their own" (p. 99).

Similarly, in a historical examination of higher education, John R. Thelin (1982) has noted: "One searches in vain for cases where programs designed to promote proximity among students and faculty achieved enduring success" (p. 162). Likewise, in discussing the possibility of an "incongruence" between students and their college settings, Tinto (1993) writes: "it is evident that student interaction with faculty appears to play a central role in individual judgments of intellectual congruence" (p. 53). Further, he observes: "Departure also arises from individual isolation, specifically from the absence of sufficient contact between the individual and other members of the social and academic communities of the college" (pp. 55–56).

From an institutional-theory perspective, the power of residentiality in retention and socialization achieved is well attested to in those organizational structures which do appear to support persistence. Astin (1986) summarizes: "The pattern of choices that maximizes the student's chances of finishing college comprises attendance at either a private university or a public four-year college, living on campus in a dormitory or fraternity or sorority house, a part-time job on campus, scholarship or grant support, membership in campus organizations or participation in extracurricular activities, deferring marriage, and the best grades possible" (p. 174). Indeed, the power of these forces and of residency itself for those who begin higher education at the community college level is noted by Baker and Velez (1996), who cite Dougherty (1994): "Critics claim that community colleges actually hinder their students from transferring to four-year colleges because they often lack supportive student peer groups and dormitories and usually have an antiacademic atmosphere in which the faculty have low expectations of their students" (Baker and Velez 1996, pp. 90–91).

On the other hand, the power of residentiality as a structured property in student departure is attested to in evidence that the foreign territory of the college is typically replete with deeply institutionalized elements that may prolong stranger-ness and that may preserve both noncontact and an intellectual incongruence between students and faculty. Indeed, the territorial passage may well be most problematic for those who see another idea (of equalized opportunity through higher education) as becoming one of society's priority values. As Astin (1982, p. 25) has phrased it, the educational "pipeline" in America experiences serious and disturbing "leakage" at the college stage—in that large numbers of minority-group members do not persist to degree completion (see also Justiz, Wilson, and Björk 1994). Tellingly, Tinto (1993) concludes, on the same topic: "Having the requisite skills for persistence is one thing. Being able to apply them in perhaps strange, unfriendly settings is another" (p. 73).

3. Might the puzzle of student departure be mitigated by structural or strategic choice toward retention in higher education?

One major focus in institutional theorizing has been on the phenomenon of mimetic behavior—that is, the tendency of organizations to mirror dominant practices in their institutional fields. New institutional thinking has hypothesized that "organizations seek legitimacy and obtain it by conforming to prevailing institutional norms for practice" (Goodrick and Salancik 1996, p. 1). Isomorphic forces have been discovered at work in higher education in research into budgetary retrenchment (Gates 1997); publication productivity (Dey, Milem, and Berger 1997); academic research cultures (Finnegan and Gamson 1996); faculty reward structures (Fairweather 1993); and fund-raising (Harris 1990).

However, institutional theorizing is also very much interested in examining and understanding organizational discretion. The realization is that despite the press toward mimicry, individual organizations can be expected to exercise varying degrees of strategic choice (in responding to their own special environments). Views differ on how much discussion of strategic choice is possible, however, and just what the outcome-producing power of discretion might be, amid the pressures of isomorphism. An opportunity is at hand, we would suggest, for some significant advances in understanding the choice-amid-mimicry side of institutionalized organizations—through further research into the retention/departure puzzle.

It is interesting that despite attempts by colleges to advertise and to compete a bit vis-à-vis retention, there is little in the extant literature on specific discretionary and strategic choices around this value. There is evidence, of course, that student departure tends to vary by institutional sector, with commuter and two-year colleges displaying poorer retention rates than four-year colleges and universities (Tinto 1993; Baker and Velez 1996; NCES 1997). There is also evidence that even when there is a weighting for differing entry characteristics, student retention rates can vary in accordance with such basic institutional qualities as public or private, sectarian or nonsectarian. Dey and Astin (1989) note, for example: "A student entering a private university is almost twice as likely to complete a bachelor's degree within four years as is one entering a public college (53.5 versus 23.3 percent)" (p. 3). It would appear, then, that the sector itself may carry a set of heavy constraints, within which there may be very different and often only limited opportunities for organizational choice or maneuver.

Recognizably, the community college sector has been caught directly on the horns of a strategic choice dilemma. Community colleges are credited with serving as agents for channeling students away from more elite educational and career opportunities and lowering their aspirations to control entry into professional and managerial occupations. Institutions "cool out" students, according to Clark (1960a), or institutionally "manage ambition," according to Brint and Karabel (1989). Nonretention here is a strategic (possibly institutionalized) organizational choice.

Nevertheless, community colleges, often called "democracy's colleges," have also taken seriously the responsibility of providing educational opportunities to the masses through their open-access admissions policies—a claim four-year institutions cannot make (Cohen and Brawer 1996). Students of all ages and socioeconomic backgrounds continue to take advantage of academic and vocational programmatic offerings, often with the intent of gaining the skills and knowledge they need but not necessarily completing a certificate, an associate degree, or transfer requirements. More significantly, in responding to community needs community colleges recognize that *not* all students enter with the intent to complete programmatic requirements but rather to take specific, limited courses that meet their personal and/or professional goals. Hence, the expectation that all students who enroll in community college will and should be retained until they complete associate degree requirements is a false expectation; nonretention here is a choice (perhaps a "demand") variable in quite another direction.

Vitally underexplored at this time is just how an intersection of strategic choices at the organizational level might operate against strategic choices at the individual/vocational level. Departure, reentry, job preparation, skills improvement, and near or full completion versus cooling-out, termination of study, and noncompletion are dynamics heavily at work in the community college sector, with decidedly little evidence thus far regarding the structural choices colleges could make to affect these dynamics.

Perhaps the closest the bulk of literature comes to identifying clearly a "strategic choice" variable in student retention in higher education is in Dey and Astin's (1989) comparisons by institutional selectivity. The authors summarize: "With few exceptions, the higher the selectivity of an institution (as measured by admissions test scores) the higher the retention rate" (Dey and Astin 1989, p. 3). Similarly, Tinto (1993) observes: "It is quite apparent that higher selectivity is associated with lower rates of first-year attrition among beginning full-time students. For instance, the most selective institutions lose only 8.0 percent of their beginning full-time students before the start of the second year whereas open-enrollment institutions lose 45.5 percent of their full-time students" (p. 16).

However, just as Dey and Astin (1989) mention some "exceptions," Tinto (1993) also goes on to indicate that within any category of selectivity there is "a wide range of institutional rates of first-year attrition." He summarizes: "Though highly selective institutions, as a group, have the lowest rate of first-year attrition, not all institutions in that group have lower rates of attrition than do all institutions in the next lower category of selectivity" (p. 16).

As a second, key question in understanding strategic choice: Just what are the "exceptions," the attrition outliers; and what organizational structures/strategies might possibly connect with a beyond-expectancy rate of student retention? Although the information to date is from shaky to nonexistent in answering such outlier questions, it is interesting that scholars analyzing different parts of the higher-education scene do discuss the saliency of common strategizing themes. Tinto (1993), for example, draws specific attention to the importance of informal faculty contact with students—particularly contacts "seen as warm, receptive, and wide-ranging in character, that is, not restricted solely to the formalities of academic work."

He concludes: "Rewarding contact with them [the faculty] is an essential element in student development" (p. 166).

Similarly, in a national study of black college students Allen, Epps, and Haniff (1991) present some evidence of comparatively higher retention rates among predominately black colleges—while simultaneously observing that student involvement, participation, and contact with faculty tend to be unusually strong on traditionally black campuses. Additionally, Davis (1991) observes: "Black students on white campuses who have good relations with faculty have never seriously considered dropping out of school and have greater satisfaction with their campus lives" (p. 154). And Kidwell (1992), Tierney (1992b), and others address the successes of tribal colleges in retaining Native American students, numbers of whom may already have dropped out of mainstream higher education. In language differing little from Tinto's, in describing one college Tierney (1992b) notes: "In keeping with tribal traditions and expectations, organizational participants at Home College promote a learning environment where the success of all students is of primary concern. In doing so, participants enable students to develop strong social bonds with other constituents of the college and thus enhance their chances for success" (p. 124).

It is fascinating that while contact could be emerging as importantly strategic in student retention, it could well be losing power as an institutionalized characteristic of higher education. In recent large-data-set research Milem, Berger, and Dey (1997) discovered that faculty members in nearly every category of higher education (e.g., research universities, doctoral universities, comprehensive institutions, liberal arts colleges, two-year colleges) are spending *more* of their time engaged in both research *and* teaching. The authors also discovered that the added time devoted to teaching and research could be at the cost of "the time that faculty spend advising students and in other out-of-class contact with students." They summarize: "Across all institutions there was a statistically significant decrease in the amount of time faculty spent advising and counseling students" (Milem, Berger, and Dey 1997, p. 14).

Summary and Conclusion

Questions such as the above offer significant promise in extending a knowledge of the discretionary side of the institutionalization construct. The exceptions, or the outliers, in student retention offer a unique opportunity to explore a little-known side of organizational theorizing wherein deep and persistent structures of organizational behavior, often seemingly impermeable or inviolate, may indeed be found to be manipulable after all, with significant outcome consequences.

We have suggested that student departure (or from an organizational perspective, the phenomenon of nonretention) may well be an institutionalized characteristic of higher education. Institutionalized characteristics tend to be those that are widely shared among members of the same field of organizations and indeed may often be products of organizational mimicry or isomorphism. Institutionalized characteristics also tend to be connected to some deeply structured qualities of organizations—part of that which is taken for granted or the way things are organizationally. These characteristics often tend to persist over time, despite concerted efforts toward change. Although persistent, institutionalized characteristics also tend, nevertheless, to be at the cutting edge of adaptive issues between organizations and their environments—often as key elements in ongoing negotiations of legitimacy with those environments. Indeed, student departure would likely receive much less attention as a puzzle were it not for the broadly shared sense in higher education that retention is increasingly a matter of public-relations concern.

Despite its possible role in legitimization, the puzzle of student departure could very well reflect an inadequate institutionalization to date of those organizational mechanisms that serve effectively to integrate, or bring a sense of membership (Hurtado and Carter 1997), to potentially departing students. Indeed, such mechanisms and the personnel in charge of them may often be marginalized in the organization. On the other hand, as a second observation, student departure may be an institutionalized feature of higher education, reflecting deep organizational cultures of after-admission selectivity and a negotiate-thy-own-way tradition of socialization into the college community. It is also possible, finally, that isomorphic forces in the student retention realm have been held at bay by some categories of higher-education organizations—organizations departing at some peril from powerful sets of homogenizing forces, with patterns of outlier behavior that are yet poorly appreciated and understood to date in retention inquiry.

Curiously, it is the behavior of these outlier organizations (vis-à-vis student retention) that may soon prove to be of central theoretical interest in the further use and development of new institutional analyses of higher education. There have been few studies thus far of what Kraatz and Zajac (1996) label "illegitimate" organizational behavior and change in higher education. These would be behaviors or changes in ways that are contrary to the demands of the institutional environment. Prevailing hypotheses are that organizations acting in institutionally illegitimate or nonisomorphic ways will tend to suffer harmful consequences.

While the numbers are small and the evidence thus far is not well focused, there are indications that many historically black colleges and universities (HBCUs) have resisted higher education's homogenizing tendencies (see Berger 1997). As mentioned earlier, there is some evidence that, when there are controls for both college size and selectivity, African American students who attend HBCUs are decidedly *more likely* to complete their degrees (Astin, Tsui, and Avalos 1996). Indeed, HBCUs do not experience the negative effects on retention that are "associated with other (nonblack) colleges that also happen to be nonselective" (Astin, Tsui, and Avalos 1996, p. 30). Astin and his colleagues conclude, enigmatically, that there is "something about the HBCUs' environment that enables them to overcome the usual negative effects that characterize most other nonselective institutions" (Astin, Tsui, and Avalos 1996, p. 30).

What that "something" is or might be remains very much a part of the puzzle surrounding student departure. Again, in many ways the entire community college sector is itself an outlier. Increasingly to be found are community college programs that advocate a celebratory, bidirectional socialization process (Van Maanen 1984; Rhoads and Valadez 1996; Tierney 1997; Laden 1998). These typically incorporate culturally specific curricula which have been especially successful in retaining students of color. Certainly, tribally controlled community colleges and historically black- and Hispanic-serving two-year colleges are noted as the gateways into higher education for many students of color. Faculty mentoring, financial aid, and alternative methods of education that focus on the culture, philosophy, and history of these students are believed to add to students' sense of self-worth and beliefs that they belong and are capable of academic success at the institution and beyond (Justiz, Wilson, and Björk 1994; Townsend 1999).

That there may indeed be "something" in this, in instructive ways for new institutional theorizing, can also be gleaned from work on Latino students' college experiences. Hurtado and Carter (1997) discovered that a sense of belonging within the college culture is much strengthened for Latino students if there is a redefined notion of residentiality at work—with on-campus socialization joining a strong sense of belonging—and maintained in external-to-campus affiliations, particularly social-community and religious organizations. The authors conclude: "Perhaps one reason why Latino students who belong to these organizations have a stronger sense of belonging is because they maintained connections with these external campus communities that they were familiar with before they entered college" (Hurtado and Carter 1997, p. 338).

In sum, it may be from such outlier and institutionally illegitimate circumstances as these that we begin to learn something about the structural choices necessary to improve student retention. On a larger scale, the strategies of the outliers may well suggest a need for renewed attention generally to questions of organizational boundaries and their management—a question at the heart of Theodore Mitchell's (1997) recent work. External demands, notes Mitchell, once buffered and deflected as much as possible, are now tending to reach deeply into the lifeways and fundamental structures of higher education. Higher education is now having to learn to bridge as much as it buffers. All of this, he concludes, is contributing to a "muddying of the university's identity," as new institutional linkages are now in order "between the internal life of the university and the demands of society" (Mitchell 1997, p. 289).

References

Allen, W. R., E. G. Epps, and N. Z. Haniff (eds.). 1991. *College in black and white.* Albany: State University of New York Press.

Astin, A. W. 1982. *Minorities in American higher education.* San Francisco: Jossey-Bass.

Astin, A. W. 1985. *Achieving educational excellence: A critical assessment of priorities and practices in higher education.* San Francisco: Jossey-Bass.

Astin, A. W. 1986. *Preventing students from dropping out.* San Francisco: Jossey-Bass.

Astin, A. W., and J. W. Henson. 1977. New measures of college selectivity. *Research in Higher Education* 6 (September): 1–9.

Astin, A. W., L. Tsui, and J. Avalos. 1996. *Degree attainment rates at American colleges and universities: Effects of race, gender, and institutional type.* Report by the Higher Education Research Institute, Graduate School of Education, University of California, Los Angeles, September.

Attinasi, L. C., Jr. 1994. Is going to college a rite of passage? Paper presented at the annual meeting of the American Educational Research Association (AERA), New Orleans, La., April.

Baker, T. L., and W. Velez. 1996. Access to and opportunity in postsecondary education in the United States: A review. *Sociology of Education:* 82–101.

Berger, J. B. 1997. The relationship between organizational behavior at colleges and student outcomes: Generating a quantitatively grounded theory. Ph.D. diss., Department of Educational Leadership, Peabody College, Vanderbilt University.

Blau, P. 1973. *The organization of academic work.* New York: Wiley.

Braxton, J. M., A. V. Sullivan, and R. M. Johnson, Jr. 1997. Appraising Tinto's theory of student departure. In J. C. Smart (ed.), *Higher education: A handbook of theory and research,* vol. 12, pp. 107–164. New York: Agathon Press.

Brint, S., and J. Karabel. 1989. *The diverted dream: Community colleges and the promise of educational opportunity in America, 1900–1985.* New York: Oxford University Press.

Clark, B. R. 1960a. The "cooling-out function" in higher education. *American Journal of Sociology* 65: 569–576.

Clark, B. R. 1960b. *The open door college: A case study.* New York: McGraw-Hill.

Cohen, A. M., and F. B. Brawer. 1996. *The American community college.* 3d ed. San Francisco: Jossey-Bass.

Covaleski, M. A., and M. W. Dirsmith. 1988. An institutional perspective on the rise, social transformation, and fall of a university budget category. *Administration Science Quarterly* 33: 562–587.

Davis, R. B. 1991. Social support networks and undergraduate student-success-related outcomes: A comparison of black students on black and white campuses. In W. R. Allen, E. G. Epps, and N. Z. Haniff (eds.), *College in black and white,* pp. 143–157. Albany: State University of New York Press.

Dey, E. L., and A. W. Astin. 1989. *Predicting college student retention: Comparative national data from the 1982 freshman class.* Report of the Higher Education Research Institute, Graduate School of Education, University of California, Los Angeles, March.

Dey, E. L., J. F. Milem, and J. B. Berger. 1997. Changing patterns of publication: Accumulative advantage or institutional isomorphism? *Sociology of Education* 70 (October): 308–323.

DiMaggio, P. J., and W. W. Powell. 1991a. Introduction. In W. W. Powell and P. J. DiMaggio (eds.), *The new institutionalism in organizational analysis,* pp. 1–38. Chicago: University of Chicago Press.

DiMaggio, P. J., and W. W. Powell. 1991b. The iron cage revisited: Institutional isomorphism and collective rationality in organizational fields. In W. W. Powell and P. J. DiMaggio (eds.), *The new institutionalism in organizational analysis,* pp. 63–82. Chicago: University of Chicago Press.

Dougherty, K. J. 1994. *The contradictory college: The conflicting origins impacts and futures of the community college.* Albany: State University of New York Press.

Fairweather, J. S. 1993. Faculty reward structures: Toward institutional and professional homogenization. *Research in Higher Education* 34 (5): 603–623.

Finnegan, D. E., and Z. F. Gamson. 1996. Disciplinary adaptations to research culture in comprehensive institutions. *Review of Higher Education* 19 (2): 141–177.

Gates, G. S. 1997. Isomorphism, homogeneity, and rationalism in university retrenchment. *Review of Higher Education* 20 (3): 253–275.

Goodrick, E., and G. R. Salancik. 1996. Organizational discretion in responding to institutional practices: Hospitals and cesarean births. *Administrative Science Quarterly* 41 (1): 1–28.

Harris, J. T. 1990. Private support for public, doctorate-granting universities: Building a theoretical base. *Review of Higher Education* 13 (4): 519–538.

Hauptman, A., and P. Smith. 1994. Financial aid strategies for improving minority student participation in higher education. In M. J. Justiz, R. Wilson, and L. G. Björk (eds.), *Minorities in higher education,* pp. 78–106. Phoenix, Ariz.: American Council on Education and Oryx Press.

Hunter, B. (ed.). 1997. *The statesman's yearbook.* New York: Macmillan.

Hurtado, S., and D. F. Carter. 1997. Effects of college transition and perceptions of the campus racial climate on Latino college students' sense of belonging. *Sociology of Education* 70 (October): 324–345.

Jencks, C., and D. Riesman. 1968. *The academic revolution.* Garden City, N.Y.: Doubleday.

Justiz, M. J., R. Wilson, and L. G. Björk. 1994. *Minorities in higher education.* Phoenix, Ariz.: American Council on Education and Oryz Press.

Kamens, D. H. 1977. Legitimating myths and educational organization: The relationship between organizational ideology and formal structure. *American Sociological Review* 42 (April): 208–219.

Kidwell, C. S. 1992. Higher education issues in Native American communities. In D. J. Carter and R. Wilson (eds.), *Minorities in higher education,* pp. 239–257. Washington, D.C.: American Council on Education.

Kraatz, M. S., and E. J. Zajac. 1996. Exploring the limits of the new institutionalism: The causes and consequences of illegitimate organizational change. *American Sociological Review* 65 (5): 812–836.

Laden, B. V. 1998. An organizational response to welcoming students of color. In J. S. Levin (ed.), *A riddle or a sea of change?: Organizational change in the community college. New directions for community colleges,* pp. 102, 31–41. San Francisco: Jossey-Bass.

Meyer, J. W., and R. Rowan. 1977. Institutionalized organizations: Formal organizations as myth and ceremony. *American Journal of Sociology* 83: 340–363.

Meyer, M. W., and L. G. Zucker (eds.). 1989. *Permanently failing organizations.* Newbury Park, Calif.: Sage Publications.

Milem, J. F., J. B. Berger, and E. L. Dey. 1997. Faculty time allocation: A longitudinal study of change. Paper presented at the annual meeting of the Association for the Study of Higher Education (ASHE), Albuquerque, N.M., November.

Mitchell, T. R. 1997. Border crossings: Organizational boundaries and challenges to the American professoriate. *Daedalus* 126 (4): 265–292.

National Center for Education Statistics (NCES). 1997. *Findings from the condition of education 1997: Postsecondary persistence and attainment.* No. 13. Washington, D.C.: U.S. Department of Education.

Newcombe, T. 1943. *Personality and social change.* New York: Holt.

Rhoads, R. A., and J. R. Valadez. 1996. *Democracy, multiculturalism, and the community college.* New York: Garland Publishing, Inc.

Rudolph, F. 1962. *The American college and university.* New York: Knopf.

Scott, W. R. 1987. The adolescence of institutional theory. *Administrative Science Quarterly* 32 (4): 493–511.

Selznick, P. 1957. *Leadership in administration.* New York: Harper & Row.

Snyder, T. (ed.). 1993. *120 years of American education: A statistical portrait.* Washington, D.C.: U.S. Department of Education, Office of Educational Research and Improvement, National Center for Educational Statistics.

Statistical Abstracts of the United States. 1996. *The national databook.* Austin, Tex.: Hoover's Business Press.

Thelin, J. R. 1982. *Higher education and its useful past.* Rochester, Vt.: Schenkman Books.

Tierney, W. G. 1992a. An anthropological analysis of student participation in college. *Journal of Higher Education* 63 (6): 603–618.

Tierney, W. G. 1992b. *Official encouragement, institutional discouragement: Minorities in academe—the Native American experience.* Norwood, N.J.: Ablex.

Tierney, W. G. 1997. Organizational socialization in higher education. *Journal of Higher Education* 68 (1): 1–16.

Tinto, V. 1982. Limits of theory and practice in student attrition. *Journal of Higher Education* 53 (6): 687–700.

Tinto, V. 1993. *Leaving college: Rethinking the causes and cures of student attrition.* 2d ed. Chicago: University of Chicago Press.

Townsend, B. K. (ed.). 1999. *Two-year colleges for women and minorities.* New York: Garland Publishing, Inc.

Van Maanen, J. 1984. Doing new things in old ways: The chains of socialization. In J. L. Bess (ed.), *College and university organization: Insights from the behavioral sciences,* pp. 211–247. New York: New York University Press.

Zajac, E. J., and M. S. Kraatz. 1993. A diametric forces model of strategic change: Assessing the antecedents and consequences of restructuring in the higher education industry. *Strategic Management Journal* 14: 83–102.

Zucker, L. G. 1987. Institutional theories of organization. *Annual Review of Sociology* 13: 443–464.

Conclusion

Reinvigorating Theory and Research on the Departure Puzzle

John M. Braxton

The seventy-year history of research on the problem of college student departure belies the current state of knowledge and understanding of this phenomenon.* We are beginning to make substantial progress in our understanding of the roots of college student departure. Research testing Tinto's near-paradigmatic interactionalist theory has yielded robust empirical support for four logically interconnected propositions (Braxton, Sullivan, and Johnson 1997).** These four propositions take the following narrative form. Students enter college with various characteristics that affect their initial levels of commitment to the institutions in which they are enrolled. Their initial levels of commitment also affect their levels of commitment (subsequent commitment) to their institutions that form as a consequence of attendance. Their levels of subsequent institutional commitment are also positively influenced by their degree of integration into the social communities of the college or university. Moreover, the greater their degree of

---

*The study of college student departure has been the object of research for over seventy years as evidenced by reviews of literature by Summerskill (1962), Tinto (1975), and Pantages and Creedon (1978).

**Aggregate support is based on all tests of a given proposition. Thus, tests carried out in different types of colleges and universities and different groups of students are included. Empirical support was defined as strong if 66 percent or more of three or more tests of a proposition was statistically significant. Put differently, strong affirmation also means that support for a given proposition was replicated in two-thirds or more empirical tests of it.

subsequent institutional commitment, the greater the likelihood of student persistence in college.

These empirically rooted relationships are logically interconnected and occur in a logical, temporal sequence. Moreover, these four vigorously empirically backed relationships constitute reliable knowledge that partially explains the college student departure process. Our knowledge and understanding remain incomplete because social integration remains unexplained. As a consequence, Braxton, Sullivan, and Johnson (1997) recommend serious revision of Tinto's interactionalist theory.

In the introduction of this volume scholars are given the choice of seriously revising Tinto's theory or abandoning it and developing altogether new theoretical perspectives on college student departure. Although critics of Tinto's theory such as Attinasi (1989), Tierney (1992), and the authors of chapters in part 2 of this volume urge the development of new theoretical perspectives, it is my strong belief that Tinto's theory should be seriously revised and that the foundation for such revision should be the four reliable relationships described above. This assertion is made for two reasons. First, given the long history of inquiry on college student departure, it is fatuous to abandon four empirically reliable relationships that partially account for college student departure. Second, these four relationships fit two criteria for the construction of theory: the theory should include pertinent research findings, and the theory should account for research findings (Chafetz 1978; Schrag 1967).

Inductive Theory Revision

A proposal is put forth for the revision of Tinto's interactionalist theory that not only uses the four reliable relationships as an underpinning but also builds on economic, organizational, psychological, and sociological theoretical perspectives. The process advocated here occurs at two levels: the level of individual research studies, and the level of induction of underlying constructs from these individual research studies carried out using all four of the theoretical perspectives. At base, an inductive approach to the revision of Tinto's theory is advanced. Inductive theory construction begins with empirical research on a particular phenomenon (Wallace 1971). From various studies conducted on a focal phenomenon, patterns of generalizations and understandings emerge. Put differently, "conceptual factor analyses" of the findings of these empirical studies are conducted to derive new concepts, generalizations, and understandings. These concepts, generalizations, and understandings, in turn, provide the basis for the development of a formal theory amendable to empirical investigation. By extension, revision of an extant formal theory can occur through such an inductive process.*

More specifically, both qualitative and quantitative research methods are suggested for studying the influence of constructs obtained from differing theoretical perspectives on college student departure in general and social integration in particular. At one level this approach resembles theory elaboration given that constructs are derived from other theories to account for the focal phenomenon. However, the ultimate aim of empirical treatments of such "helper" theories is to develop a more powerful explanatory theory of college student departure. From the pattern of findings of such empirical treatments of differing theoretical orientations, scholars will be able to glean new concepts and generalizations that may be used either to revise Tinto's interactionalist theory or to formulate an entirely new theory of college student departure. As a consequence, this later process parallels theory integration, which entails the combination of two or more sets of logically connected propositions to form a larger set of interconnected propositions to create a new theory (Thornberry 1989). The distinction, however, is that the process recommended herein uses empirically supported constructs rather than constructs that may or may not have been subjected to empirical treatment. The foundation for either outcome would be the four empirically reliable relationships derived from the 1975 formulation of Tinto's theory.

Tinto (1986) recognizes the limits of his interactionalist theory and points to its failure to account for the influence of external communities (e.g., families, neighborhoods, and secondary schools) and organizational attributes of colleges and universities on college student departure decisions. Moreover, other scholars note its failure to adequately account for the effects of individual psychological processes (Eaton and Bean 1995) and economic forces such as student finances and financial aid (Cabrera, Stampen, and Hansen 1990; Cabrera, Nora, and Castañeda 1992).

Given such shortcomings, the process of inductive theory revision urged here should entail empirical investigations—qualitative and quantitative—that discern the influence of various constructs derived from   economic, organizational, psychological, and sociological theoretical frameworks on college student departure decisions in general and social integration in particular. Some possible empirical directions are suggested for

---

*Tinto's interactionalist theory, as formulated in 1975, offers an illustrative example of inductive theory construction.

each of these theoretical orientations. These directions are not meant to be exhaustive, but rather are offered with the intent of inviting scholars to identify other theoretical perspectives and concepts.

Economic

Cost/benefit analyses comprise the basis for economic theoretical perspectives on college student retention, as shown in chapter 2 of this volume by St. John, Cabrera, Nora, and Asker. Cost/benefit analyses entail a weighing of costs and benefits associated with remaining in a particular college or university. In chapter 2 the authors recommend that future studies of departure include such constructs as ability to pay, perceptions of aid, family resources, tuition, and student aid. Such constructs may directly influence social integration, institutional commitment, and departure decisions. In addition to pursuing these suggestions, scholars are urged to focus on the crux of the economic perspective: the cost/benefit analysis process. We need knowledge and understanding not only of the various types of costs and benefits used by students but also of how they weigh the costs and benefits of departing/remaining at a particular college or university. Without such knowledge, the ability of the economic perspective to contribute to the revision of Tinto's theory through inductive reasoning processes will not be realized.

Organizational

The influence of organizational characteristics and processes on college student departure characterizes the organizational perspective on college student departure (Tinto 1986, 1993). Organizational structure and organizational behavior provide distinctions for ways in which organizations affect students and their departure decisions (Berger and Braxton 1998). Tinto (1986) points to such structural properties of organizations as bureaucratic structure, institutional size, faculty-student ratios, and institutional resources and goals as organizational characteristics that might affect college student departure decisions. Other such characteristics include admissions selectivity and control. Empirical work using such structural characteristics of organizations and their effects on social integration and college student departure are necessary for the revision of Tinto's theory using the organizational perspective on retention.

The forms of organizational behavior that might affect social integration and college student departure decisions include the presidential and administrative styles of colleges and universities (Berger and Braxton 1998). Given that such styles affect students' adjustment to and satisfaction with college, presidential and administrative styles may influence the college student departure process (Astin and Scherrei 1980). The four models of organizational functioning that represent ideal types of colleges and universities—bureaucratic, collegial, political, and anarchical—described by Birnbaum (1988) may also be hypothesized to foster or impede social integration and student departure decisions. Research demonstrating the effects of these organizational models on various student outcomes (Berger 2000) strongly suggests such a hypothesis. In addition, research shows that such organizational attributes as institutional communication, fairness in the administration of rules and policies, and participation of students in decision making also exert influences on social integration and departure (Braxton and Brier 1989; Berger and Braxton 1998). In order to revise Tinto's theory using the organizational perspective, these various forms of organizational behavior should be the focus of empirical inquiries.

Regardless of whether organizational structure or behavior is the focus, scholars studying such effects on college student departure decisions need to conduct such inquiries in a wide range of colleges and universities. Although studying departure in a wide range of institutions is the desideratum of research on college student departure, it is particularly important to the study of the influence of organizational structure and behavior on college student departure because of the need to maximize the variability in structure and behavior of colleges and universities as organizations.

Psychological

The basic thrust of the psychological theoretical perspective on college student departure is to determine psychological characteristics and processes that distinguish persisters from departers (Tinto 1986, 1993). Psychological characteristics and processes occur at the levels of the individual and the environment. In chapter 3 of this volume Bean and Eaton describe four psychological theories: attitude-behavior theory, coping behavioral theory, self-efficacy theory, and attribution (locus of control) theory. From these four they construct a set of formulations that can serve as a "helper" theory to add explanatory power to the four strongly backed relationships of Tinto's theory.

In addition to these four psychological theories, biculturalism constitutes another psychological characteristic worthy of empirical treatment. In chapter 7 of this volume Rendón, Jalomo, and Nora assert that biculturalism and its antecedent bisocialization may play a role in the departure process for minority students. Biculturalism refers to the ability of minority individuals to learn and function simultaneously in both the predominately white culture and in the culture of their racial/ethnic group (Valentine 1971; Polgar 1960). As a consequence, biculturalism may influence the social integration and retention of college students who are members of racial/ethnic minority groups. Although scholars such as Rendón, Jalomo, and Nora view social integration as problematic for minority students, research demonstrates that social integration exerts a positive influence on the retention of students who are members of racial/ethnic minorities (Pascarella 1985; Stoecker, Pascarella, and Wolfle 1988; Nora and Cabrera 1996). Thus, social integration remains a viable construct for minority students despite the problematic assumptions underlying the notion of social integration.*

The influence of the process of dual socialization on biculturalism also needs investigation. Dual socialization is influenced by the extent to which two cultures overlap (de Anda 1984). Although dual socialization is sociological, it is presented here because it putatively affects biculturalism, a psychological construct. The six dimensions of dual socialization that may affect biculturalism, identified by de Anda (1984), are listed by Rendón, Jalomo, and Nora in chapter 7. Scholars are urged to study both the influences of the six dimensions on the biculturalism of students who are members of racial/ethnic minority groups and the role biculturalism plays in the college student departure process.

Other psychological perspectives meriting consideration are Astin's (1984) theory of involvement and such student development theories as Chickering (1969) and Chickering and Reisser's (1993) seven vectors of student development, Perry's (1970, 1981) scheme of intellectual and ethical development, King and Kitchener's (1994) reflective judgment model, and Baxter Magolda's (1992) formulations regarding the intellectual development of students. Milem and Berger (1997) show some support for the extension of Astin's theory of involvement to college student departure as they found that involvement with peers and involvement in social activities influence social integration, subsequent institutional commitment, and intent to reenroll. Sullivan (1996) also postulates that Chickering's seven vectors of student development and Perry's stages of cognitive and ethical development

---

*The problematic assumptions may be more apparent than real, as evidenced by a close inspection of the items measuring social integration. Social integration is typically measured using the "interactions with peer group" scale developed by Pascarella and Terenzini (1980). This scale assesses the degree of social affiliation a student experiences. Thus, the underlying assumptions of this scale do not assume the need for minority students to assimilate into the predominately white student social communities of a given college or university.

influence the departure decisions of college students in general and social integration in particular. Moreover, it seems reasonable that the formulations of King and Kitchener and Baxter-Magolda might also be extended to account for student departure in general and social integration in particular.

A key question regarding future research using the various psychological perspectives advanced herein is whether the influences of these psychological processes on student departure decisions are invariant across different types of colleges and universities and different student groups. In past research using the psychological perspective, the type of psychological characteristics that were influential were dependent on the setting for the research and the samples used in the research (Cope and Hannah 1975; Tinto 1986).

College climate offers a psychological perspective at the level of the environment. In chapter 4 of this volume Baird posits that students' perceptions of the climates of colleges and universities shape their behaviors, which, in turn, influence their integration into the social systems of a given college or institution. Efforts to develop approaches to assessing the climates of colleges and universities yield consensus on some environment dimensions. Baird suggests that friendliness or cohesiveness of the student culture and a sense of shared identity are particularly salient dimensions that may affect the college student departure process in general and social integration in particular. The logic of the assessment of college climates suggests that colleges and universities vary on these two dimensions as well as on other dimensions.

Scholars interested in focusing on the effects of college climate on college student departure should study such effects across different colleges and universities in order to assure variability on environmental dimensions. In conducting such research, scholars should consider the use of the College and University Environment Scales (CUES) developed by Pace (1969) to assess the climate of a given college or university. At another organizational level, residence halls also possess climates that may affect social integration and the departure decisions of students. For such assessments, scholars should consider the use of the University Residential Environment Scales (URES) developed by Moos (1979). In chapter 4 Baird discusses the various issues associated with the assessment of college climate. A fuller treatment of such issues and approaches to the assessment of college environments can be found in Baird's 1988 work.

Sociological

The influence of various social forces on the retention or withdrawal of students from college is the focus of the sociological perspective on college student departure. At base, Tinto's interactionalist theory is sociological. However, it is only one of a range of possible ways of accounting for the effects of the social environment on student departure. Other social forces can emanate from the structure of larger society, student peer groups, and the classroom.

Bourdieu's (1973, 1977) theory of social reproduction offers a particularly promising set of constructs for studying the influence of the social structure of larger society on the process of college student departure. Of particular importance to such a formulation is the notion of cultural capital. Cultural capital possesses only symbol values and represents the type of knowledge valued by elite members of society. In chapter 6 of this volume Berger advances a set of propositions for examining the influence of cultural capital on college student departure in general and social integration in particular. The crux of these propositions is that students are more likely to remain enrolled in a given college or university if their level of cultural capital is comparable to the level of cultural capital of the social and organizational systems of that college or university. Put differently, wide discrepancies in such levels of cultural capital are likely to result in student departure. Accordingly, Berger advances four propositions: two at the level of the institution and two at the level of the student. Given our recommendation to seriously revise Tinto's theory using the four strongly backed relationships as a foundation, the two student-level propositions—propositions 3 and 4—are most relevant to such efforts. Berger states proposition 3 as "Students with higher levels of cultural capital are most likely to persist at institutions with correspondingly high levels of organizational cultural capital." In contrast, proposition 4 reads, "Students with access to lower levels of cultural capital are most likely to persist at institutions with correspondingly low levels of organizational cultural capital." Each of these propositions has subpropositions that address academic and social integration.

The measurement of cultural capital looms as a problem for scholars wishing to test Berger's propositions regarding the role of cultural capital in college student retention. Berger suggests some ways in which this elusive construct can be measured in quantitative studies.

Student peer groups constitute the core of the social communities of colleges and universities. Hence, these groups also function as mechanisms for social integration (Tinto 1975). Because a peer group is any group with which a student may seek membership and approval (Newcomb 1966), individual students may belong to more than one peer group at any given time during their college careers (Kuh 1995). Tinto (1993) also acknowledges the multiple communities and peer groups in which students may belong.

Student peer groups also form cultures that shape the formation of the groups as well as influence the groups' attitudes, values, and behaviors (Kuh and Whitt 1988; Kuh 1995). Although in chapter 10 of this volume Kuh and Love champion the construction of a new theory of college student departure based on a cultural perspective, they advance two propositions—propositions 4 and 5—that can be extended to account for social integration and college student departure. At base, these propositions are organized around the students' cultures of origin and the cultures of various student groups. Proposition 4, which currently reads, "The probability of persistence is inversely related to the cultural distance between a student's culture(s) of origin and the cultures of immersion," can be altered as follows: Social integration is inversely related to the cultural distance between a student's culture(s) of origin and the culture of immersion. Proposition 5, which in its current form reads, "Students who traverse a long cultural distance must become acclimated to dominant cultures of immersion or join one or more enclaves," can be modified to postulate: Students who traverse a long cultural distance must become acclimated to dominant cultures of immersion or join one or more enclaves to achieve social integration. The alteration of these two propositions is consistent with the underlying assumptions of the cultural perspective on student peer groups. In fairness to Tinto, it should be noted that he advanced similar propositions about the effects of centrality and marginality on student departure decisions (Tinto 1993, p. 124).

Social forces also wield an influence on college classrooms. Tinto (1997) contends that such social forces flow from student learning communities. In chapter 5 of this volume Tinto describes the characteristics of student learning communities. Learning communities are characterized by the block scheduling of students in the same courses and the organization of course content around a particular theme that relates the various courses that are block scheduled. Collaborative learning as a pedagogical technique also marks student learning communities. Through research on first-year learning community programs, Tinto in chapter 5 identifies two undergirding social forces that serve to connect the college classroom with student departure: the development of supportive peer groups, and the sharing of learning experiences that connect the academic and social lives of students. Increased involvement and learning as a consequence of participation in student learning communities is a third underlying force. Tinto builds on these underlying forces and links them to student persistence. His formulations speak to how college classrooms can be reorganized to influence student persistence.

The three undergirding forces inherent in learning communities should be operationalized to determine their effects on student departure decisions in general and social integration in particular in a wide variety of college classrooms. The goal of such research is to determine the utility of these forces to efforts to seriously revise Tinto's theory using the four strongly backed relationships as a foundation.

Other Recommendations for Research

Our knowledge and understanding of the departure puzzle will be advanced if scholars pursue the process of inductive theory revision recommended in this chapter—a process that uses the four strongly backed propositions of Tinto's theory as its foundation. However, the complexity of this puzzle is recognized. Overcoming the limits of Tinto's interactionalist perspective through inductive theory revision may not be sufficient for the comprehension of such complexity. Accordingly, some additional lines of inquiry on college student departure that fall outside the parameters of the inductive theory revision process are recommended and described here.

1. Tinto's core construct of academic integration, which has failed to garner strong empirical support, should be reconceptualized along the lines suggested by Braxton and Lien in chapter 1 of this volume. More specifically, Braxton and Lien suggest that academic integration should be viewed as comprising two components: academic normative integration and intellectual isolation. They offer ways in which these two indexes of academic integration might be operationalized. Studies employing these reconceptualized indexes of academic integration may yield strong empirical affirmation for the influence of academic integration on subsequent institutional and goals commitments and on student persistence.

2. Van Gennep (1960) posits that three distinct stages or rites of passage characterize the movement of individuals from one social group to another. Tinto (1993) extends Van Gennep's rites of passage to the process through which students establish membership in the communities of colleges and universities. He postulates that college students must successfully pass through three stages in order to successfully establish membership in such communities. These three stages are separation, transition, and incorporation. In chapter 7 of this volume Rendón, Jalomo, and Nora describe these stages.

Tinto's formulations regarding these stages have received more conceptual criticism (Rendón, Jalomo, and Nora, chapter 7; Tierney 1992) than empirical treatments. However, Elkins, Braxton, and James (2000) provide empirical support for Tinto's formulations regarding the separation stage. Consequently, studies focusing on the transition and incorporation stage, as well as replications of the research by Elkins, Braxton, and James, are justified. Elkins, Braxton, and James recommend that such research should focus on the underlying processes of transition and incorporation and their linkage to student departure decisions. Although separation and transition account for early departure decisions (Tinto 1993), these stages may also function as "helper theories" to elaborate the four strongly backed propositions of Tinto's 1975 theory in general and social integration in particular.

3. The linkages between the college choice process and college student departure warrant inquiry. In chapter 9 of this volume Stage and Hossler advance a set of theoretical formulations that connect the formation of a predisposition to attend college with college departure. Stage and Hossler refer to their formulations as a "student-centered theory of persistence" as they focus on the personal agency of students in the processes of college choice and college departure.

Research testing their formulations might establish linkages between college choice and student persistence that might assist college and university administrators in their efforts to manage the enrollments of their institutions. Through an understanding of such linkages, we might also deepen our understanding of the perceptions students hold of the various social communities that make up colleges and universities.

4. In chapter 11 of this volume Tierney asserts that "at risk" students are more likely to persist if their identities are affirmed and incorporated into the cultures of colleges and universities. He offers a model for interventions designed to achieve such a purpose. Five tenets comprise this model: collaborative relations of power; connections across home, community, and schooling; local definitions of identity; challenge over remediation; and academic support.

Scholars should devote some attention to the role such a model plays in fostering the retention of at-risk college students. More specifically, scholars should focus on the influence of each of the tenets of this model on student identity and student departure decisions. These tenets may be intentional aspects of various programs for at-risk students or characteristics of the academic and social communities of colleges and universities selected for study.

5. In chapter 12 of this volume Laden, Milem, and Crowson point to types of colleges and universities that are "outliers" to the institutionalized pattern of high student departure. Put differently, some types of institutions experience retention rates higher than might be predicted for them. Laden, Milem, and Crowson cite historically black colleges and universities and tribal colleges as such outlier institutions. The college student departure process in such outlier institutions should be the focus of scholarly inquiry.

Guidelines for Future Research on Departure

Following is a set of guidelines for conducting research using the various theoretical perspectives previously described as well as the other recommendations for research.

1. Studies using constructs from each of the theoretical perspectives should be conducted across the full range of colleges and universities. Such studies should also be carried out using different groups of students based on gender, racial/ethnic, and traditional age/nontraditional age. Such studies are necessary for the rigorous testing of these constructs (Zetterberg 1965). Both qualitative and quantitative studies should follow this particular guideline.

2. Multiple replications of studies conducted in different types of colleges and universities and with students who are members of various racial/ethnic groups also are needed. Replications are necessary for scholars to assess the reliability of the influence of a given construct.

3. When possible, scholars should design studies that simultaneously test alternative theoretical perspectives. Through the simultaneous testing of two or more theoretical perspectives, we gain what Platt (1964) labels "strong inference." The task of revising

Tinto's theory through the inductive theory process outlined here would also be greatly simplified.

4. The measurement of social integration, subsequent institutional commitment, and student persistence as well as constructs derived from each of the four theoretical perspectives should be consistent across studies testing the influence of these constructs. This guideline pertains primarily to quantitative studies.

5. Scholars need to make careful distinctions among antecedents of social integration, social integration, and the outcomes of social integration. Social integration reflects a student's experience with the social communities of a college or university. Such experience manifests itself in a student's sense of normative congruence and affiliation with members of the social communities of a college or university (Durkheim 1951; Tinto 1975). Thus, antecedents of social integration are social activities or interactions with members of the social communities that shape a student's perception of his/her degree of social integration. Tinto (1975) points to informal peer group associations and extracurricular activities as antecedents or mechanisms of social integration, whereas outcomes of social integration are perceptions or behaviors that occur because of a student's degree of social integration. Hurtado and Carter's (1997) sense of belonging construct offers a good example of an outcome or consequence of social integration.

Issues Needing Resolution

The inductive theory revision process raises three issues that need to be resolved by scholars of the college student departure process.

1. The purpose of the inductive theory revision process described herein is to develop a revised or new theory that builds on studies conducted across the four theoretical perspectives. Put differently, the components of a revised theory will contain not only elements of the four strongly backed relationships, but also new constructs that emerge from the admixture of empirically supported constructs derived from research focusing on the four theoretical perspectives. Because the new constructs that are conceptualized

emerge from theoretical perspectives having possibly different underlying assumptions, the process advanced is similar to the process of theory integration as described by Thornberry (1989). More specifically, theory integration involves the development of a more inclusive explanation of the focal phenomena that is based on a larger set of interconnected propositions that are derived from the combination of two or more logically related propositions (Thornberry 1989). Elliot (1985), however, contends that the new theory must maintain the underlying assumptions of the theories that were combined. Some scholars may accept Elliot's argument, whereas others may reject it. For scholars accepting Elliot's assertion, the question that emerges is: Should the differing underlying assumptions of empirically backed constructs that are combined to revise Tinto's theory be taken into account and reconciled in the formulations of the revised theory?

2. Is it the aim of the process of inductive theory revisions advanced here to generate grand theory or theories of the middle range?* Is it possible to develop a revised theory that accounts for departure across the full range of colleges and universities and across different groups of students? Grand theory would obtain from invariant findings, whereas theories of the middle range would result from different patterns of findings across these various research settings. In the case of middle-range theories, we might develop theories of college student departure for particular types of colleges and universities and for different types of students. For example, we might develop such theories of the middle range as a theory of college student departure from community colleges or a theory of African American college student departure.

---

*Merton (1968) makes a distinction between grand and middle-range theories. Grand theory seeks to explain a wide range of phenomena at a high level of abstraction, whereas middle-range theories account for a limited range of phenomena at a lower level of abstraction. Although college student departure is a singular phenomenon within the broader category of the college student experience, these terms are extended to depict college student departure theory as a grand theory if it seeks to explain departure across a wide range of settings and groups of students. Moreover, middle-range seems appropriate to describe specific theories that account for college student departure in particular types of colleges and universities and for particular types of students.

3. Is it possible to reconcile explanatory theory with critical theory? Tierney's (1992) critique of Tinto's interactional theory leads many scholars to view explanatory theory and critical theory as two trains in the night going in opposite directions and incapable of any meaningful dialogue.

Tierney and Rhoads (1993) identify marginalization and emancipation as key facets of critical theory. Critical theorists such as Giroux (1983) maintain that society marginalizes and oppresses groups through hierarchies that array themselves on the basis of race, ethnicity, gender, and sexual orientation. The idea of critical theory is to emancipate such groups from their oppression. Tierney and Rhoads also point to the union of theory and research as another key aspect of critical theory. They posit that the fundamental assumption of this key aspect is rooted in the Marxian imperative "to comprehend the world in order to change it" (Marcuse 1972, p. 216).

Through explanatory research, an understanding of the basis for oppression of college students because of their race, ethnicity, gender, and/or sexual orientation can obtain. Put differently, emancipation of such students can emanate from an understanding rooted in an explanatory theory developed through the process of inductive theory revision. Such an understanding stems from a process that includes multiple theoretical perspectives. Thus, scholars of the college student departure process should come to view the relationship between explanatory theory and critical theory in this manner.

Concluding Thoughts

The directions for research outlined in this conclusion as well as in the other chapters of this volume provide a robust foundation for scholars of the college student experience in general and college student departure in particular to rethink the departure puzzle. Such reworking also serves to reinvigorate theory construction and empirical inquiry in this important area.

The testing of Tinto's 1975 theoretical formulations rested on the scholarly efforts of many individuals. Likewise, the scholarly efforts of multitudes of scholars will be required to carry out the process of inductive theory revision recommended here, the other recommendations for research advanced in this conclusion, and the research directions suggested in other chapters of this volume. Through the efforts of many scholars, theory and research on the departure puzzle will be reinvigorated, and an enhanced comprehension of this puzzle will also result. However, such progress will be greatly constrained if the guidelines advanced here for conducting research are not followed and if the issues needing resolution as outlined in this chapter are not addressed.

References

Astin, A. W. 1984. Student involvement: A developmental theory for higher education. *Journal of College Student Personnel* 25: 297–308.

Astin, A. W., and R. Scherrei. 1980. *Maximizing leadership effectiveness.* San Francisco: Jossey-Bass.

Attinasi, L. C., Jr. 1989. Getting in: Mexican Americans' perceptions of university attendance and the implications for freshman year persistence. *Journal of Higher Education* 60: 247–277.

Baird, L. L. 1988. The college environment revisited: A review of theory and research. In J. C. Smart (ed.), *Higher education: A handbook of theory and research,* vol. 4, pp. 1–52. New York: Agathon Press.

Baxter Magolda, M. B. 1992. *Knowing and reasoning in college: Gender-related patterns in students' intellectual development.* San Francisco: Jossey-Bass.

Berger, J. B. 2000. Organizational behavior at colleges and student outcomes: A new perspective on college impact. *Review of Higher Education* 23: 177–198.

Berger, J. B., and J. M. Braxton. 1998. Revising Tinto's interactionalist theory of student departure through theory elaboration: Examining the role of organizational attributes in the persistence process. *Research in Higher Education* 39: 103–119.

Birnbaum, R. 1988. *How colleges work.* San Francisco: Jossey-Bass.

Bourdieu, P. 1973. Cultural reproduction and social reproduction. In R. Brown (ed.), *Knowledge, education and cultural change,* pp. 189–207. London: Collier Macmillan.

Bourdieu, P. 1977. *Outline of a theory of practice.* Translated by Richard Nice. Cambridge, U.K.: University Press.

Braxton, J. M., and E. M. Brier. 1989. Melding organizational and interactional theories of student attrition. *Review of Higher Education* 13 (1): 47–61.

Braxton, J. M., A. V. S. Sullivan, and R. M. Johnson. 1997. Appraising Tinto's theory of college student departure. In J. C. Smart (ed.), *Higher education: A handbook of theory and research,* vol. 12, pp. 107–164. New York: Agathon Press.

Cabrera, A. F., A. Nora, and M. B. Castañeda. 1992. The role of finances in the persistence process: A structural model. *Research in Higher Education* 33 (5): 571–593.

Cabrera, A. F., J. O. Stampen, and W. L. Hansen. 1990. Exploring the effects of ability to pay on persistence in college. *Review of Higher Education* 13 (3): 303–336.

Chafetz, J. S. 1978. *A primer on the construction and testing of theories in sociology.* Itasca, Ill.: F. E. Peacock Publishers.

Chickering, A. W. 1969. *Education and identity.* San Francisco: Jossey-Bass.

Chickering, A. W., and L. Reisser. 1993. *Education and identity.* San Francisco: Jossey-Bass.

Cope, R., and W. Hannah. 1975. *Revolving college doors.* New York: John Wiley and Son.

de Anda, D. 1984. Bicultural socialization: Factors affecting the minority experience. *Social Work* 29 (2): 101–107.

Durkheim, E. 1951. *Suicide.* Translated by J. A. Spaulding and G. Simpson. Glencoe, Ill.: The Free Press. Originally published as *Le Suicide: Etude de Sociologie.* Paris: Felix Alcan 1897.

Eaton, S. B., and J. P. Bean. 1995. An approach/avoidance behavioral model of college student attrition. *Research in Higher Education* 36 (6): 617–645.

Elkins, S. A., J. M. Braxton, and G. W. James. 2000. Tinto's separation stage and its influence on first-semester college student persistence. *Research in Higher Education* 41: 251–268.

Elliott, D. 1985. The assumption that theories can be combined with increased explanatory power: Theoretical integrations. In R. F. Meier (ed.), *Theoretical methods in criminology,* pp. 123–150. Beverly Hills, Calif.: Sage.

Giroux, H. A. 1983. *Theory and resistance in education.* South Hadley, Mass.: Bergin and Gavey.

Hurtado, S., and D. F. Carter. 1997. Effects of college transition and perceptions of the campus racial climate on Latino college students' sense of belonging. *Sociology of Education* 70: 324–345.

King, P. M., and K. S. Kitchener. 1994. *Developing reflective judgment: Understanding and promoting intellectual growth and critical thinking in adolescents and adults.* San Francisco: Jossey-Bass.

Kuh, G. D. 1995. Cultivating "high stakes" student culture research. *Research in Higher Education* 36: 563–576.

Kuh, G. D., and E. J. Whitt. 1988. *The invisible tapestry: Culture in American colleges and universities.* ASHE-ERIC Higher Education Report, no.1. Washington, D.C.: Association for the Study of Higher Education.

Marcuse, H. 1972. *Studies in critical philosophy.* Translated by J. De Bres. Boston: Beacon Press.

Merton, R. K. 1968. *Social theory and social structure.* New York: The Free Press.

Milem, J. F., and J. B. Berger. 1997. A modified model of student persistence: Exploring the relationship between Astin's theory of involvement and Tinto's theory of student departure. *Journal of College Student Development* 38: 387–400.

Moos, R. H. 1979. *Evaluating educational environments.* San Francisco: Jossey-Bass.

Newcomb, T. M. 1966. The general nature of peer group influence. In T. M. Wilson and E. K. Wilson (eds.), *College peer groups: Problems and prospects for research,* pp. 2–16. Chicago: Aldine.

Nora, A., and A. F. Cabrera. 1996. The role of perceptions of prejudice and discrimination on the adjustment of minority students to college. *Journal of Higher Education* 67 (2): 119–148.

Pace, C. R. 1969. *College and university environment scales: Technical manual.* 2d ed. Princeton, N.J.: Educational Testing Service.

Pantages, T. J., and C. F. Creedon. 1978. Studies of college attrition: 1950–1975. *Review of Educational Research* 48 (1): 49–101.

Pascarella, E. T. 1985. Racial differences in factors associated with bachelor's degree completion: A nine-year follow-up. *Research in Higher Education* 23 (4): 351–373.

Pascarella, E. T., and P. T. Terenzini. 1980. Predicting freshmen persistence and voluntary dropout decisions from a theoretical model. *Journal of Higher Education* 51 (1): 60–75.

Perry, W. G. 1970. *Forms of intellectual and ethical development in the college years: A scheme.* Troy, Mo.: Holt, Rinehart and Winston.

Perry, W. G. 1981. Cognitive and ethical growth: The making of meaning. In A. W. Chickering and Associates (eds.), *The modern American college: Responding to the realities of diverse students and a challenging society.* San Francisco: Jossey-Bass.

Platt, J. R. 1964. Strong inference. *Science* 146: 347–353.

Polgar, S. 1960. Biculturation of Mesquakie teenage boys. *American Anthropologist* 62: 217–235.

Schrag, C. 1967. Elements of theoretical analysis in sociology. In L. Gross (ed.), *Sociological theory: Inquiries and paradigms,* pp. 220–253. New York: Harper and Row.

Stoecker, J., E. T. Pascarella, and L. M. Wolfle. 1988. Persistence in higher education: A 9–year test of a theoretical model. *Journal of College Student Development* 29: 196–209.

Sullivan, A. S. 1996. Integrating student development and attrition models: Psychological and sociological perspectives as complementary frameworks. Paper presented at the annual meeting of the Association for the Study of Higher Education, Memphis.

Summerskill, J. 1962. Dropouts from college. In N. Sanford (ed.), *The American college: A psychological and social interpretation of the higher learning,* pp. 627–657. New York: John Wiley and Sons.

Thornberry, T. P. 1989. Reflections on the advantages and disadvantages of theoretical integration. In S. F. Messner, M. D. Krohn, and A. E. Liska (eds.), *Theoretical integration in the study of deviance and crime,* pp. 51–60. Albany: State University of New York Press.

Tierney, W. G. 1992. *Official encouragement, institutional discouragement: Minorities in academe—the Native American experience.* Norwood, N.J.: Ablex.

Tierney, W. G., and R. A. Rhoads. 1993. Postmodernism and critical theory in higher education: Implications for research and practice. In J. C. Smart (ed.), *Higher education: A handbook of theory and research,* vol. 9. New York: Agathon Press.

Tinto, V. 1975. Dropout from higher education: A theoretical synthesis of recent research. *Review of Educational Research* 45: 89–125.

Tinto, V. 1986. Theories of college student departure revisited. In J. C. Smart (ed.), *Higher education: A handbook of theory and research,* vol. 2, pp. 359–384. New York: Agathon Press.

Tinto, V. 1993. *Leaving college: Rethinking the causes and cures of student attrition.* 2d ed. Chicago: University of Chicago Press.

Tinto, V. 1997. Classrooms as communities: Exploring the educational character of student persistence. *Journal of Higher Education* 68 (6): 599–623.

Valentine, C. A. 1971. Deficit, difference, and bicultural models of Afro-American behavior. *Harvard Educational Review* 19 (4): 137–157.

Van Gennep, A. 1960. *The rites of passage.* Translated by M. Vizedon and G. Caffee. Chicago: University of Chicago Press.

Wallace, W. 1971. *The logic of science and sociology.* Chicago: Aldine-Atherton.

Zetterberg, H. L. 1965. *On theory and verification in sociology.* Totowa, N.J.: Bedminster Press.

Contributors

Eric H. Asker is a doctoral candidate in the School of Education, Indiana University. His dissertation research focuses on graduate student persistence. He previously held positions in the military, business, and consulting. Asker is a graduate of the U. S. Military Academy and received an Ed.M. from the University of California, Davis, and an M.B.A. from the University of California, Los Angeles.

Leonard Baird received his B.A., M.A., and Ed.D. from the University of California, Los Angeles, the last in 1966. He began his career as a research psychologist at the American College Testing Program (1966–1969), then joined Educational Testing Service (1969–1983), eventually serving as a senior research scientist. From 1983 to 1994 he was a professor and director of the Office of Research in Higher Education at the University of Kentucky. In 1994 he joined the faculty of the Ohio State University as a professor in the Higher Education and Student Affairs Program and as editor of the *Journal of Higher Education*. His research and scholarly interests have focused on the assessment of college environments and climates, the examination of the effects of those environments and other experiences on student growth and development, the nature of the socialization and personal experiences of graduate and professional school students, and the assessment of student outcomes.

John P. Bean is an associate professor in the Department of Educational Leadership and Policy Studies at Indiana University, Bloomington. Coauthor of *The Strategic Management of College Enrollments* (Jossey-Bass, 1990), he has studied and published in the area of college student retention for more than years. He regularly teaches doctoral courses in educational policy analysis, organizational theory, and research methods. Current research interests include ethical issues in college student retention and the metaphors and values affecting faculty members.

Joseph B. Berger is an assistant professor in the Department of Educational Policy, Research, and Administration at the University of Massachusetts— Amherst. He earned his Ph.D. from Vanderbilt University in 1997. His dissertation was recognized by the Association for the Study of Higher Education with the Irvin Lee "Bobby" Wright Dissertation of the Year Award.

Much of his teaching and research has focused on the impact of organizational behavior on undergraduate student outcomes, with particular emphasis on studying undergraduate persistence. He is the author of numerous book chapters and journal articles and is a consulting editor for *Research in Higher Education*.

John M. Braxton is an associate professor of education and is the coordinator of the Higher Education Administration Program in the Department of Leadership and Organizations at Peabody College, Vanderbilt University. His research interests center on the college student experience, the sociology of the academic profession, and academic course-level processes. He has published more than forty-five refereed journal articles and book chapters on topics related to these areas of research interest. His current scholarly interests include research and theory development pertaining to college student departure, scientific misconduct, and the normative structure of undergraduate college teaching. Recent articles and book chapters on these topics have appeared in the *Journal of Higher Education, Research in Higher Education, Science, Technology and Human Values,* and *Higher Education: Handbook of Theory and Research.* Professor Braxton also has edited two other books: *Perspectives on Scholarly Misconduct in the Sciences* (Ohio State University Press) and *Faculty Teaching and Research: Is There Conflict Conflict?* (Jossey-Bass). He and Alan E. Bayer also wrote the book *Faculty Misconduct in Collegiate Teaching* (Johns Hopkins University Press). Professor Braxton serves as a consulting editor for the *Journal of Higher Education* and *Research in Higher Education* and is a member of the national review panel for the ASHE-ERIC Higher Education Report series. He also serves as series editor for the Vanderbilt Issues in Higher Education book series published by the Vanderbilt University Press.

Alberto F. Cabrera holds a Ph.D. in Educational Administration from the University of Wisconsin—Madison) and is an associate professor of education and a research associate in the Center for the Study of Higher Education. Prior to joining the center, Dr. Cabrera served as a faculty member at the State University of New York—Albany and at Arizona State University—West Campus. He was the coordinator for planning and analytical studies for the University of Houston and served as research associate in the Center for the Study of Higher Education and Finance at the University of Wisconsin—Madison. He specializes in research methodologies, college students, minorities in higher education, and economics of education. Dr. Cabrera has consulted with the Hispanic Association of Colleges and Universities (HACU), the Cooperative Institutional Research Program at University of California, Los Angeles, the American Council on Education, the Western Interstate Commission for Higher Education, and the U.S. Department of

Education and with several universities. His work on the role of finances on college persistence and on determinants of default behavior has received the best paper awards from the Southern Association of Colleges and Universities and the Southern Association of Institutional Researchers. In 1993 the Association for the Study of Higher Education granted him the Early Career Scholar Award because of his contributions to the understanding of the determinants of college persistence. Dr. Cabrera's research has been released in such top tier outlets as *Research in Higher Education, Review of Higher Education,* the *Journal of Higher Education,* and *Economics of Education Review,* among others. He also serves on the editorial boards of *Research in Higher Education, Review of Higher Education,* and the *Journal of Higher Education*

Robert L. Crowson, a researcher and lecturer for more than thirty years, is a professor of education with the Department of Leadership and Organizations, Peabody College, Vanderbilt University. His research interests center on organizational theory, study of urban education, the politics of education, and school-community relations. His most recent book is *Community Development and School Reform* (forthcoming, fall 2000). Crowson received his Ph.D. from the University of Chicago.

Shevawn Bogdan Eaton received her Ph.D. in Higher Education from Indiana University and is the director of ACCESS, an academic services program at Northern Illinois University. She is also the program evaluator for the university's special admissions program and focuses her research on the retention of specially admitted students.

Don Hossler is a professor of educational leadership and policy studies and is currently the vice chancellor for Enrollment Services at Indiana University, Bloomington. His areas of specialization include college choice, student financial aid policy, enrollment management, and higher education finance. Hossler has consulted with more than thirty colleges, universities and related educational organizations including: the College Board, Educational Testing Services, the University of Cincinnati, the Mennonite Board of Higher Education, Inter-American University of Puerto Rico, the Pew Charitable Trust, the University of Missouri, the University of Alabama, and the U.S. General Accounting Office. Recently he conducted research and served as an expert witness in the *Knight v. Alabama* desegregation case. Hossler is the author, or coauthor, of eight books and monographs and more than forty articles and book chapters. His books include *Mapping the Higher Education Landscape* and *The Strategic Management of College Enrollments.* His most recent book, *Going to College: How Social, Economic, and Educational Factors Influence the Decisions Students Make,* was published by Johns Hopkins University Press in 1998. Professor Hossler is currently the editor of the *CASE International Journal of Educational Advancement*. He has received national awards for his research and scholarship from the American College Personnel Association and the National Association of Student Personnel Administrators.

Romero Jalomo, Jr., is assistant professor of higher education administration at New York University. His research examines the transition to college and first-year experiences including campus climate issues that influence student involvement on campus.

Robert M. Johnson, Jr., has published articles on retention theory, linguistics, and teaching and learning. He is currently the dean of Information Services and chief information officer at Rhodes College in Memphis, Tennessee.

George Kuh is professor of higher education at Indiana University, Bloomington. He directs the College Student Experiences Questionnaire Program and the National Survey of Student Engagement funded by the Pew Charitable Trusts, an annual survey of college first-year and senior students that is cosponsored by the Carnegie Foundation for the Advancement of Teaching. A past president of the Association for the Study of Higher Education, Kuh has written extensively and made hundreds of presentations on topics related to college and university cultures, student engagement, assessment, and institutional improvement and has consulted with more than 130 educational institutions and agencies in the United States and abroad.

Berta Vigil Laden is a visiting scholar in the School of Education at Stanford University. Her research focuses on higher education and policy issues of culture, ethnic identity, access and equity, persistence, retention, transfer, and completion for racial/ethnic students and faculty in two- and four-year colleges. Recent articles and book chapters include "Mentoring Relationships for Students of Color: The Puente Project as an Exemplary Celebratory Socialization Model," "Hispanic-Serving Two-Year Colleges," and "Job Satisfaction and Faculty of Color in Academe: Individual Survivors or Institutional Transformers?," which was co-authored with Linda Serra Hagedorn. Laden received her Ph.D. from Stanford University.

Leigh A. Lien is a Ph.D. candidate in higher education at Vanderbilt University. Her dissertation topic focuses on the influence of academic and social integration of undergraduates on their psychosocial development. Her research interests also include how campus culture and organizations influence student experience and retention.

Patrick Love is an associate professor in higher education administration and student personnel at Kent State University. He coordinates the master's program in higher education administration and student personnel. He earned his Ph.D. in Higher Education and Student Affairs from Indiana University in 1990 and his M.S. in Counseling Psychology and Student Development from the University at Albany in 1981. His areas of scholarship and research include organizational influences on college student learning; intellectual, social, and emotional influences on learning; gay, lesbian, and bisexual college student experiences; and organizational culture as applied to higher education. In 1997 the College Student Personnel Association of New York State presented him with its award for Outstanding Contribution to the Profession, and in 1999 the National Association of Student Personnel Administrators (Region IV—East) honored him with its award for Outstanding Contribution to Student Affairs through Teaching.

Jeffrey F. Milem is an associate professor in the College of Education at the University of Maryland. His research focuses on the impact of college on students, racial dynamics in higher education, the educational outcomes of diversity, and the condition and status of the professoriate. Recent publications include "The Benefits of Racial and Ethnic Diversity in Higher Education," coauthored with Kenji Hakuta, for the American Council on Education's *Minorities in Higher Education, 1999–2000: Seventeenth Annual Status Report* and *Enacting Diverse Learning Environments: Improving the Campus Climate for Racial-Ethnic Diversity,* coauthored with Sylvia Hurtado, Alma Clayton-Pedersen, and Walter R. Allen. Milem received his Ph.D. from the University of California, Los Angeles.

Dr. Amaury Nora is a professor of higher education and the associate dean for research and faculty development in the College of Education at the University of Houston, Texas. His research focuses on college persistence, the role of college on diverse student populations across different types of institutions, the development of financial aid models that integrate economic theories and college persistence theories, graduate education, and theory building and testing. His inquiries have not only contributed to traditional lines of research on college persistence but have opened research on women and minorities in community colleges. Nora has been a visiting professor at the University of Michigan at Ann Arbor, summer 1990, and Penn State University, summer 1991. As an associate professor of higher education at the University of Illinois at Chicago, Dr. Nora also served as a research associate for the National Center on Postsecondary Teaching, Learning and Assessment, funded by the U.S. Department of Education. He has also served as a consultant to the American Council of Education, the Ford Foundation, the Hispanic Association of Colleges and Universities, the U.S. Department of Education, and he is currently a reviewer for the National Research Council in Washington, D.C. Nora has served on the editorial boards of *Research in Higher Education,* the *Review of Higher Education,* the *Journal of*

Higher Education, and the *Journal of College Student Retention: Research, Theory, and Practice* and as program chair for the 1999 Annual Meeting of the Association for the Study of Higher Education. He was the recipient of the Association for the Study of Higher Education's 1991 Early Career Scholar Award and the College of Education 2000 Research Excellence Award. Nora has published numerous book chapters and articles in referred journals, including the *Review of Higher Education,* the *Journal of Higher Education, Research in Higher Education, Higher Education: Handbook of Theory and Research, Community College Review, Education and Urban Society, Journal of College Student Development,* and *Educational Record.*

Laura I. Rendón is the Veffie Milstead Jones Endowed Chair at California State University—Long Beach. She is also professor of educational leadership and policy studies at Arizona State University—Tempe. Dr. Rendón is a Fetzer Institute fellow participating in a program designed to develop and sustain the capacity of individuals to inform their work through the inner life of spirit and the outer life of action and service. She is currently developing a spiritual model of teaching, learning, and research in higher education. Dr. Rendón is past president of the Association for the Study of Higher Education, and her work focuses on issues of access to college for underrepresented student groups, as well as student recruitment and retention in higher education. She holds a Ph.D. in Higher Education administration from the University of Michigan.

Edward P. St. John is a professor in the Department of Educational Leadership and Policy Studies at Indiana University, where he also serves as director of the Indiana Education Policy Center and coordinator for the Higher Education Program. Dr. St. John has focused his research on a range of topics related to educational reform and the financing of higher education. He has published numerous studies of the impact of student financial aid on college choice and persistence in *Research in Higher Education,* the *Journal of Higher Education* and other research journals. He authored *Prices, Productivity, and Investment,* (ASHE/ERIC Higher Education Study, 1994) and edited *Rethinking Tuition and Student Aid Strategies* (Jossey-Bass, 1995). Previously he has been a professor at the University of Dayton and the University of New Orleans. He also held policy analyst positions with the U.S. Department of Education and the Missouri Department of Education and served as a senior manager in the consulting industry. He holds an Ed.D. from Harvard and M.Ed. and B.S. degrees from the University of California, Davis.

Frances Stage is professor of educational leadership and policy studies at Indiana University, Bloomington, and is currently senior fellow at the Na-tional Science Foundation. Her areas of specialization include college student learning, especially math and sciences and student participation in math/science majors. Stage is author or coauthor of eight books and more than seventy articles and book chapters focusing on college students and the methods used to study them. She is lead author of the ASHE/ERIC monograph *Creating Learning Centered Classrooms: What Does Theory Have to Say?* Stage is currently vice president for the Postsecondary Education Division of the American Educational Research Association and has won awards for research and scholarship from the Association for the Study of Higher Education and the American Educational Research Association.

William G. Tierney is the Wilbur-Kieffer Professor of Higher Education and director of the Center for Higher Education Policy Analysis at the University of Southern California. His most recent book is *The Responsive University: Creating High Performance Colleges and Universities* (Sage, 1999). He writes frequently on issues of access, equity, organizational culture and socialization, and higher education policy.

Vincent Tinto received his Ph.D. in education and sociology from the University of Chicago. He is currently Distinguished University Professor at Syracuse University and chair of the higher education program. He has carried out research and has written extensively on higher education, particularly on student retention and the impact of learning communities on student growth and attainment. He is the author of a theory of student leaving that has become the benchmark by which research on student attrition is judged. More important, it has dramatically influenced views of how institutions affect the leaving of their students. His book from the University of Chicago Press, *Leaving College: Rethinking the Causes and Cures of Student Attrition*, second edition, describes that theory and shows how it can be applied to the formulation of institutional policies to enhance student retention. He has consulted widely with federal and state agencies, independent research firms, foundations, and two- and four-year institutions of higher education on a broad range of higher educational issues, not the least of which concern the retention and education of students in higher education. He serves on the editorial boards of several journals and with various organizations and professional associations concerned with higher education. He chaired the national panel responsible for helping establish the first national center for research on teaching and learning in higher education and served as associate director of the National Center on Postsecondary Teaching, Learning, and Assessment, funded by the U.S. Office of Education. His current research focuses both on the impact of learning communities on the academic achievements of first-year students in differing educational settings and on the character of doctoral persistence in differing fields of study.

Index